Healing
Children's Grief

Healing
Children's Grief

Surviving a Parent's
Death from Cancer

Grace Hyslop Christ

New York • Oxford
OXFORD UNIVERSITY PRESS
2000

Oxford University Press

Oxford   New York
Athens   Auckland   Bangkok   Bogotá   Buenos Aires
Calcutta   Cape Town   Chennai   Dar es Salaam   Delhi
Florence   Hong Kong   Istanbul   Karachi   Kuala Lumpur
Madrid   Melbourne   Mexico City   Mumbai   Nairobi   Paris
São Paulo   Singapore   Taipei   Tokyo   Toronto   Warsaw

and associated companies in
Berlin   Ibadan

Published by Oxford University Press, Inc.,
198 Madison Avenue, New York, New York, 10016
http://www.oup-usa.org

Library of Congress Cataloging-in-Publication Data

Christ, Grace Hyslop.
   Healing children's grief : surviving a parent's death from cancer / by Grace Hyslop Christ.
      p. cm.
   Includes bibliographical references.
   ISBN 0-19-510590-7 (alk. paper) — ISBN 0-19-510591-5 (pbk. : alk. paper)
      1. Grief in children. 2. Grief in adolescence. 3. Bereavement in children. 4.
   Bereavement in adolescence. 5. Parents—Death—Psychological aspects. 6. Children and
   death. 7. Teenagers and death. I. Title.

BF723.G75 C58 2000
155.9'37'083—dc21   99-015342

Printing (last digit): 9 8 7 6 5 4 3 2 1

Printed in the United States of America
on acid-free paper

This book is dedicated to the families of the parents who died.
Their stories are a legacy of healing they left for all of us.

Contents

List of Tables and Figures

Foreword

There is always the unforgettable moment when the biopsy result is relayed by the surgeon, "I am sorry to say that our fears have come true—the biopsy shows that you have cancer." You reach out your hand to your spouse, your head becomes blurred, there are tears. In a moment, the physician intervenes, "but there are many things that we can now offer. . . ." A parent's first thoughts are not with his or her own fate, or not only that. Quickly, it is with the fate of Seth, Deborah, William, Elisabeth . . . with infants and children who need you as the very source of their own lives, with older children whose weddings you will miss, with grandchildren who you will not see at confirmation and bar mitzvah.

Cancer is a family affair: to be diagnosed as having cancer immediately is to reinforce one's roles—obligations and hopes—among those one loves and is loved by. These relations become hyper-cathected—they become more charged, meaningful, precious—as time becomes more precious. For those for whom the new and improved treatments have failed, who are now face to face with the Angel of Death, the entire meaning of their lives and of their last days will be measured by these relationships which they, and those around them, will try to make as ideal as possible.

The systematic, scientific study of this complex process offers many opportunities for studying the deepest feelings between spouses and between parents and their children. A great deal has been written about the psychology of death and dying, and this literature has allowed clinicians and families to cope much better with this natural and yet awful process. Much less is known about the impact of death from illness on those who survive, especially on children. The phenomena of grief, mourning, and the capacity for depression during childhood have been enduring interests not only among clinicians but also theorists of child development. What are the cognitive preconditions for children to understand the process of death and its irreversibility? How do children experience the loss of the functions provided by a parent and the loneliness, pains and longings from the separation? What allows a child to give up hope and yet hold on to wonderful memories; to remain in love and yet, also, to say a final, psychological goodbye; to be loyal to mom and yet allow dad to date and bring another woman into their family?

In this volume, Grace H. Christ demonstrates how systematic research can enrich and be enriched by clinical sensitivity, and how theory can guide and be advanced by the careful, empirical study of individual children and families. She has used the unique perspective that is offered to clinicians to be with families at their most intimate times because we offer our care. She has used this privileged position to describe the major variables that shape a child's experience of the dying and death of a parent. Her research highlights the major influence of the child's psychological, developmental position or stage.

Each phase of life has distinctive modes of mental organization that shape the way a child experiences and understands what he or she is feeling and going through. To understand a child's response to the illness and death of a parent, and how he or she copes during the next months and years, the clinician must appreciate these general psychological issues as well as the specific features of the child's inner and outer life. Dr. Christ's examination of these psychological stages and the interactions with the other factors reveals that patterns can be explicated that are of use in clinical intervention. An important innovation was finding a way to group children by developmentally derived ages rather than by more arbitrary biological markers. This clarified the changes in their mourning and in the emergence of anticipatory grief as children matured, the changes in what they experienced as most stressful, the type of parental support they needed, the defenses they utilized, and the changing role of peers in their adaptive efforts. Dr. Christ's study of children whose parents are dying provides important new information for the construction of theories about children's adaptation to the traumatic experience of expected death from medical illness (and all that accompanies this in technological medicine and in specific family situations).

The careful documentation of children's adaptation to a parent's death from cancer is also a model of research that can be extended to the consideration of other variables. The current study selected children from intact, middle class families. Dr. Christ notes that there may be other phenomena in families where the only parent is dying or where families are also burdened by socioeconomic and other burdens. Unfortunately, the AIDS epidemic has placed many children in just this situation. Children whose mothers are dying of AIDS—fortunately, fewer children today than just a few years ago—are often burdened by just these additional stresses. Yet, even here, clinicians have been able to see how useful it is for mothers to be actively engaged in the planning for their children after their death. Sometimes, this process involves sharing the child with their selected caregiver during the months of illness, and thus creating for the child the surrogate parent. At the same time, we have seen how useful it is for children to be allowed to remain as engaged with their mothers during the process, to develop their own psychological legacies in which their mothers are idealized and appreciated for what they offered.

The current study of children of parents dying in a tertiary care hospital, where the highest quality of care is offered, also provides an important comparison for future research on other cohorts of children whose parents die in far less controlled and compassionate situations. Death may come when care is less competent, or unexpectedly during childbirth or routine surgery. It very often comes without warning—in accidents, from suicide, during warfare, as a result of natural catastrophes. Each of these situations can now be framed on the basis of the findings of the current study in which death—never lovely, of course—occurred with warning and in the context of the best treatment that clinicians can offer.

It should be a consolation to the families that were involved in this research project that their personal suffering has left a scientific and clinical legacy that will help other boys and girls. At times, the obligations of the researcher and the ethical commitments of the clinician are seen as two contrasting and opposing forces. This research demonstrates that this is a false splitting. Dr. Christ shows that clinical engagement and systematic research are synergistic and mutually enriching. The care these children and families received was improved by their involvement in research; authentic clinical research will continue to improve our understanding and abilities to be helpful. Remarkably, this volume is both deeply moving—as we must all be moved at the deepest core of our experiences by the fantasies of the child's loss of a parent—and remarkably sober. To work with people dying from cancer and their families demands these special aptitudes for pleasure in life and calm, thoughtful acceptance of what lies beyond our ability to control. For the scientific insights and compassionate care of Dr. Christ and her colleagues, and for those clinicians who are continuing to be presences in the lives of children and families in hospitals and clinics that care for individuals with cancer, all of use owe a great debt of gratitude.

DONALD J. COHEN, M.D.
Director, Child Study Center
Irving B. Harris Professor of Child
  Psychiatry, Pediatrics and Psychology
Yale University School of Medicine

Acknowledgments

There were many people who participated in the intervention research, the preparation of the book, and who contributed to my thinking and ideas. First and foremost are the families to whom this book is dedicated. They shared with us their most painful experiences, their sorrows and their joys. We are grateful to them for their courage and their commitment to helping other parents who must take their journey. Theirs is indeed a legacy of healing.

There were several people who played unique roles and without whom the book could not have been created. Dr. Karolynn Siegel, friend and colleague, was the principal investigator on the Childhood Bereavement Intervention grant that provided the information on which the book is based. Throughout the many years of our close working relationship, her brilliant research leadership, insight, and foresight have been invaluable.

Dr. Adolph Christ, child psychiatrist, is also my life's partner and best friend. His conceptual, experiential, editorial, and critical contribution to this book were essential to its completion.

I also want to thank Dr. Susan Krause, a social work educator and clinician who provided special inspiration, encouragement, and wise insights into the dynamics of the situation during those early years when so little was known. She generously and informally shared with us from both her professional and personal experiences providing the kind of grounding in the actual process that we needed.

There were many people involved with interviewing and supervising the intervention over the seven years of the grants; others managed and analyzed the data, and helped with conceptualization and publication. I am grateful for their enormous commitment and contribution.

The supervisors who worked closely with me to carry out our emerging vision of the intervention included Dr. Rosemary Moynihan who provided guidance and wisdom for many years. Margaret Adams-Greenley supervised during the early years of the program and Dr. Barbara Freund supervised during the later years. Lois Weinstein, supervised the research evaluators.

The interviewers were all experienced social workers, three remained throughout most of the seven years of the grant: Deborah Langosch, Shelly Hendersen, and Diane Sperber. Others participated for shorter periods: Diana Brown, Frances Camper, and Nan Younger. Their careful recording of interviews and case notes was invaluable. We so desperately wanted to know what we were only in the process of discovering about interventions that would help and those that might hinder the adaptive processes of these families. The work was intense because to be effective required a level of empathic connection to the family's tragic circumstances that inevitably stirs the deepest fears in all of us. As one interviewer said, "To talk with a child about the probable death of a parent is an awesome task." But we knew we could not avert our gaze if we were to be helpful. Other members of the research team who were involved in the data management and analysis from the beginning included Dan Karus, Drs. Frances Mesagno, and Vicki Raveis.

Special thanks is also owed to the social work staff at the hospital during the years of the study. They provided information, guidance, counsel, and important illustrations as they helped to identify and recruit families into the intervention. Their efforts to interpret the intervention to other disciplines were very effective.

This work was supported in part by grants from the National Institute of Mental Health (MH41967), the American Cancer Society (PRB-24-A), the van Ameringen Foundation, the Society of Memorial Sloan-Kettering Cancer Center, and by the Project on Death in America of the Open Society Institute.

There were other individuals who helped in the actual writing of the book. Dr. Mindy Fullilove, colleague and friend, unstintingly shared her extensive knowledge and experience in qualitative analysis as well as her deep understanding of the human experience. Along with Leslie Green and the other members of the "Tuesday Writing Group" at the Columbia University School of Public Health, they provided invaluable counsel, critique and encouragement during all phases of the shaping and editing of the book.

Dean Ronald Feldman and Associate Dean Peg Hess at the Columbia University School of Social Work provided support and encouragement which was deeply appreciated. Their early vision about the importance of this work was often clearer than my own.

Two people were extraordinary in the editorial assistance they provided with earlier versions of the book, Elizabeth Bowman and Dr. Doral Alden. Others who read various versions and provided critique and consultation included Athena Stevens, Cynthia Tinapple, Drs. David Fanschel, Helene Jackson, Carole Lebeiko, William Worden, and the "blind reviewers."

Finally a special thanks to Jeffrey Broesche and Benjamin Clark at Oxford. Their enthusiastic support and interest in the book, and excellent skill was so helpful in resolving problems that emerged.

Introduction

This book concerns 88 families and their 157 children who coped with the terminal illness and, ultimately, the death of a parent. It presents a qualitative analysis which complements the quantitative findings reviewed in Chapter 2 of how the families and children responded to these events during the 6 months preceding and the 14 months after the patient died. Five developmentally separable age groups emerged from the data, and the groupings clarified the many ways in which children's development shaped their responses. Because we talked with them, their parents, and their siblings at length, we were able to use exact words, gestures, and processes to describe interactions between family members, to go beyond the numbers to tell the previously untold story of how the children and their families actually responded to and survived the tragedy. As will become apparent, the majority of the children successfully adapted to the loss of their parent.

There is an emerging consensus that childhood mourning is defined as the (successful and unsuccessful) adaptive process children experience following the death of a parent (Furman, 1974; Osterweis et al, 1984; Worden, 1996). Grief, on the other hand, refers to the painful personal feelings associated with the death, while bereavement is an umbrella term that includes overall adaptation to the death. These are the definitions that are used in this book.

Healing children's grief occurred not only by relieving those painful feelings that are so central to their experience of such a family tragedy but also by helping them to adapt to and integrate this new reality. The healing occured in part through continuous interactions with family and others throughout the process of the parent's illness, death, and reconstitution; interactions that informed prepared, and guided the child. Equally important were interactions that resonated with children's feelings; encouraged, supported, and gave solace, meaning, and value to their experiences. Because these processes are interactive, they were significantly advanced by the parents' attending to their own mourning. It was only when parents did so that they were able to attend to the grief and mourning of their children. Such interactions, both helpful and unhelpful, are described in this book.

Healing children's grief also included the construction of a legacy created by continuously revising the image of their dead parent. As such, the legacies represented complex reconstructions of children's relationship with a parent who was no longer present for day-to-day interactions but who nonetheless remained a constant reality in their lives. It reflected the incorporation of the children's own memories, experiences, wishes, and fantasies, added to by the memories, experiences, wishes and fantasies of siblings and the surviving parent, as well as the eulogies community members delivered during memorial services.

Finally, healing children's grief took place through the reconstitution of individual and family life following the death. The long, slow process of reestablishing relationships to each other and to the world without the living presence of the parent who died was complicated by differences in the way children and adults expressed their grief. These new bonds, born in sorrow, were integral to children's healing.

I dedicated this book to the families because I believe that the parents who died would have appreciated it. In fact, the terminally ill parents permitted their families to participate in the intervention that generated the narratives in the book, although many of them knew they would not live to see the results. I like to think that this book is a legacy of healing those parents left for all of us.

The families participated in a parent guidance preventive intervention that was implemented over a period of seven years. All the ill parents in the sample were treated at Memorial Sloan-Kettering Cancer Center in New York City, where they were recruited during the terminal stage of their illness, approximately six months before they died. Most of these patients and their families were randomly assigned to a parent guidance intervention; the others, as part of a true experiment, received a supportive, reflective intervention.

The families who participated in these interventions had several characteristics that distinguished them from participants in other studies. First, the deaths of all the parents were anticipated, unlike the causes of death, such as accidents, suicide, or homicides, discussed in other studies. This distinction is relevant because unanticipated deaths may cause more complex stress responses (Pynoos, et al. 1995). Second, the participating families were able to reach out beyond their own community hospitals for health care; most were middle class and, because all were two-parent families, the surviving parents were available to participate in the intervention after their spouse's death. (Their demographic characteristics are summarized in Chapter 4). Most children did not have a history of severe mental illness. Although these unique factors limit our ability to generalize the findings to families who have lost a parent from causes other than cancer, they do clarify a pattern of responses observed in a clearly defined and relatively homogeneous sample of families.

Although recent research has yielded a host of important quantitative findings about bereaved children, which are reviewed in Chapter 2, these studies have not provided knowledge of how children's development affects their responses. There are few detailed descriptions of how children and their families interacted while coping with day-to-day stresses during the parent's terminal illness and death and during the period of bereavement after the death. This information would have been extremely useful to us in our clinical work with other families during the illness of a young parent.

For these reasons, I embarked on a qualitative analysis of the data obtained from the participating families from over 1000 audiotaped interviews, as well as notes from telephone contacts, the psychologists' evaluations, the interviewers and their supervisors. This approach yielded a more complete understanding of the processes involved in the parent's terminal illness and death and the reconstitution of the families after the death. In Tremblay's words (1998, p. 436), it permitted me to undergo a "molecular analysis of 'grief work,'" which included grief-related interactions between children and their parents. Both quantitative and qualitative methods are necessary to begin understanding an issue as complex as how a child copes with the death of a parent.

Personal as well as professional motivation has led me to focus on this issue. When I was growing up, I heard a great deal about why my Aunt Hazel was not only my mother's aunt but, in a sense, her mother as well. My biological grandmother died at age 26 from Hodgkin's disease leaving three young children, 5-year-old Ruth (my mother), 3-year-old Grace, and 1-year-old Paul in the care of Aunt Hazel and her husband, Carl. Two years later five year old Grace died from pneumonia, and the family's sense of tragedy deepened. Thus, I heard many times about the sad plight of children who tried hard throughout their lives to become as perfect as they imagined their dead mother and sister had been. That effort was, in part, a consequence of the reconstitution of my mother's experience.

Four aspects of my professional experience as a social worker shaped my thinking about the impact on children of a young parent's death. The first was a developmental perspective derived from my work with psychiatrically disturbed children. The perspective I gained from that experience was reinforced by participating in Dr. Margaret Mahler's nursery for autistic and psychotic children in the late 1960s. At the time, Dr. Mahler, a psychoanalyst and researcher, was assembling clinical data from normal and disturbed children that led her to identify the individuation-separation sequence of emotional development (Mahler, et al. 1975).

Next, I worked with the families of adolescents who were hospitalized in the Payne Whitney Psychiatric Clinic at The New York Hospital-Cornell Medical Center in New York City. Dr. James Masterson, director of the adolescent inpatient unit, was influenced strongly by Dr. Mahler's insights regarding early development. He viewed the central dynamic of these seriously disturbed adolescents as arising from their early problems involving individuation and separation from the maternal figure (Masterson, 1972). In short, a developmental perspective, albeit primarily psychoanalytic, was an influential part of my understanding of mental health and mental illness.

The third important influence was my clinical work and research with cancer patients and their families at Memorial Sloan-Kettering Cancer Center where I was director of the Social Work Department for 12 years. There, I observed the stress reactions of patients and their families that reflected a broad range of normative and more troubled responses to extraordinary stresses. As a result, I searched for methods of providing meaningful interventions for the patients and families who faced this difficult situation. The turmoil, the progressively worsening crises, and the fear of the inevitable end had a powerful effect on these people. Especially wrenching for staff emotionally were young families with a terminally ill parent. We believed that we could do more to support, make life better for, and heal surviving parents, children, and the patient's middle-aged parents. In other words, the patient's terminal illness appeared to be a crucial time for intervention with these families.

Although there was no precedent for a research component in a clinical social work department (Christ, 1993), two remarkable people, Barbara Berkman, DSW, and Karolynn Siegel, Ph.D, helped convert the idea into a reality. First, Dr. Berkman consulted with us and began training social work clinicians to think from a research perspective, to present papers at national conferences, and to publish their work. Within two years, Dr. Siegel joined the Department of Social Work as director of research and began the systematic process of converting clinical ideas into a reality through research grants. One result was the parent guidance intervention project, which yielded the data and the findings reported here. (Dr. Berkman is currently Helen Rehr and Ruth Fizdale Professor of Health and Mental Health, Columbia University School of Social Work. Dr. Siegel is currently Director of the Center for the Psychosocial Study of Health and Illness, Columbia University School of Public Health.)

In 1992, I joined the faculty at the Columbia University School of Social Work, where I came to understand the process of bereavement through case studies while teaching graduate students in social work about grief, loss, and bereavement. In classes, the students present a broad range of cases involving different kinds of loss experienced by clients seen in dozens of community and health care agencies in the New York metropolitan area. These cases provided me with a rich context in which to compare the experiences of these clients and patients with my more focused experience with young families that have lost a parent to cancer.

STRUCTURE OF THE BOOK

This book begins with the story of Rachel, who was not a participant in the intervention study. Shortly after I arrived at Memorial Sloan-Kettering, three-year-old Rachel's father died. We followed her case until she left for college at age 18. The other children and families described in the book were followed for about 18 months. Thus, they provide an important understanding of the more immediate consequences of the tragedy of losing a parent. I have included Rachel's story because it provides a longer-term perspective on the impact of a young parent's death. It also underscores the need for longer-term follow-up studies.

Chapters 2 through 4 describe the theoretical context for and the methods used in the analysis. Chapter 2 summarizes the relevant literature on childhood bereavement and compares it with stress associated with trauma and divorce. Chapter 3 summarizes the stages of the cancer experience and the theories that helped us understand the developmental context of the children's and adolescents' reactions and behaviors. Chapter 4 describes the sample of children and families, the methods used in the qualitative analyses, and the model of outcome derived from the analyses.

Chapters 5 through 14 present the findings of the qualitative analyses of the information provided by the families. As described in Chapter 4, the 157 children were divided into five age groups on the basis of common developmental characteristics. Two chapters are devoted to children in each age group. The first chapter in each group describes the patterns and differences in the children's responses and ends with specific recommendations gleaned from the more successful interactions between child and parent. The second chapter provides extensive descriptions of the experiences of two families. These narratives elaborate the interactions of the family members, the many stresses they confronted, and the methods they used to cope with the family tragedy. Each narrative chapter concludes with a discussion about the different patterns of adjustment among the children when last seen and the factors associated with the outcome of each child. Finally, Chapter 15 summarizes salient findings presented throughout the book. This was done to provide an overview of the ways development shaped the children's experiences and their more or less successful adaptation to this family tragedy.

INTENDED AUDIENCE

The book is intended for a variety of audiences. One audience consists of colleagues—researchers and teachers whose work on childhood and adolescent bereavement has been and continues to be helpful and inspiring.

Another audience consists of professionals and students who provide services to children and their families. Comparing the responses of children with similar developmental characteristics provides a sense of how the children cope over time. Thus, the summary of developmental theories in Chapter 3 and the more detailed discussions about development at the beginning of each set of chapters focusing on a specific age group may help readers gain a keener understanding of how important a child's development is with regard to how he or she experiences the stress associated with a parent's death.

Finally, another audience consists of family members, friends, teachers, religious leaders, and other members of the community who know children who have lost a parent and have the opportunity to help them. These individuals may be especially interested in Chapter 1 and 5 through 14. Although the recommendations at the end of each clinical chapter are written for family members as well as professionals, each group is likely to use the recommendations in different ways. For families, the recommendations may guide their thinking and actions. For professionals, they can serve as guides for developing approaches that will help families faced with specific barriers to their process of adaptation. The purpose of the book is to offer information about children's experiences and the inventive solutions that families and friends devised to respond knowledgeably, confidently, and effectively to children and adolescents facing the loss of a parent.

1

❦

Mother and
3-Year-Old Daughter

"I Was a Tear on My Father's Cheek."

One family started me on the road of looking for possible ways of helping families in which a parent is dying from cancer. At the time, I was director of social work at Memorial Sloan-Kettering Cancer Center in New York City. I choose to tell this family's story because the family members continued to communicate with me for 15 years and thus gave me a glimpse of the change in the child's relationship with the dead parent through different stages of cognitive and emotional development. In addition, the plight of the child's sensitive and intelligent mother, her fine intuition, her quick responses to suggestions, and her daughter's excellent progress inspired me to pursue my interest in both helping and studying the process of bereavement in children.

Joel and Lisa Klein were young, really too young, not for the normal things that people do, but for dying. Both were 27 years old. They met when they were in college and decided to postpone their marriage until they had finished school. Joel and Lisa were in that enviable moment when careers begin, when dreams and excitement about the future temper the day-to-day drudgery. Both were elated when Rachel was born, confident that they could manage both careers and child rearing with the help of many friends and close family members.

DIAGNOSIS AND TREATMENT

When Rachel was 1 year old, Joel seemed uncharacteristically tired. Lisa noticed nodes on his neck, and he subsequently found hard lumps under his arms. His physician looked concerned and ordered a number of tests, some of which, such as the bone marrow aspiration, were painful. Both Lisa and Joel were frightened but kept their feelings to themselves. They tried to reassure one another by recalling that fatigue and swollen lymph nodes were symptoms of mononucleosis and that everyone in college seemed to get the "kissing disease." Rachel seemed out of sorts, crying and fussing when she was supposed to be crawling, saying words, exploring her world, and trying to stand. Each parent cried when alone.

1

Joel and Lisa met with the physician together. His voice had sounded omi-nous on the telephone, but he had simply said that he wanted to see them in per-son to review all the test results. Neither remembered the ride to his office, and they were ushered in immediately when they arrived. "Leukemia," he said, "and not the slow-growing type." It was good that both of them were there because each of them shut out different parts of what the physician said about the treatments, the side effects, and the statistics. Each felt a numbness and sense of unreality they had never experienced before. The physician recommended that they consult a well-known and highly respected oncologist who specialized in leukemia.

Joel's treatments were uncomfortable, leading to severe and seemingly unending nausea, hair loss, and weight loss. One nurse told Joel it was a good thing he was so sick because it meant that the drugs were having an effect. Joel responded positively to the treatment, and for six ecstatic months, he and Lisa told each other they had beaten the odds, never mind what the oncologist had said. Because they were a likable, engaging couple, all the physicians, nurses, and social workers who knew them treated them as peers and friends as well as patient and wife, and joined in their optimism. Both Lisa and Joel had close friends, with whom they expressed their worries and cried. At the end of six months, Joel's remission ended.

There was a second round of treatments, then a third. Both generated hope, but secretly Joel and Lisa felt a little less optimistic each time. By now Rachel was 2 $1/2$ years old, and Joel and Lisa no longer talked hypothetically about Joel's death. Death had become a heart-wrenching certainty.

TERMINAL STAGE

Rachel was almost 3 years of age when Lisa visited the social worker on Joel's hospital floor for advice about how to manage Rachel, who was reacting to Joel in a way that puzzled and upset both parents. Several weeks earlier, when Joel was admitted to the hospital in crisis, Lisa and Rachel visited him, and he imme-diately began to cry. Lisa also cried, and both parents hugged Rachel, who became upset. This had happened a couple of times. Subsequently, when Rachel went to the hospital, she refused to go into Joel's room and seemed afraid of and angry with him. When the social worker suggested that Rachel was over-whelmed and frightened by their intense emotions because she was too young to share those feelings or to understand that her father was dying, Lisa and Joel stopped including Rachel in their intense grief.

Lisa described how she and Joel had to work out their communication with Rachel about the illness. In the final few weeks before he died, Joel told Lisa he wanted to protect Rachel from seeing his deteriorating condition by having her live with his parents "until I'm better." Although Lisa struggled with a desire to honor her dying husband's wishes, she thought it would be better to be honest with Rachel and to include her at that critical time. "If I lied to Rachel and said that everything would be fine, she'd never trust me again." She and Joel decided to be honest and direct with their daughter and to be neither overly optimistic nor pessimistic. When Rachel asked, "Will this (new medicine) make you better,

Daddy?" he responded, "I really don't know, Rachel. I hope so; the doctor thinks it will make me *feel* better."

Lisa wisely handled the ambiguity of Joel's illness and treatment by pointing out to Rachel the subtle changes in Joel's functioning, thus validating the reality of his physical decline. At one point, Lisa went out to dinner with friends and told Rachel she could stay home with her father. "But Daddy can't take care of me," she said, obviously aware of her father's weakness and debilitation. Lisa explained that family friends would be with them so that Rachel would feel safe.

Lisa reflected on communicating with Rachel about her father's changing physical condition this way: "I think the key to communicating was answering her questions about the illness and treatment as they were happening, rather than having to explain a sudden illness crisis that wasn't attached to any concrete thing for her.

"I understand why parents are reluctant to tell their young children about a parent's terminal illness. The hardest part for me was realizing that I couldn't protect Rachel from the pain of her father's death. It hurts to watch my child in pain. But then I realized that it isn't a choice of whether she will hurt or not, but whether I will know about it."

Rachel was a strong-willed child, and her parents valued and reinforced her emerging independence. For example, in the following episode, Rachel expressed her displeasure with her mother openly:

"I came home from the hospital sad and exhausted and reprimanded Rachel for some minor misdeed. She began to cry, and I realized that my anger was displaced. So I apologized and told her that I was just tired and upset because Daddy was so sick. Then I began to cry. I thought we were having a good cry together, and I felt much better.

"However, the next day Rachel said: 'Remember yesterday I was crying? You were crying too. I was crying first. Two people aren't allowed to cry at the same time.'

"My first impulse was to say, 'I'm sorry. I'll never do that again.' But then I thought better of it and said: 'You know, Rachel, Mommies are allowed to be sad too, and they are allowed to cry too. I'm strong and I can take care of you, but sometimes I hurt too.'"

Rachel struggled with the many forced separations caused by Joel's illness. These included separations not only from her father but, most important to children of her age, separations from her mother. In addition, there was a distinct change in the affective tone of the relationship between Rachel and her mother as Lisa struggled with the emotional highs and lows that are ubiquitous during a loved one's unpredictable but relentless course of terminal illness. Rachel was distressed during this period and complained about the many times she was sent to neighbors or friends when Lisa was at the hospital caring for Joel.

DEATH AND FAMILY RITUALS

When Joel died, Lisa was prepared to address the four key issues that need to be clarified for young children:

- The body stops functioning when a person dies.
- Death is irreversible; the parent will not come back.
- Death is different from what happens on television; dead people do not come back again on reruns.
- Death has an emotional context: The people who loved the dead person not only feel sad but also angry or afraid.

In this context, Lisa's conversation with Rachel proceeded as follows:

"Something very sad happened today. Daddy died. He isn't going to be here any more."

"When is he coming back?"

"He can't walk any more. He can't talk. His heart stopped, and he isn't going to *be* any more."

"Where is he?" she asked.

"People who cared a lot for him are giving him a bath and putting special clothes on him so he can be buried." Lisa then took Rachel's man doll, found a box, and showed her how a burial worked.

"When is he coming back?"

"Well, Rachel, when people die they don't come back. We remember them and we think about them, but they don't come back."

Rachel still wasn't satisfied. She challenged her mother's story, "Edith came back on Archie Bunker. Why can't Daddy come back?"

"Edith was on television. That was a picture, and we have pictures of Daddy we can look at, but the pictures are not him."

"Can Daddy move in the box?"

"When you are dead, you don't move anymore."

"But when is Daddy coming home?"

"Daddy isn't coming home. He will never come home. We love him and we will miss him, but he can never come home again."

At that point, Rachel began to cry, and Lisa joined her. After two or three minutes, Lisa felt that Rachel was beginning to understand that her father was dead. But the next day, Rachel again asked when he was coming home.

Rachel attended her father's funeral and walked with Lisa and other family members from the synagogue to the burial site. When she became restless during the funeral, Joel's sister took her with her own children for some lunch.

A few days after the death, Rachel said angrily: "Daddy didn't say good-bye to me. Why didn't he say good-bye?"

"I don't know. He didn't say good-bye to me either." But after thinking about the question, Lisa prepared a better answer for when Rachel asked the question again several days later. She was becoming accustomed to the repetitive nature of her daughter's questions. This time she said: "You know, Rachel, Daddy didn't say good-bye because he didn't want to leave us. He loved us very much and he didn't want to die, so he couldn't say good-bye."

BEREAVEMENT AND RECONSTITUTION

Several weeks after Joel's death, Rachel came home unhappy from preschool and announced: "I don't have a daddy, but everyone else has a daddy." The 3-year-old class tormentor had teased her about not having a daddy when all the other children had one. She then began asking Lisa to get another daddy, which seemed to signal her transition into the phase of reconstituting the family.

A few weeks later, Rachel said to her mother: "I'll be your husband."

"Only a man can be a husband, Rachel. You are my daughter, and I really want you to be my daughter."

"Edith (the housekeeper) can be your husband."

"Edith is a lady. As I told you, a husband has to be a man."

Rachel thought about this for a while, then said, "Samuel (Lisa's best friend's husband) can be your husband."

"Samuel already has a wife—Judith."

"Judith can get another husband."

"Marriage is forever. I can't marry another person's husband. What I need to do is go out with different men until I find the right person. That won't be easy."

Lisa then described some of the attributes she was looking for, to which Rachel added, "And he needs to be funny, and he needs to be a good daddy."

"Yes. But for right now, it's just going to be you and me. But we can have a lot of fun, and I can take care of you while I'm looking for a husband and a daddy for you."

At last, Rachel seemed satisfied, but a few days later, she asked, "Did you find a husband yet?"

Several months after Joel's death, Lisa encouraged Rachel to recall some of the good times she had had with her father at the hospital: for example, having a meal with him on his bed when he felt well enough.

"Eating egg salad with Daddy was fun," Rachel said, "but staying with Elana (a family friend) was not fun!"

"Why?"

"I wanted to stay with you."

"I know," Lisa said, somewhat defensively, "but I had to stay at the hospital and take care of Daddy."

Another incident that occurred during this period suggested to Lisa that Rachel now understood and accepted the permanence of Joel's death. When Rachel and her 2-year-old cousin were playing, he asked her, "Where is your daddy?" but she didn't respond. But when he asked again, "Where is your daddy?" she said emphatically, "My daddy got sick, he got medicine that made his hair fall out, he went to the hospital, and then he died." "Oh," said the cousin.

About a year after Joel's death, Lisa felt she was ready to begin dating. However, she decided that Rachel had gone through enough traumatic separations and didn't want to subject her to a series of such experiences while she dated. "Until I'm fairly sure that the relationship has a good chance of going somewhere, I'm not going to involve my child and subject her to a series of unnecessary rejections. She has Joel's brothers, who care about her, and the husbands of some of our friends."

Typical of children in her age group, Rachel remained preoccupied with her need for Lisa to find a new daddy for her, and she expressed resentment about Lisa's need to date. Lisa explained, "Dating is a necessary part of finding the right daddy for you and the right husband for myself. It isn't easy, but I need to date to find out what a person is like."

Rachel thought for a while, then said: "Don't date at night. Date when I am in school."

Rachel stopped talking easily about her father a year or two after his death. When Lisa mentioned him, Rachel often adamantly announced that she did not want to talk about him. As time went on, Lisa worked hard to complete an advanced degree and planned a career that would give her maximum flexibility and time to bring up Rachel. Dating was easy compared with thinking about a permanent relationship, which always made her anxious. If one husband had died, it could happen again. The trauma of an unexpected tragedy that occurs at such a young age is difficult to shake.

CASCADE OF EVENTS

Rachel's relationship with Joel's family became distant rather quickly when Lisa began dating, and it became even more distant when, four years after Joel's death, Lisa told his family that she planned to marry again. Rachel was 7 years old at the time. Joel's family felt that they didn't understand their daughter-in-law as well without Joel. She was involved with different people and pursuits from theirs, and now she was moving out of their suburban village. They often disapproved of Lisa's values and goals, but said little; they simply didn't see her as much. Although they invited her and Rachel to their home on holidays, she often went to visit her own family in the South instead. Their relationship with Rachel became much more formal, with little real personal content or understanding. However, they did attend Lisa's second wedding.

Before the wedding, Rachel spoke about Joel to her prospective stepfather, Robert, because she wanted him to understand something that was extremely important to her: "I like you very much, and I want you to be my stepfather, but there is one thing you should know. You will always be Number Two in my heart, and my father will always be Number One." Robert understood and worked hard to be accepted by Rachel as completely as possible. Many children express this sense of loyalty to their biological parent and retain a special and primary place for that parent when the surviving parent dates or plans to be married. It was also hard for Rachel to accept Robert because she felt jealous sometimes. She and Lisa had been "a team" for four years, and now she had to share that special relationship.

When Rachel entered first grade, at age 6 she was a bright, highly verbal, engaging, and socially adept child who showed no evidence of having any unusual problems concerning separation. Throughout grade school, she was viewed as an appealing, social child who had exceptional verbal skills. She did well in a competitive private school that drew top students in the area. In the fifth grade, she began to expect herself to do even better, to earn the very highest grades in all subjects. She felt disappointed in herself when it became clear to her that her skills in mathematics were not at the same level as her verbal abilities. That summer, she went away to camp and loved it. She showed no symptoms of distress at parting when she left.

When Rachel was 10 years of age, Lisa gave birth to a son, and Rachel was overcome with jealousy. She openly expressed her resentment about the time Lisa spent caring for her brother and insisted that she was neglected and rejected. Her grades took a nose dive, and she blamed this on her brother's presence.

In the sixth grade, Rachel was fortunate to have a male teacher who recognized and enjoyed her outstanding verbal and writing skills and encouraged her to develop them. Rachel was buoyed up by his acknowledgment, and her school performance was much better for a while. She became interested in writing poetry and wrote a poem entitled, "I Was a Tear on My Father's Cheek." She was in the midst of establishing a different, more mature relationship not only with her mother and stepfather but also with her deceased father. The poem seemed to reflect her evolving sense of her relatedness to him as she began the developmental process of forming a separate, independent identity. This relatedness was based on her memory and experience, but also on the memory of others who spoke of him. She also became interested in boys, and they certainly were interested in her. She was vivacious, enthusiastic, and able to hide her insecurities. Rachel had her mother's ability to organize and function at a highly productive level while experiencing severe internal distress.

When Rachel's brother was about 3 years old, it became apparent that he had language problems—another stress on this family system. Rachel was 13 years old at the time and was aware of her mother's increasing preoccupation with obtaining professional evaluations that might clarify the nature of her son's problem so she could arrange for his care. The stress only increased as she and Robert consulted specialist after specialist.

Unhappily for everyone, Lisa and Robert finally separated when Rachel was 14 years old. Although Rachel had resented Robert at first, she had become fond of him; in fact, she had adopted his surname in addition to Joel's. Robert had given her the stable family she had always thought she wanted. When Lisa and Robert separated, Rachel was furious, feeling abandoned and rejected because she was losing a father all over again. Robert remained a responsible provider and was emotionally supportive and involved with Rachel to the extent the separation allowed. Because Rachel felt loyal to Robert as well as to her mother, she even lived with him for a time. Lisa agreed to this because she was prepared to do anything that would help Rachel feel better about herself.

Meanwhile, Lisa struggled to divide her time among her son's special needs, her need to expand her career to compensate for the financial losses caused by the divorce, and her attempts to understand and respond to Rachel's anger and sense of loss. Rachel's depression was becoming another nightmare for Lisa.

Suddenly, Joel's family precipitated another family crisis. Upset because Lisa had remarried and moved from their community and because Rachel had added her stepfather's surname to theirs, they decided to remove Rachel from the family's will and exclude her from holiday celebrations. Thus, Rachel experienced additional feelings of abandonment and loss.

This coalescence of events precipitated a crisis in Rachel's depression, and she entered therapy. Lisa was frightened, but she carefully followed the therapist's advice about how to manage Rachel, and she was relieved when Rachel slowly began to improve. Rachel was able to make good use of therapy, and her school performance improved dramatically. She received the straight As she had always wanted, became the editor of the school newspaper, and was chosen for other leadership positions in her school. In her senior year, she was accepted by a prestigious college, which would take her away from home. She also had a boyfriend who shared her artistic interests. She was quite anxious about being separated from her mother and her boyfriend when she went away to college.

Lisa was extremely proud of Rachel's successes and increased self-esteem and was excited about her current choice of a writing career. Yet she worried about Rachel's ability to manage the separations and the possibility that her earlier problems would reappear under the stress of doing college work and being away from home. Rachel's first year at college was a highly successful one.

CONCLUSION

Although the tremendous stress that Lisa and Rachel Klein experienced is obvious, both of them also had great strengths. How did these stresses and strengths balance out? Does losing a parent at a young age—especially when the loss is coupled with the inevitable separations, the well parent's sadness and dejection during the patient's terminal illness and after the death—represent a trial by fire to which some children succumb, whereas others become stronger? Does the loss result in a psychological deformity that will forever poison every close relationship?

Rachel's experience and the experiences of many other children who will be described in this book suggest a different perspective about the effect of a parent's death on a child. The death of a parent is clearly not just a single event, stress, or trauma. For the young child, it is more like a family tragedy that changes much that existed before and shakes a child's basic trust and sense of psychological predictability. It is a tragedy that requires the child to undergo a major psychological reconstitution after the death. The process of reconstitution reflects not only the family tragedy but also the child's stage of development when the tragedy occurred and the quality of the buffers provided by the surviving parent and other people in the child's life. It seems obvious that some changes that occur in children as a consequence of the parent's death remain, probably for life. However, the reconstitution is affected also by subsequent events, including a broad range of secondary stressors that occur as a consequence of the death or in addition to it.

Perhaps the concept of the "cascade" of events will improve our understanding of children's reactions in these situations over time and through different stages of development. The "cascade" is a process involving a number of events that may have a cumulative effect. Each stressful event may affect the child's self-esteem or self-confidence, which in turn shapes (and often distorts or exaggerates) the individual's perception of or response to subsequent events.

The parent's death shakes young children's emerging sense of trust in the inalienable right to the comfort and security provided by a loving parent and the emerging sense that 'the world is my oyster.' Added to this is the fact that a young child's ability to process and understand an event such as death is limited. Helpful rationalizations and explanations such as "Mother loves me even though she can't be with me because someone else needs her even more" and "Every occurrence is unique unto itself, and future occurrences should not be judged on the basis of previous but unrelated events" are not available at this stage of development. Even cause and effect as a concept does not really exist, certainly not when it is used to explain an absence that causes such pain. Emerging trust, security, confidence, and self-esteem as a mirror of the esteem the young child senses from others—all these emerging good things may be altered significantly by the family tragedy.

The reconstitution that takes place after a parent's death is not like putting Humpty Dumpty together again. The surviving parent's ministrations, preparation, love, support, and ability to understand and respond to the child's despair are buffers that mitigate some of the ravages of the family tragedy and provide anchors that the child can use to construct a new *Weltschauung,* a view of the world that incorporates the reality of the loss. Although providing all these things to the child is tremendously difficult for a grieving parent, Lisa Klein managed to do it remarkably well.

Do vulnerabilities remain, even when the surviving parent desperately attempts to eliminate them in an effort to return the child to the person he or she was before the death? Rachel's vulnerability seemed specific and almost predictable, given her age and developmental stage when the family tragedy occurred. Her 'cascading responses' to the subsequent stressful events in her life focused on loss as the theme of her young life: *loss* of her father, *loss* of her mother when she took care of Robert, *more loss* of her mother after the birth of a brother who needed an extraordinary amount of attention, *loss* through divorce of a stepfather she had grown to love, and *loss* of her father's family, which rejected her. Some of these events—the surviving parent's dating and remarriage, a new sibling, a less exclusive relationship with the surviving parent—cannot and should not be prevented. However, when these anxiety-producing life events are preceded by a major family tragedy such as a parent's death, the child's perceptions and reactions may be altered no matter how well reconstituted the family relationships are during the first year or so after the death. Children who experience early loss may overreact to future losses much like the body responds to an allergen. The strength of the reaction is probably influenced by a child's temperament, previous life experiences, and the quality of the surviving parent's support.

Even at the end of Rachel's story, when she was doing exceptionally well, we saw that her world view continued to be shaped by the family tragedy. Her anxiety about going away to college revealed an apprehension that she might never be able to return home or might not have a loved one at home to return to. This suggests that her "lenses" have been changed forever. "Ground" by the family tragedy and reconstitution and "re-ground" by subsequent events, the lenses may distort her view of separations for life. Alternatively, however, her view of other events and other human conditions may be sharpened as a consequence of this tragedy. As she continues to have positive, successful experiences, she may develop a view of herself as being less vulnerable to loss and more able to survive and overcome.

Rachel's narrative allows a conclusion not possible in the other cases that will be presented. An event, even one as dramatic and tragic as a father's death, may still be just a single tragic event. To gain a better perspective on the power of such an event in shaping a life requires careful prospective information. I have a 14-month window into the lives of some children following the death of their parent. The glimpse into Rachel's 15-year window is humbling to the scientist seeking to predict future reactions based on previous events. But perhaps a predictive algorithm is not the best model for understanding the import of an event on future events. As will become clear in subsequent chapters, the outcome and adjustment of the children after 14 months, were powerfully influenced by other circumstances and other events, which perhaps had an effect even more powerful than the death of the parent. That is the message that Rachel's narrative underscores—the need to develop long-term, prospective narratives, which may gradually help us understand the importance of a stressful event at a particular point in the development of an individual.

2

Childhood Bereavement Studies

I recently saw Charlie Rose interview an eminent author on a Public Broadcasting System program. This author described a personal experience that had been crucial in his life. When he was 4 or 5 years old, he was sent away from home to stay with relatives. When he came home a few months later, he was told his mother was away on a trip but would return—soon. He remembers asking a few times when she was coming back, but something about his father's and grandparents' response when they said 'soon' dissuaded him from pursuing the topic. As the months became years, he often cried alone at night and wondered what he had done to keep his mother away. Many years later, he discovered that she had died of cancer. He described his anger at his family for having subjected him to such cruel uncertainty as a child—uncertainty that filled him with guilt and self-recrimination. This type of story is not uncommon: It exemplifies the belief still permeating our culture that children should be protected from painful information.

The studies that are summarized in this chapter underscore the support children feel when they are informed and are an integral part of the family, which does not withhold important information from them. Four relevant areas are reviewed: (1) the evolving models proposed to explain the complexity of how children cope with bereavement, (2) the relevance of models of traumatic stress to childhood bereavement, (3) the retrospective and prospective studies of adult and child bereavement, and (4) the relationship between divorce, traumatic death, and anticipated death. These perspectives help us to understand the variations in the findings from different studies and to clarify the significance of this research. I hope this book will add to the information that may gradually replace mistaken beliefs about children's grief—beliefs that may interfere with a child's optimal coping with the family tragedy of a parent's death from cancer.

EVOLVING BEREAVEMENT MODELS

Early Psychoanalytic Theories

The 'scientific' examination of the process of mourning began with Sigmund Freud's classic paper on mourning and depression (Freud, 1915/1957). In addition to his psychoanalytic work with emotionally disturbed adults, his under-standing of mourning was influenced by his self-analysis after his father's death (Freud, 1905). Freud believed that the task of mourning required the gradual freeing up or withdrawal of psychic energy that had been attached (cathected) to the internal representation of the dead parent so that psychic energy would be available to form new attachments. The inability to form such attachments, he hypothesized, would result in melancholia (depression). Because children whose parent died were viewed as incapable of engaging in such an arduous, psychological mourning task, they were vulnerable to later psychopathology.

Many other authors built on and amplified Freud's insight, based on their psychoanalytic work with adult patients (Abraham, 1927; Shafer, 1968; Volkan, 1981). Others added insights from the psychoanalysis of emotionally disturbed children (Freud, 1960; Furman, 1974). For example, Erna Furman observed that children as young as 3 years old had the capacity to mourn because they had attained object permanence (the ability to accept emotionally that they were separate from the parent and that the parent continued to exist even when not physically present). She also believed that parents could support a child through this process in ways that would not compromise the child's later development. Furman's book, which includes pertinent personal communications from Anna Freud, remains an excellent resource on psychoanalytic thinking about childhood grief.

Modifications of Psychoanalytic Views

John Bowlby (1969, 1973, 1980), who was originally a psychoanalyst, was influenced by his observations of how children between the ages of 1 and 3 years reacted when separated from their mother. He observed that their responses to separation strongly resembled those of bereaved adults: protest, followed by despair, then apathy. His observations were bolstered further by a careful synthesis of accumulating studies of children separated from their parents (Freud & Burlingham, 1974; Heinicke, 1956; Robertson, 1953; Spitz, 1946).

Bowlby (1980) also drew on Furman's case descriptions of children who were seen in a psychoanalytically oriented therapeutic nursery and concluded that infants as young as 6 months experienced grief reactions when separated from a parent, thereby challenging the validity of traditional psychoanalytic conclusions that children could not grieve. He also observed that adults often had difficulty communicating accurate information to children about the loss of their parent and that they had difficulty coping with children's open and con-frontational thoughts and feelings about the loss. Bowlby proposed that even a young child could mourn a lost parent under certain favorable conditions, including a reasonably secure relationship with both parents before the loss, prompt receipt of accurate information about what had happened, encourage-ment to ask relevant questions, the opportunity to participate in funeral rites, and the comforting presence of the surviving parent.

Bowlby (1980) and others (Kliman, 1965; Silverman & Worden, 1992a; Worden, 1996), questioned the idea that emotional detachment (i.e., decathexis from the lost parent) was the desirable outcome for anyone, whether child or adult.

They found that most children retained a psychological relationship to the lost parent, a relationship that underwent revision at different stages of development and with changing life events. Furthermore, they found that this process seemed to be one that was largely adaptive for children. The life events shared by Rachel Klein in Chapter 1 illustrate these insights.

Three Models of Adaptation to a Parent's Death

A broad range of individual case studies and quantitative research have been carried out over the past three decades. In reviewing these studies, Clark and colleagues (1994) suggested two models that characterized retrospective studies with adults: the blunt trauma model and the shock-aftershock wave model. In addition, they proposed a third model—the cascade model—that might better account for children's adaptation over time.

Blunt Trauma Model

The blunt trauma model was reflected in the earlier, more traditional perspectives concerning childhood bereavement. In this model, parental death was conceptualized as a single event: a discrete blow that was "bounded in time, powerful in impact, and more disruptive for children than adolescents" (Clark, et al., 1994, p. 128). The focus was on the nature of the event and the child's developmental stage when the event occurred. This approach was reflected in a range of mostly retrospective studies that tried to identify a connection between adult psychopathology and the loss of a parent during childhood. Although some investigators were able to find such connections (Bowlby, 1980; Brown, et al., 1986; Finkelstein, 1988; Furman, 1974; Rutter, 1966; Tweed, et al., 1989), others disputed their existence (Berlinsky & Biller, 1982; Osterweis, et al., 1984; Van Eederwegh, et al., 1982). This disagreement challenged the simplistic and linear reasoning of an approach that looked for a specific event in childhood to explain adult psychopathology.

Shock-Aftershock Wave Model

In a series of retrospective studies, researchers were able to shed light on the process that links early parental death and adult depression (Bifulco, et al., 1987; Brown et al., 1986; Harris, et al., 1986; Harris, et al., 1987). They found that the quality of care after loss of the mother mediated the relationship between the loss in childhood and depression in adulthood. This finding suggested that a specific type of insufficient care may be an underlying factor related to later vulnerability. Saler and Skolnick (1992) had similar findings from a more recent retrospective study. Children who were allowed to speak openly about the death with the surviving parent and other family members and who received a high level of care and affection from the surviving parent appeared to be protected against later depression.

These studies emphasize the role of multiple intervening factors that have a continuing impact on the developing child over time. Furthermore, they support the observation that a parent's death is not the single event that determines the later outcome of that experience. Specific situational factors that may play a crucial role in children's adjustment also must be investigated. Finally, changes take place within a child as he or she experiences and reexperiences grief during successive stages of developmental. Thus, Clark and his colleagues (1994) referred to this process as a series of shocks and aftershocks.

Cascade of Events Model

In a further refinement, researchers have focused on an expanded view of the long-term developmental effects of a parent's death and how these effects emerge in the child. Parental death may result in later psychopathology, or what Rutter (1994) called a "carry forward" of the effects of the stress and adversity. Precisely how these processes occur over time is unknown; thus, the subject is clearly an important one for future research.

Other researchers (Clark et al., 1994; Garmezy, 1983; Krupnick, 1984) suggested that the term "cascade" would aid in understanding the interactions of the child's stage of development, the specific meaning of the parent's death to the child, subsequent life stressors, and the child's characteristics of vulnerability and resilience, which potentially exacerbate or buffer the effects of stressors at a particular point in the child's development. Psychopathology may result from the heightened vulnerability set in motion at the time of the parent's death. In addition, the death may trigger a cascade of significant life changes that influence the child's psychological development for a lifetime as well as immediately.

TRAUMATIC STRESS

Is the anticipated death of a parent from cancer a 'traumatic event' as trauma is currently defined? The literature on childhood bereavement and the literature on children's responses to traumatic stress have developed in parallel, but the interaction between the two subjects has been limited (Figley, et al., 1997). Earlier bereavement theorists often spoke of a parent's death as inevitably a traumatic event, a designation that was challenged by stress theorists who viewed traumatic stresses as requiring specific types of behavioral responses and reactions (Eth & Pynoos, 1985a; Eth & Pynoos, 1985c).

The last two decades have been especially rich in studies exploring the significant parameters of children's traumatic stress and its psychopathological companion—posttraumatic stress disorder (Pynoos, et al., 1995; Terr, 1995). The explosion of professional awareness of childhood traumatic stress, such as sexual and physical abuse, as well as catastrophes such as fires, shootings, hostage situations, and floods, have yielded data that have spawned complex models of traumatic stress. Pynoos and colleagues (1995) formulated an elegant model of childhood traumatic stress in which the posttraumatic distress is derived from the traumatic experience and from subsequent traumatic reminders and secondary stresses.

Although the death of a parent from cancer is a painful psychological experience that may have lifelong repercussions for children, there may be quantitative as well as qualitative differences in children's responses to experiences involving the death of a parent through dismemberment, suicide, or homicide (Cerel, et al., 1999). Some children who have had such experiences evidenced the range and intensity of traumatic reactions that are consistent with a diagnosis of posttraumatic stress disorder (DSM IV, 1994). Such traumatic stress reactions include agitated or disorganized behavior; intense fear, horror, and/or helplessness; traumatic re-experiencing of the event; avoidance of stimuli associated with the event; or persistent symptoms of increased arousal. A frequently described impediment to children's grief after a traumatic death is preoccupation with the circumstances of the death, sometimes the gruesome image of the body (Nader, et al., 1990; Pynoos, et al., 1991; Pynoos, et al., 1995).

Relevance to Bereavement Models

In what way might traumatic stress models be relevant to childhood bereavement? Although the experiences of traumatic stress and anticipated parental death result in quite different responses, concepts of proximal and distal secondary stressors (Cicchetti, et al., 1993; Pynoos, 1992) and proximal and distal traumatic reminders (Pynoos et al., 1991; Pynoos et al., 1995) are relevant to childhood bereavement models. A proximal secondary stressor or traumatic reminder is defined as one that occurs within the first year after the stressful event, a distal secondary stressor or reminder is defined as one that occurs more than a year after the stressful event.

Secondary Stressors

A number of predictable events that occur after the parent's death may also cause stress because of their psychological relationship to the parent's absence, illness, or death. These events are referred to as secondary stressors, and they occur as a consequence of the impact of the primary stressor or take on special significance because of the original stressor. An example of this concept arising from an anticipated death might include the following: when separation is a significant developmental stage-related stressor during the 6 months before or during the 12 months after the death; when a child returns to school or preschool; when a parent goes to work or even leaves the house to go shopping. These experiences can invoke proximal secondary stress because the event activates the young child's fear of separation, which played such a prominent role during the terminal stage of the dead parent's illness. However, when the surviving parent begins dating, remarries, or has additional children, or when the child reaches adolescence and goes away to college, all of which are psychologically related to separations, earlier separation anxiety may be reactivated and hence be a distal secondary stressor.

Anticipatory Stressors

Anticipatory stressors are not a part of extant traumatic stress or bereavement models. I include them here to clarify similarities and differences from the more traditional proximal and distal secondary stressors, which do play a significant role in traumatic stress models. Anticipatory stressors during the terminal stage of illness could take the form of anticipatory fears about the parent's possible death. The stress during the terminal stage of a parent's illness includes the increasing awareness that the parent could or probably will die. This awareness may constitute such an anticipatory stressor.

Traumatic Reminders

Proximal reminders following the anticipated or traumatic death of a parent (Pynoos et al., 1991; Pynoos et al., 1995) might include, for example, Father's Day or Mother's Day, the dead parent's birthday, and even family holidays such as Christmas and Thanksgiving. Distal reminders may occur as the child continues the ongoing renegotiation of the relationship to the dead parent through successive stages of development.

It is estimated that about one-quarter of parental deaths of children under 17 years of age are unexpected (World Health Organization, Office of Publications, 1991). It may be necessary to separate this group of potentially more traumatic deaths (sudden deaths, accidents, suicides, and homicides) from anticipated deaths to compare the reactions and responses of the children. However, due to the difficulty of obtaining a large enough study sample, some research has included both types of death, often without sufficient statistical power to allow a comparison of responses to these two potentially very different experiences. Studying children's responses and outcomes to a death of a parent from cancer offers the possibility of clarifying similar or different symptom constellations when death can be anticipated.

STUDIES OF BEREAVED CHILDREN

When it became apparent that bereaved children's responses needed to be studied as they were occurring rather than relying only on later recollections (Osterweis et al., 1984), several prospective studies using nonclinical samples and comparison or control groups were developed. Tremblay and Israel (1998) and Sandler and colleagues (1992) provide excellent critiques of their findings and methodology. The major findings from these studies are summarized here.

Prospective studies, most of which include both sudden and anticipated parental deaths, suggest that the majority of children experience elevated levels of a range of symptoms such as depression, anxiety, somatic complaints, and behavior problems both before the death in the case of anticipated death and in the short-term aftermath of a parent's death (Christ et al., 1993; Christ, et al., 1994; Siegel, et al., 1996a; Siegel et al., 1992). These findings suggest that children may constitute a vulnerable population at increased risk for social impairment and/or psychopathology not only during the immediate postbereavement period, but extending into adulthood as well (Berlinsky & Biller, 1982; Brown, et al., 1986; Finkelstein, 1988; Kaffman, et al., 1987; Kranzler, et al., 1983; Osterweis, et al., 1984; Siegel, et al., 1992; Tweed, et al., 1989; Van Eederwegh, et al., 1982; Weller, et al., 1991; Worden, 1996).

On the other hand, there is an unresolved question. Some studies have found that bereaved children are comparable to their normal peers approximately one year after a parent's death, as judged by many commonly used indicators (Saldinger, et al., 1999; Sanchez, et al., 1994; Siegel, et al., 1996a; Silverman & Worden, 1992a; Van Eederwegh, et al., 1982; Worden, 1996). A range of methodological issues may have affected these outcomes: (1) Most samples include predominantly intact middle-class families, and exclude children with a psychiatric history. The strengths and resources available in these families may have impacted favorably on the children's adjustment process. A more socio-economically diverse sample of bereaved children could yield a different adjustment profile among the children. (2) Some studies have relied on standardized measures of anxiety and depression. It is possible that the manifestations of problematic adjustment to the loss of a parent are more subtle than those assessed by such measures. Incorporating other measures, such as a clinical diagnostic assessment, might more comprehensively identify children who experienced difficulty adjusting to parental death. (3) Some studies used only the parent's report of the children's behavior. In bereavement situations, parents, especially fathers, have been found to underreport their child's depressive symptoms (Sanchez et al., 1994). (4) There are no long-term evaluations of these samples. A longer-term follow-up may be necessary to identify children who are at increased risk of experiencing a delayed grief reaction to parental death. Indeed, a recent study reported that serious emotional/behavioral problems attributed to the experience of parental death doubled from one year to two years postdeath (Worden, 1996).

These findings continued to underscore the importance of the complex and often highly stressful events that follow parental death as being at least as, if not more important, in determining the child's adjustment than the death itself. They also provided more detailed findings about the events that resulted in poorer or better outcomes (Arthur & Kemme, 1964; Cohen, et al., 1977; Raveis, et al., 1999; Sandler, et al., 1992; Worden, 1996). Such events included the parent's neglect, the surviving parent's severe depression, an unhappy relationship between the child and the parent, the lack of parental warmth, perceived open communication with the surviving parent, and the parent's active coping style (Gray, 1989; Kranzler, et al., 1989; Raveis, et al., 1999; Silverman & Worden, 1992a; Worden, 1996). Three additional moderating and mediating factors are background characteristics, factors associated with the parent's death, and attributes of the family environment (Raveis, et al., 1999).

Background Characteristics

Background characteristics of the child, the deceased parent, and the family may potentially have an impact on the process and outcome of a child's grief (see reviews: Berlinsky & Margolin, 1982; Osterweis, et al., 1984; Sandler, et al., 1988; Tremblay & Israel, 1998)). Age and gender of the child (Elizur & Kaffman, 1982; Gray, 1987; Worden, 1996) and the gender of the deceased parent (Arthur & Kemme, 1964; Cohen, et al., 1977; Van Eerdewegh, et al., 1985; Worden, 1996) are identified most consistently as possible factors contributing to the child's adjustment. Children younger than five years (Bowlby, 1980; Elizur & Kaffman, 1982; Elizur & Kaffman, 1983; Rutter, 1966) and those in early adolescence (Fristad, et al., 1993; Gray, 1987; Raphael, 1982; Van Eerdewegh, et al., 1985; Wolfenstein, 1966) appear to be especially vulnerable to poor adjustment after a parent's death. Raveis et al. (1999) found that the younger children in a group ranging in age from 7 to 17 years were more likely to have higher trait anxiety during bereavement than were older children.

Some researchers have found that girls are more vulnerable to adverse consequences after the loss of a parent (Birtchnell, 1972; Black, 1978; Brown, et al., 1977; Van Eederwegh, et al., 1982), whereas others have observed that boys have a more difficult time adjusting (Fristad et al., 1993; Lifshitz, et al., 1977). Still others report no gender differences (Kaffman & Elizur, 1983). These inconsistent findings may be explained in part by the importance of a gender match between the child and the parent who has died. Investigations have documented that such factors as the child's gender and the deceased parent's gender may operate in conjunction with each other to increase the child's risk, as in a gender match between the bereaved child with the dead parent for girls younger than 11 years or for adolescent boys (Rutter, 1966; Van Eederwegh, et al., 1982). However, other studies have found no effects, or only modest effects, of a gender match on bereaved children's adjustment (Worden, 1996).

Factors Associated with the Parent's Death

Studies have consistently found that when the death is sudden and unexpected and there is no opportunity to prepare the child for the death, subsequent adjustment can be more problematic, at least in the period immediately following the death (Furman, 1983; Kaffman, et al., 1987; Kranzler, et al., 1990; Krupnick, 1984; Parkes, 1972/1986; Worden, 1996). Most studies include both anticipated deaths (generally from cancer) and unanticipated deaths (generally from heart attacks, strokes, or accidents) (Weller, et al., 1991; Worden, 1996). Some have included deaths by homicide and suicide, as well (Worden, 1996). One study included only fathers who had died a traumatic death while in the military (Kaffman, et al., 1987). Trauma theory suggests that these experiences might be different for children than anticipated deaths and that the traumatic stress reactions to the death may impede, delay, or distort children's grief process. In a comparison of 26 suicidally bereaved children with 332 non-suicidally bereaved children Cerel, et al. (1999) reported the former were more likely to experience anxiety, anger and shame and have more behavioral and anxiety symptoms throughout the first two years after the death than the non suicidally bereaved children. The admixture of bereaved children with children suffering from a possible traumatic stress reaction complicates the interpretation of these findings.

When the death is from an illness, such as cancer, and can be anticipated, other factors related to the illness and the associated situation have been thought to have an impact on the child's adjustment: for example, the duration of the illness (Black & Urbanowicz, 1987), advance knowledge of the impending death or the degree to which the child was aware that the parent would die (Black & Urbanowicz, 1987; Polack, et al., 1975; Wolfenstein, 1966; Worden,

1996). Changes in the family's lifestyle during the parent's chronic illness, the ill parent's absence or withdrawal from family functions, and household economic changes also have been suggested as factors that may have an adverse effect on a child's functioning before the death period (Christ, et al., 1993; Compas, et al., 1994; Lewis, et al., 1993; Siegel, et al., 1992). These stresses and changes can continue into the period immediately after the death, potentially negating the benefits of knowing in advance about the death.

The series of childhood bereavement studies conducted at Memorial Sloan-Kettering Cancer Center focused on the pre- as well as the postdeath period. Children reported higher levels of depression and anxiety during the parent's terminal illness than did children in a community sample—levels of depression and anxiety that were reduced after the death (Christ, et al., 1991; Siegel, et al., 1992; Siegel, et al., 1996). These findings suggested that the terminal phase of a parent's illness may be a period of greater psychological stress for children than is the period after the actual loss.

What has not been reported is how children are affected by observing a parent's gradually deteriorating condition during the terminal illness, a parent dying at home rather than in a hospital or hospice, or the stress caused when children or adolescents are left in sole charge of an incapacitated parent. Clinical experience indicates that these are not unusual situations. The responses to such situations are described in the clinical chapters of this book.

Studying the responses of children before the parent's death is challenging. Death is a clearly defined point of entry for research assessments, whereas the period before the death is more unpredictable in its duration and definition. Accruing patients during this often tumultuous period is extremely difficult because it requires cooperation and an excellent working alliance with the patients' physicians, who are understandably reluctant to anticipate death by three to six months. It also is extremely difficult for parents and children to commit to a study during this critical and highly stressful time, even when an intervention is promised. Christ and her colleagues (1991) found that highly trained and sensitive staff were required to make the extensive number of telephone contacts needed to arrange each interview. However, an important understanding of the stress caused by a parent's death may be missed if the period before the death is not included in future studies.

Attributes of the Family Environment

The quality of the child-care and the child's relationship with the surviving parent have emerged as among the mediators identified most consistently as affecting the course and outcome of the child's bereavement (Bifulco, et al., 1987; Breier, et al., 1988; Gray, 1987; Harris, et al., 1987; Lutzke, et al., 1997; Parker & Manicavasagar, 1986; Saler & Skolnick, 1992; Sandler et al., 1992; Sood, et al., 1992; Strength, 1991; Tennant, 1988; Worden, 1996). More active coping and less depression are attributes of surviving parents that contribute to the better functioning of children after a parent's death (Kranzler, et al., 1990; Worden, 1996). Other attributes of the family environment that have been most consistently and strongly related to the children's adjustment include parental warmth and family cohesiveness (Bifulco, et al., 1987; Harris, et al., 1987; Lutzke, et al., 1997; Parker & Manicavasagar, 1986; Saler & Skolnick, 1992; Sandler, et al., 1992; Sood, et al., 1992; Strength, 1991; Tennant, 1988).

A recent analysis of data from the Memorial Sloan-Kettering bereavement study found that the child's perception of the surviving parent's level of openness in general communication was highly correlated with the child's level of distress (Raveis, et al., 1999). This finding was consistent with the considerable amount of clinical data indicating that healthy adaptation to parental loss is more likely to occur when family relationships are characterized by a sharing of information and the open expression of feelings about the deceased (Becker & Margolin, 1967; Black, 1978; Cohen, et al., 1977; Furman, 1974; Kaffman, et al., 1987; Rosenthal, 1980; Walsh, 1998; Worden, 1996). This finding also is consistent with findings that family communication patterns about a parent's death and the events leading up to it are potentially important mediating factors in children's adjustment to a parent's death (Black & Urbanowicz, 1987; Furman, 1974; Furman, 1978). When family relationships are characterized by a sharing of information and the open expression of feelings about the deceased, a child's healthy adaptation to parental loss is more likely to occur (Black & Urbanowicz, 1987; Cohen, et al., 1977; Kaffman, et al., 1987). On the other hand, it is conceivable that a child's perception of open communication with the surviving parent may reflect an underlying positive quality in the relationship that leads to better adaptation.

Children also are affected by the stability of family circumstances and the availability of social support for them and surviving parents (Elizur & Kaffman, 1983; Gray, 1987; Kranzler, et al., 1990; Silverman & Worden, 1992b; Tremblay & Israel, 1998). When a parent is dying, children react to inconsistencies in the family's daily environment and to unpredictability in the family's daily routine (Furman, 1974; Osterweis, et al., 1984; Rutter, 1983), as well as to changes that occur after the parent's death: for example, economic changes (changes in income level), a new residence, a new school, and the surviving parent's remarriage (Black & Urbanowicz, 1987; Brown, 1961; Cohen, et al., 1977; Finkelstein, 1988; Hilgard, et al., 1960; Kaffman & Elizur, 1983; Osterweis, et al., 1984; Rutter, 1966; Rutter, 1983; Worden, 1996). Bereaved children in families with high incomes and those in which the parents perceived their finances as adequate were less likely than those from less affluent families to exhibit symptoms of anxiety and to have learning problems (Worden, 1996). These findings emphasize further the possibility of different outcomes among children in different socioeconomic samples.

In summary, the responses of children followed in prospective studies showed that there is indeed a great deal of complexity in responses. First, it is not the parent's death alone but the type of care the children receive before and after the death that is a significant factor in the outcome. Added to that are other factors, ranging from the surviving parent's depression and loss of family income, the child's perception of open communication, and a second marriage that the child cannot accept. Findings from both retrospective and prospective studies suggest that bereaved children's eventual adjustment is affected not only by external factors—the most important of which may well be the surviving parent's ability to support the child's coping efforts—but also the changes that take place within the children over time as they experience and re-experience grief and mature in various domains (Edelman, 1994; Harris, 1991; Silverman, 1986; Silverman, 1989; Worden, 1996).

TRAUMATIC AND ANTICIPATED DEATH AND DIVORCE

In what way might the loss by divorce be similar to or different from the anticipated or unanticipated death of a parent? Child guidance groups in schools often include children who have experienced these types of losses. Their commingling does not seem to reduce the therapeutic efficacy of such interventions. Clearly, these experiences pose difficult challenges. There are similarities as well as important differences in factors that influence the outcomes from these three experiences (Hetherington, 1993; Kalter, 1990; Mishne, 1984; Pynoos, 1992; Sandler, et al., 1988; Saucier & Ambert, 1982; Wallerstein & Blakeslee, 1989; Worden, 1996).

In general, children whose parents divorce are more negatively affected by parental conflict, the loss of economic support, and a feeling of guilt and rejection. Boys appear to be more negatively affected than girls; they are usually raised by their mother after divorce, and that gender mismatch can be difficult. In addition, support from the extended family and the community is often compromised. Children whose parent dies are affected by closed communication patterns in the family, by an inadequate relationship with the surviving parent, or both. However, support from the extended family and the community may be more available to bereaved children than to children of divorce.

Perhaps most important is the predominant stress in each situation and the most prevalent reaction of children facing the situation. In divorce, the unique stress is divided loyalties; in parental death, it is the death; in trauma, it is the shock and the threat. In divorce, the primary affective responses are anger, guilt, and sadness. In parental death, the primary responses are grief and apprehension. And in traumatic death, the unique responses include terror, intrusive reminders, and hyperarousal. All three situations share loss and change as stressors, and grief, anxiety, sadness, loss of self-esteem, and loss of sense of control as shared responses. The similarities and differences in the reactions of children to the three classes of events are summarized in Table 2.1

SUMMARY

The death of a parent is never an easy experience for young children and adolescents—nor is it a benign one. We have learned that even very young children benefit from preparation and timely information that facilitates making a modicum of sense out of a horrible situation. To provide this information, both parents and professionals have had to overcome their own cultural and personal barriers. We now understand that children grieve, although they do so differently from adults, and they need the opportunity to grieve by receiving timely

Table 2.1
Death, Divorce and Traumatic Stress: Differences and Similarities

Experience	Unique major stresses	Unique major responses
Death of parent	Death	Grief, apprehension
Divorce	Divided loyalties	Anger, guilt, sadness
Traumatic death	Shock, threat reminders	Terror, intrusive reminders, hyper-arousal
Shared stresses and responses	SHARED STRESSORS: Loss, change	SHARED RESPONSES: Grief, anxiety, sadness, loss of self esteem, loss of sense of control

and appropriate information; younger children need a model of how to grieve. As we have expanded our knowledge base, we have begun to understand that it is not only death, or even the particular death itself, that may be the most significant factor in the child's ultimate adjustment, but the supports the child receives, most importantly from the surviving parent. More recently, we have found that it is not only the death but also the events that precede the death that may pose the most difficult challenge when death can be anticipated.

It is increasingly apparent that the concept of detachment, ridding oneself of emotional ties to the dead, does not describe the course of mourning for children. We are beginning to understand how a child's relationship with the dead parent changes as the child matures.

Today, there is compelling evidence that the death of a parent is better understood by a cascade model than by a single-event model. But what about the notion that the death of a parent is a traumatic stress? There, too, the evidence suggests that there are significant differences between the predominant outcome in bereavement and the outcome after a traumatic death. That doesn't mean that some factors proven to be relevant in the traumatic stress model are not useful for developing a more comprehensive predeath-postdeath model of bereavement. A bereavement model may benefit from borrowing aspects of the traumatic stress models, such as bereavement reminders and proximal and distal secondary stressors. Although the similarities of bereavement to divorce are greater than those for traumatic death, important differences suggest different areas for intervention and for mediation of stress specific to divorce.

Studies using a stress-and-coping model have identified a variety of risk and protective factors for and strengths and vulnerabilities in bereaved children. Several ways in which these factors interact with each other over time have been suggested. However, the strength of their correlations is generally insufficient to make them useful on an individual case basis (Rutter, 1989).

What is missing in the literature is the kind of detailed description of children's and family's experiences that might clarify for families and clinicians how bereavement is expressed within families over time. We must also look at the responses of all those in the child's environment to see which result in better rather than poorer outcomes. As an administrator, supervisor, and researcher, I was keenly and sometimes painfully aware of our limited knowledge as we implemented our interventions. But these interventions, which involved multiple contacts with families and careful documentation, produced the information base that provided the needed descriptions and analyses.

We also need a clarification of the relationship of development to the way children cope with stressful experiences. The developmentally specific sections in this book, together with the children's clinical outcomes, represent an effort to translate the quantitative research findings into clinically relevant and informative descriptions, which gain in specificity when related to the children's development. The goal is to improve our understanding of the various ways in which these factors interact, the patterns that emerge, and the processes that result in better outcomes. Finally, this study provides descriptions of children's reactions during the terminal stage of a parent's illness, descriptions of how development influences children's coping, and a sample that excludes all unexpected deaths that potentially result in traumatic stress.

3

Stages of the Illness and Child Development

Two dimensions provide a frame for our understanding children's responses and outcomes. One is the family's responses as the illness progresses through its various stages, the second is the sequential, developmental changes that occur as the child ages. These two factors form a structure within which the complex interactions that affect each child's adjustment to this family tragedy can be studied.

PSYCHOSOCIAL STAGES OF CANCER

The anxiety experienced during the course of a cancer illness waxes and wanes. Points of severe stress are predictable and define the different stages. Understanding these stages helps to clarify the family's reactions and to plan psychosocial interventions. Each stage requires specific, adaptive tasks that challenge both patient and family (Christ, et al., 1991).

Initial Psychosocial Stages of Cancer

The initial stages of cancer include the diagnosis, treatment, termination of treatment, normalization, survivorship, recurrence, and experimental treatment. For many, survivorship or 'cure' is the final stage they will experience. For others, the recurrence, metastasis, or the development of a second cancer, sometimes related to the treatment of the first cancer, means a changed prognosis. Now, with newer treatments, even that course can lead to survivorship. For this book, patients were invited to participate only when their illness progressed beyond these initial stages of cancer into the terminal stage of their disease.

Diagnosis

For young adults, a cancer diagnosis constitutes a powerful and abrupt confrontation with mortality. While coping with the specter of an untimely death and a numbing sense of disbelief, patients find that they must give up the comforting aspects of psychological denial because they must make important treatment decisions.

Treatment

The treatment for cancer in young patients is intensive and aggressive because the disease tends to be aggressive, and the young person's general good health permits more aggressive treatment. The side effects are commensurate with intensive treatment, and include severe nausea and vomiting, fatigue, hair loss, weight loss, precipitous drops in blood counts, and toxicity from the drugs that can be life threatening. Families with young children are thrown into chaos as the patient's treatment schedule takes priority and the healthy spouse struggles to adjust to the new roles and functions required by the presence of an ill spouse.

Survivorship

With advanced medical treatments, increasing numbers of cancer patients can anticipate remission, cure, or at least longer control of their disease. However, even survivorship extracts a price: social and psychological rehabilitation remain among the most difficult issues for cancer survivors (Christ, 1987; Gotay, 1987; Koocher, 1983; Kornblith, 1998; Mellette & Franco, 1987; Siegel & Christ, 1995; Tebbi & Mallon, 1987). The powerful, life-threatening impact of cancer diagnosis and treatment makes returning to former roles and responsibilities difficult. The idea that cancer survivors can resume their lives unchanged after successful treatment is not consistent with the experience of the majority of survivors (Christ, et al., 1995). Instead, the illness often creates a major discontinuity in their lives, culminating in lasting changes in how they perceive themselves and their future (Cella, et al., 1987; Fobair, et al., 1986).

Recurrence and Metastasis

If the patient's expected life span is suddenly cut short by a recurrence or metastasis, the family's emotional reactions can be as severe as those experienced when a patient progresses steadily to the terminal stage after the initial diagnosis (Worden, 1991). Most patients in either situation experience disappointment, anger, and, especially troublesome, guilt: "If I had taken better care of myself," they wonder, "could I have prevented the cancer from progressing?" They struggle with feelings of bitter disappointment, helplessness, hopelessness, and grief, but taking the next steps of deciding on new treatments and planning for their family's future well-being means that they must master these feelings quickly. At this point, however, treatments are likely to be more aggressive and intensive and to have more potential for severe side effects.

Experimental Protocols

When proven treatments are ineffective, patients must explore experimental treatment options, the efficacy and potential side effects of which are far less predictable than conventional treatments. Often, the patient, family, and medical staff disagree about what course to pursue. Physicians may also disagree with each other in the absence of standardized approaches. Some patients described in this study became frantic about prolonging their lives at this stage and were impatient with the extreme care and slower pace at which experimental protocols are implemented. Some began searching for alternative, nonscientifically based therapies; a few combined alternative or complementary therapies with experimental treatments.

End Stages of Cancer

This study follows patients and their families through the three late stages of cancer: the terminal stage, the death, and the bereavement and reconstitution stage. Because these stages have the greatest impact on the patient's spouse and children (Christ, et al., 1994; Siegel, et al., 1996), knowledge about them clarifies the context of some of the families' reactions.

Terminal Disease

The terminal stage of cancer is a time of high psychological stress. Our experience indicated that the impact on families of the terminal phase of cancer was generally more dramatic and stressful than the period after the death. It is filled with immobilizing uncertainty, intense fear of sudden acute physical symptoms, chaotic schedules and unpredictable separations, overwhelming practical and sometimes physical demands, and increasing, unrelenting dread of the moment when the actual death occurs. As the patient's condition deteriorates, more symptoms appear. When successive treatments prove to be ineffective, all members of the family struggle to function in an intense emotional climate. It was this clinical experience that guided our research to begin studying children and their families before the death occurred. The high levels of depression and anxiety observed in children during the terminal phase is not surprising, given this scenario (Siegel, et al., 1992; Siegel, et al., 1996).

Death

Telling children that their parent has died and contemplating how they can participate in the funeral and burial rites evokes great apprehension in many parents. Although no amount of preparation can prevent their pain and shock, surviving parents can limit the destructiveness of an acute traumatic reaction that may complicate the necessary and inevitably painful mourning process by having ongoing, thoughtful dialogues with the children about events during the terminal phase as they occur. The variations in this process for children of different ages will be described in subsequent chapters. I, as well as others (Silverman & Worden, 1992a; Silverman & Worden, 1992b; Sood, et al., 1992), found that the funeral and burial rites provide children with great solace and support if they are prepared in advance and able to participate.

Bereavement and Family Reconstitution

After the patient's death, the survivors enter into a period of reconstitution, which includes both bereavement and the reorganization of family life without the patient. When these tasks are well underway, the family establishes a new homeostasis, and the children feel confident about the surviving parent's ability to take care of them emotionally and physically. For adolescents, however, conflicts regarding autonomy, responsibility, and separation can become pronounced, as we shall see in later chapters.

CONTRIBUTION OF DEVELOPMENT

Background

Although a developmental stage paradigm is the most familiar, not all scholars agree that development proceeds by invariant *qualitative* or stage shifts that provide the child new options in the new stage. Organismic models (Lewis, 1997) such as those of the psychoanalytic schools and the cognitive developmental schools all find utility in thinking of development as invariantly progressing through various stages. In marked contrast are the sociobehaviorist (Bandura, 1989; Sears, et al., 1957) and contextual models (Lewis, 1997) that represent schools of thought that find no evidence for qualitative shifts in development but, rather, emphasize an ongoing quantitative increment in development. Whereas the theorists who accept stages think of an underlying biological-genetic change that allows a qualitative shift into a new stage of development (Luria & Vygotsky, 1976), the sociobehaviorist theorists feel that all developmental changes are adequately explained by imitation, modeling, cultural requirements, and observational *bi-directional* interactions. They argue that the rules of development are not really different in the child, the adolescent, or the adult (Sears, 1951; Sears, et al., 1957). All of these schools of thought offer two perspectives. One is an interest in the driving force that underlies the changes over time, the other is the data, the observations, and the concepts that provide the material that gives rise to these theories.

My approach to development was more pragmatic: I searched for orientations that allowed a clearer depiction of similarities within but also differences between age groups. I was also interested in describing the rich and changing ecological system that seemed to play such an important part in influencing how children coped with their experiences (Bronfenbrenner, 1989). The methodology used to determine which schools of development were most relevant to this sample is reviewed in Chapter 4. Those found most relevant are briefly reviewed here.

Cognitive Development

I can not overstate just how valuable information about the illness, the treatment, and its course was to all 157 children and adolescents whose experiences are chronicled in this book. The age of the child, or, more precisely, the cognitive developmental attributes of the child, provides essential information about how to inform a child because it provides information about **how** the child thinks and processes information. One approach to understanding the progression of cognitive development, of how children's thinking changes over time, is that provided by Piaget and his group (Flavell, 1963; Flavell, 1977; Ginsburg & Opper, 1979; Inhelder & Piaget, 1958; Piaget, 1952). They described four sequential stages through which thinking matures. These include the **sensori-motor,** the **pre-operational,** the **concrete operational,** and the **formal operational** stages of development. The ages given here to span Piagetian stages of cognitive development are traditional (Flavell, 1963), and not applicable to most samples of children. The population Piaget used in his experiments were children of academicians enrolled in his school. Piaget was interested in discovering invariant sequences, not in determining ages that spanned stages (Ginsberg and Opper, 1979).

Sensori-Motor Stage

The **sensori-motor** stage of development, spanning birth to age 18 to 24 months, is not relevant to our sample. However, the contrast to the next, the **pre-operational,** stage is useful. By 18 months, the **sensori-motor** child can crawl, walk, smile, bond, be lovable, even solve problems using trial and error tactics as long as all the pieces necessary for the solution of the problem are within the visual field. What the infant lacks is the ability, perhaps the wiring to the potential memory bank, to know, or more accurately, to remember, that what is not immediately visible continues to exist. The development of this type of memory is one of the landmarks that distinguishes the **sensori-motor** from the **pre-operational** child. Another is the ability to symbolize. We see the fruits of this capacity in the development of (symbolic) language, in the ability to engage in imaginative (symbolic) play, and in the ability to imitate later, that is, after the person being imitated is gone (deferred imitation).

Pre-Operational Stage

This stage spans ages 2 to 7. The preschool and most of the early school children described in this book fall within the **pre-operational** stage of development. **Pre-operational** thinking strategies to understand the illness, its course, and the symptoms evidenced by the parent are always used by 3 to 5 year olds, almost always used by 6 to 8 year olds and almost never used by 9 to 11 year olds. Importantly, **pre-operational** thinking involves magical-animistic-correlational thinking. A child at the pre-operational stage "knows" that thoughts cause events ("I don't like to talk about what can happen to Dad because if I do it will happen). The child also "knows" that if two events are temporally related, they are causally related ("I spilled milk, Dad slipped and broke his leg, then he got cancer, so I caused his cancer"). What creates more problems for the parent is that the child's thinking is not *reversible*, that is, the child can not backtrack. When such a child confronts a mistake, as when a parent corrects a misremembered sequence, the child can not backtrack to where she first started. This is part of the reason logical explanations, even clear and simple ones, may not correct a mistaken idea. Instead, a new sequence may need to be provided so the child can then memorize (rather than understand) the correct information. As we saw with Rachel in Chapter 1, two other attributes are helpful in understanding **pre-operational** thinking: concretization and simile. Rachel's mother went through the burial sequence using dolls to concretize the burial of her father for 3-year-old Rachel. When a child has experienced the death of a pet or of a grandparent, likening the death of the parent with the other deaths can be helpful.

Concrete Operational Stage

This stage spans 8 to 13 years of age. Around seven or eight major new **concrete operational** thinking tools start to become available to the child. These include the ability to classify, to understand relations, to reverse, and gradually to conserve. The ability to classify means that with appropriate instruction the child can understand that not all tumors are cancer. Relations implies the ability to organize objects using some criterion, such as organizing sticks from largest to smallest, and inserting others into a pre-existing sequence. Unfortunately, the more abstract the concept, the less the **concrete operational** child is able to apply the principle of relations. This is one reason why it is difficult to understand why one parent with a disease dies and another with the same disease does not. The reasons, such as greater progression, involvement of critical brain centers, etc., are all perfectly true, but too abstract. The other reason for this difficulty is emotional—such factual explanations do not deal with the rage and pain of the unfairness of having lost a parent. The ability to reverse is particularly significant. When discussing a child's erroneous conclusion (e.g., I caused Dad's cancer), the ability to reverse gradually allows the child to reexamine the steps that led to the original mistaken conclusion (Dad slipped on my spilled milk), and to introduce new evidence (he slipped months *after* he got cancer) and change the original conclusion. Asking the **concrete operational** child to believe what she is told on the strength of the adult's power relationship is generally less effective. Thus the approach in correcting an erroneous conclusion with a **concrete operational** child may be quite the opposite from one helpful to the pre-operational child. With the **concrete operational** child, a much more rational, exploratory, even Socratic approach, is most helpful. With the **pre-operational** child, the rational, exploratory approach is generally confusing.

Formal Operational Stage

This stage spans age 13 to adulthood. During adolescence, the child gradually develops **formal operational** thinking abilities. Of the various attributes of this major shift, two, the ability to relate various abstract ideas or concepts to each other and the ability to conceptualize all attributes of a problem or situation at the same time, are particularly relevant. These attributes mean the adolescent is able to understand the illness and its progression in a much more profound way. A 16-year-old girl wrote several school reports the year after her mother died: the first was on Cancer and its Treatment, the second on Euthanasia, the third on Genetics and Cancer. These were accurate, factual reports. She stated she felt better after writing them because she understood what happened to her mother so much better. Through these reports she began to develop a more comprehensive understanding of her mother's illness—she began to understand genetics as one of the causes of cancer, the many different treatments for the many different types of cancer, and the role of assisted suicide as one way of thinking about dealing with unbearable pain. The **formal operational** capacity is evident in the way she was able to deal with rather abstract topics, but also in how she was able to relate these abstract topics to each other. What also emerges between the ages of 15 to 18 is a greater ability to empathize with others, to get beyond the egocentric or self-referential viewpoint of the younger adolescent. Finally, a greater facility with hypothetico-deductive reasoning is also present. Familiarity with a subject, in part independent of the stage of cognitive development, also affects the ability to understand. This is why the 16-year-old girl who had gained a significant familiarity with the subject of her mother's cancer *and* was **formal operational** in her thinking was prepared to speak with her mother's oncologist, and gained from that discussion.

Emotional Development

About a century ago, Sigmund Freud (Freud, 1905) described the sequences of psychosexual development that to this day remain the foundation of psychoanalytic developmental stages: oral, anal, phallic (genital, oedipal) (ages ~ 3–5), latency (ages ~ 6–12), and adolescence (puberty to early adulthood). Erik Erikson, who as a teacher taught the children of many of the original group of psychoanalysts in Vienna, became interested in and then graduated as a psychoanalyst in 1933. He contributed to the shift from the sexual to the psychosexual context of development and to the ontogenesis of identity. He also emphasized that each stage represents a developmental crisis or turning point, "a crucial period of increased vulnerability and heightened potential" (Erikson, 1968, p. 96). The three polarities that are most germane to the age group of the children in this study include initiative versus guilt during the oedipal stage (age 3–6), industry versus inferiority during latency (age 6–12), and identity versus role confusion during adolescence (age 13–19) (Erikson, 1963). The contributions of another psychoanalyst, Peter Blos, were especially helpful in clarifying many of the responses of the adolescents to the stresses of this experience (Blos, 1962). The name—the second individuation–separation stage of development—highlights the gradual shifts in the relationship of the child to the internalized object—the internal representation of the parent. Three stages of adolescent development (early, middle, and late adolescence) are particularly germane to our understanding of the adolescent's reactions. During **early adolescence** (puberty), the developmental task is the slow severance of emotional ties with the family. In addition, same gender friendships now take on a different meaning. The 'chum' of latency, the friend with whom one can do things, now becomes the friend one admires and loves. During **mid adolescence** (adolescence proper) the emotional growth of the youngsters continues, with the emphasis on emotional separation from parents and a deeper emotional engagement with peers, but now also of the opposite sex.

A final contribution to our understanding of emotional development comes from the relational perspective contributed to by Carol Gilligan (Gilligan, 1979; Gilligan, 1982) and members of the Stone Center (Jordan, et al., 1991). Jordan (1991) emphasized that rather than thinking of development as a move toward autonomy, separation, and independence, as is more relevant with boys, with girls the more accurate model is growth through and toward relationship. A girl's self-esteem or self-worth "is based on feelings that she is a part of relationships and is taking care of these relationships" (p 16), and her feeling of competence or effectiveness arises out of emotional connections. Especially during adolescence, the differences between boys and girls highlight the difference in the centrality of relationships.

Ecological Perspective of Development

Although the internal, cognitive and the psychological perspectives of development are helpful in understanding children's reactions to the illness and death of a parent, the reciprocal interactions with the external world are also crucial in understanding the more complex interactions. An example of this more complex perspective is Urie Bronfenbrenner's ecological model of human development (Bronfenbrenner, 1989; Bronfenbrenner, 1993). He emphasized that the "characteristics of the person at a given time in his or her life span are a joint function of the characteristics of the person and of the environment over the course of that person's life up to that time" (Bronfenbrenner, 1989: p. 190.). The child's ecological systems expand as the child matures. This is a concept captured by the four ecological systems that span the world of the child. The most intimate is the microsystem (e.g., family microsystem of child–home–parent). The next are the mesosystems that comprise the interaction of pertinent microsystems (e.g., interaction of family, school, friends, sports team). As the child matures, the next level, the exosystem, has increasing relevance. Examples of relevant exosystems are the board of education, local transportation system, policies of the local government, parent's employer(s). Finally, the most global macrosystem includes the national mass media, country of origin, cultural and subcultural characteristics. Within this system, the transitions in the ecological system, such as modifications of the mesosystem as the microsystem is changed and outgrown generally involve changes in role definitions. This perspective allows research "on differentiating the transition to see whether and what family processes may actually be responsible for the outcome" (Muuss, 1996, p. 333). Its emphasis on the processes, changes, and mutual interactions between the child and the environment enhances the utility of this ecological model in the refinement of interventions.

Place of Discontinuity in Development

The great importance of subsequent life events in obviating early adverse experiences has challenged the more "simplistic concepts of immutable events (which) need to be put aside" (Rutter, 1989, p 24). People change a good deal, and the long-term effects of early adversities are greatly influenced by subsequent life experiences (Clarke & Clarke, 1984). A recent contribution to this view is made by Michael Lewis, who challenged the very substance of organismic (psychoanalytic, cognitive) developmental theories by invoking the importance of discontinuity in a study that included an 18-year follow-up of a group of infants (Lewis, 1997). The study was based on John Bowlby's model of attachment (Bowlby, 1980), which postulates that "a person's model of her relationship with her mother determines her future social life" (Lewis, 1997, p 61). In this study, Lewis measured the quality of mother–child attachments at age one. In his follow-up at age 18, Lewis found that neither the quality of the young adults' attachment nor their mental health status bore any relation to the quality of the attachment at age one. *"If attachment classification, a much-reported impor-*

tant characteristic of early childhood adjustment, bore no relation to young adult behavior, serious doubt is cast on the likelihood of finding data for the belief that earlier events affect later ones" (Lewis, 1997, p. 62, italics in original).

The concept of discontinuity in development takes on important prognostic meaning in thinking about the long-term effects of the death of a parent during childhood. It may help parents weigh the relative importance of this tragic event in the life of their child, and of their own contribution in mitigating the adverse effects by providing a warm, nurturing support to their children.

Summary

These two large frames—the stages of the parent's illness and the changes in the child's development—allow for greater clarity in the description of the *variation* in children's reactions and responses within similar developmental attributes and illness stage frames, and *between group comparisons* with different stages of the illness and with children having earlier or more advanced developmental attributes. As will become clear throughout this book, not even the impact of a parent's death is sufficient to understand differences in the outcome as evaluated 8 to 14 months after the death. The rich interplay of the significant actors in the microsystem, the mesosystem, and the exosystem play a major role in affecting this outcome. Yet it is the details of the interaction with the child at different stages of development and, in turn, the effect of the child on the significant others that begin to refine and distinguish the most relevant information for interventions.

4

❧

Study Sample, Intervention, Bereavement Model, Methodology

SAMPLE

The 88 families described in this book included 157 children who were 3 to 17 years old when one of their parents died from cancer. Fifty-one fathers and 37 mothers received treatment for advanced cancer at Memorial Sloan-Kettering Cancer Center. All but one of these families participated in a psychoeducational intervention program that was intended to help families cope with the death of one parent. This intervention was also designed to generate data that would inform through quantitative and qualitative analyses. This book presents the findings from the qualitative analyses.

Families

Recruitment of the Sample

Staff social workers from the Memorial Sloan Kettering Cancer Center (MSKCC) identified cancer patients who were terminally ill and had one or more 7- to 16-year-old children. They discussed their possible eligibility for the study with the oncologists, who in turn referred those patients who had a 3- to 6-month expected survival time. Participation in this study was limited to families in which the well parent was proficient in English, lived within two hours travel time of the hospital, had at least one child age 7 to 16 years of age who had no history of a major psychiatric disturbance. The ill parent, who was contacted first, agreed to the participation, the well parent signed a written informed consent form, and the children also gave their assent. The 3- to 6-year-old children in our sample, except for Rachel Klein (Chapter 1), were all siblings of the 7- to 16-year-old children. About half the parents who were eligible agreed to participate in this study, and were randomly assigned to participate in the Parent Guidance Intervention (80%) or to a supportive-reflective intervention. The demographic characteristics of the sample did not differ from the demographic characteristics of MSKCC patients, except that there were more surviving fathers than would be expected in a sample of this age. The young, terminally ill mothers welcomed the opportunity for their husbands to obtain help in the eventual care of their children.

Parents' Demographic Characteristics

The mother was the surviving parent in 58 percent of the 88 families, the father in 42 percent. These were young people—33 percent of all mothers and 24 percent of all fathers were 40 or younger, while only 4 percent of mothers and 14 percent of fathers were 50 or over when they started the intervention. The majority of families were Catholic, 71 percent had some college education, 80 percent were white, and the families' median annual income when recruited from 1988 to 1994 was $53,000. This was mainly a middle-class population able to seek treatment outside their immediate community. They had characteristics not unlike patients treated at other cancer centers. These characteristics are summarize in Table 4.1

Single-parent families were not recruited for this study because the stresses and responses of children who lose their only parent are quite different from those faced by children who have a surviving parent. For the same reason, families in which a parent died from AIDS or from unexpected causes such as homicide, suicide, or accident were not recruited.

Children's Demographic Characteristics

Of the 157 children, 79 were girls and 78 boys. There were 19 in the preschool group, and 32 to 38 in each of the four older age groups.

INTERVENTION: DATA COLLECTION

Intervention Design

A psychoeducational intervention was developed to facilitate the adjustment of children to the terminal illness and subsequent death of a parent, emphasizing a parent guidance approach. More specific details about this intervention have been published (Christ et al., 1991, Siegel et al., 1990). A second goal of the project was to expand our knowledge of children's and families' responses, interactions, and needs during and after the parent's terminal illness.

After the family was informed about the intervention, agreed to participate, and signed the consent forms, two psychologists from the evaluation team scheduled a meeting with the family to administer a battery of tests and conduct an interview with each child and well parent. (This procedure was repeated 8 and 14 months after the death of the ill parent.) After the psychological assessment was completed, the family was assigned to one of a group of social workers who, along with their supervisors, made up the clinical team. One social work interviewer made an appointment shortly after the completion of the initial evaluation. If the child had checked off one of the 'thinking about self harm' questions in the psychologist's evaluation and the interventionist, in collaboration with the parent, assessed this to be a possible problem, an appointment

Table 4.1
Demographic Characteristics of Parents

	Mothers	Fathers
AGE		
>40	33%	24%
40–49	63%	63%
50+	4%	14%
RELIGION		
Catholic	52%	45%
Protestant	22%	21%
Jewish	18%	20%
Other	8%	14%
EDUCATION		
<HS	6%	5%
HS Graduation	23%	23%
College	56%	48%
Posthgrad	15%	24%
MEDIAN FAMILY INCOME: $53,000		
RACE		
White	80%	
Hispanic	7%	
Black	7%	
Mixed	5%	
Asian	1%	

with a child psychiatrist for an evaluation was offered as a part of the intervention program.

A typical intervention spanned about 14 months and included six or more 60- to 90-minute interviews during the terminal stage of the illness and six or more after the death. The sequence of interviews, most of which were carried out in the family home, included an initial interview with the well parent, but could include the patient if so desired. A separate interview was then done with each child. This was followed by an informing interview with the parent(s) in which the parent(s) was given an assessment of the children's adaptation to the crisis. Possible ways of handling emerging problems were also discussed. A family interview that included the well parent and all of the children in that

Table 4.2
Children and Adolescents in This Sample

AGE			
3–5:	11 girls	7 boys	18 children
6–8:	16 girls	16 boys	32
9–11:	18 girls	19 boys	37
12–14:	21 girls	17 boys	38
15–17:	13 girls	19 boys	32
TOTALS	79 girls	78 boys	157 children

family was then done. This was followed by two or more bi-weekly to monthly interviews. A similar schedule of interviews was followed starting 2 to 4 weeks after the death of the parent. When appropriate and requested, additional child and/or family interviews were scheduled. After the final interview, the social worker initiated bi-monthly to monthly telephone contacts with the surviving parent up to the time of the final psychological assessment (about 14 months after the death of the parent). If significant family crises emerged during the psychologist's final assessment, additional telephone contacts were initiated, and, if necessary, individual or family sessions were offered.

Interviewer training and supervision were an integral part of the project. Each of the six social workers who were part of the intervention team had at least five years' post masters experience working in a medical or mental health setting. Each social worker received extensive written and verbal descriptions about the goals of the intervention, her role in meeting these goals, the types of material that would be elicited from children and parents, and the type and quality of notes that would be kept after each scheduled and unscheduled contact. Ongoing training was provided through weekly individual and group supervisory meetings. I coordinated and supervised the clinical program.

Data Collection

When permitted, all interviews were audiotaped. The interviewer also filled out a lengthy 10- to 12-page semi-structured form following each interview. Different forms were developed for each predeath and postdeath interview that reflected the intent of that interview. These notes were used to aid in the supervisory process, but were also intended to facilitate a qualitative analysis. Detailed written notes were also kept of all telephone contacts with or about the family.

The author transcribed all interviews of 31 of the 88 families and compared the written records with the transcribed material. The families with the largest number of audiotaped sessions were selected. Additional family tapes were transcribed to insure the presence of families from each of the six interviewers.

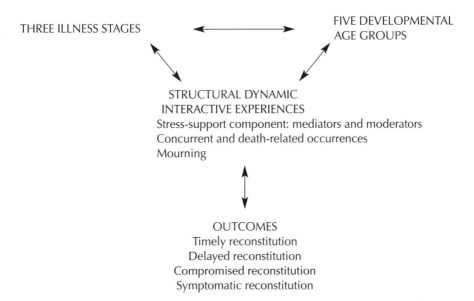

THREE ILLNESS STAGES

FIVE DEVELOPMENTAL
AGE GROUPS

STRUCTURAL DYNAMIC
INTERACTIVE EXPERIENCES
Stress-support component: mediators and moderators
Concurrent and death-related occurrences
Mourning

OUTCOMES
Timely reconstitution
Delayed reconstitution
Compromised reconstitution
Symptomatic reconstitution

Figure 4.1.   Bereavement-Outcome Model

Audiotapes for transcription were also selected to represent each of the five age groups described below.

The transcribed interviews, the interviewer summaries, and all telephone contacts were prepared for entry into the Ethnograph program for computer-assisted analysis (Seidel, et al., 1988). To facilitate retrieval of information, a problem in any very large data base (Huberman & Miles, 1998), a separate file was created for each family. For each family file, data were organized under one of four major headings: background, terminal illness, death, and reconstitution. The title of each entry included the date of the contact, the type of entry, and the name of each participant.

BEREAVEMENT OUTCOME MODEL

A bereavement outcome model emerged from the analyses of the data. It is presented here to facilitate the description of the data analysis. An outline of the four-dimensional bereavement outcome model is summarized in Figure 4.1.

Illness Dimension: Terminal Illness, Death, Reconstitution

The bereavement intervention was planned to start during the terminal illness. This decision was based on clinical experience. We found that the family members' responses differed substantially during the terminal stage of the illness from responses following the death. This clinical experience was further supported by the quantitative analyses of depression and anxiety—measures which showed that children were more anxious and depressed during the predeath period than at the end of the reconstitution stage (Siegel et al., 1996; Siegel et al., 1992).

Development Dimension: Five Developmental Age Groups

The 157 children in this sample were separated into five age groups: 3–5, 6–8, 9–11, 12–14, and 15–17 years of age. These ages were not chosen at random. A board certified child-adolescent psychiatrist and I grouped the children based on their cognitive, emotional, and social-ecological developmental characteristics as they emerged from the data. Several attempts to maximize within-group developmental similarities yielded the five age groups as the best compromise. To insure consistency, the age assigned each child was the age they attained when the parent died. Finally, as parents and educators know so well, there are differences in the maturational rates of children, some based on gender, some on socio demographic characteristics, others on innate capacities, to name only three. No effort was made to correct for slower or faster developers. Despite these limitations, the age spans were surprisingly helpful in summarizing common developmental characteristics and understanding development-specific differences in the children among these five age groups. The predominant defining characteristics that emerged for each of the age groups are summarized here and further expanded in each of the chapters subtitled "Themes."

Age 3 to 5

Cognitively, these children evidenced earlier pre-operational characteristics: They did not accept the finality of their parent's death for several weeks or months. Emotionally, separations from the primary care taker aroused separation-anxiety responses. Their social-ecological involvement was almost exclusively the family microsystem (Bronfenbrenner, 1989).

Age 6 to 8

Cognitively, these children evidenced primarily late pre-operational capacities, drawing wrong, often self-accusatory, inferences about the cause of the illness and death. They immediately understood the finality of the parent's death. Emotionally, they were more tolerant of separations, especially when prepared with explanations. The social-ecological involvement that affected their development also began to include the school. Parent-school contacts and parent invitation of peers to the death-related family rituals are examples of an important mesosystem for young children (Bronfenbrenner, 1989).

Age 9 to 11

Cognitively, these children had solid concrete operational cognitive capacities. They aggressively pursued detailed information about the illness and death that provided some sense of control and mastery. Emotionally, they could not tolerate grief, and escaped to the school, peer, and sports microsystems to avoid it. The support and acknowledgment from both parents and other adults (especially teachers) was welcomed and enhanced their self-esteem. Their development was now affected by the ecology of home, school, peers, and sports. Surviving mothers obtained help from the children's peer's fathers in sports, and fathers encouraged their daughter's contacts with peer's mothers to enhance the children's reconstitution.

Age 12 to 14

Cognitively, these early adolescents were in transition between late concrete and early formal operational capacities. Emotionally, most characteristic were pubertal-early adolescent ambivalent emotional dependence-independence manifestations. They evidenced emotional withdrawal from parents. They avoided information about the illness and their own and others' grief reactions. There was a gradual shift in the importance of their social-ecological involvement, with activities outside the home taking on more importance.

Age 15 to 17

Cognitively, these mid-adolescents evidenced fairly consistent formal operational capacities, showing more sophisticated understanding of past-present-future implications of the parent's illness. Their emotional dependence-independence was less ambivalent than that of the 12 to 14-year-olds. They sought solace and support from peers more consistently. They had a more adult-like grief. Their social-ecological horizon evinced greater understanding of and involvement with the larger community and was syntonic with their more integrated formal operational cognitive capacities.

Reviewing the transcripts of the children and their families supported the idea that the age-related cognitive, emotional, and social development, as well as the impact of their expanding ecological world was indeed important in understanding the children's responses to the illness and death. The surviving parents' ability to understand and respond to children at different developmental stages was also important. For example, many fathers had difficulty understanding their younger children's thinking processes, while many mothers had difficulty understanding mid-adolescent boys' need for emotional distance and independence.

Structural-Dynamic-Interactive Dimension

This complex dimension encompasses the various pre-existing, death-related and unrelated dynamic (stressful and stress reducing) interactions that take place between the children, their family, and the larger ecological system they live in, the quality of the grief experience, and the pre-existing attributes in the child and parent that may account for better or more compromised outcomes. For ease of description, three components will be described separately.

Stress-Support Dynamic Component

This component includes positive and negative mediating and moderating variables. In the generic stress process model, a careful definition of the types of protective and risk factors and processes is presented (Roosa, et al., 1997). These definitions are more specific than intrinsic and extrinsic factors, terms frequently used in the literature. Mediators include both risk reducers and risk enhancers, while moderators are similarly dichotomized into protective and vulnerability factors. These distinctions were helpful in improving the precision of the analyses.

Moderators are variables that impact with stressors to influence adaptation (Rutter, 1990). Moderators are not influenced by the occurrence of the stressor. Examples of moderators that enhanced a positive outcome included adequate family income and good intellectual ability in the child. Examples of moderators that detracted included poverty, recent immigration, and a temperamentally difficult child (Thomas & Chess, 1977).

Mediators, on the other hand, are those risk enhancers or reducers that *are* affected by the major stressor. One risk reducing mediator we found to be very important was the presence of positive parenting behaviors such as warmth, provision of timely information, allowing the adolescent sufficient peer time, and consistent appropriate discipline. In the chapters that follow there are a number of examples in which the surviving parent rose to the occasion and provided excellent mediation. An example of a negative or risk enhancing mediator was the presence of a pathological grief response or an increase in alcoholism in the surviving parent following the death of the spouse.

Concurrent and Death-Related Occurrences

This second component of the structural-dynamic-interactive dimension relates to the source of factors that also affect the outcome. Some sources were directly related to the illness and death experience, some, like help from neighbors or teachers, followed from this family tragedy, while others, like the death of a friend or another family member, were significant co-occurring stressors, but were not directly related to the illness or death of the parent.

The dynamic interrelationship of the structural-dynamic-interactive dimension clarified a great deal of the difference in the outcome of the children when last seen. A few, like the child's relationship with the surviving parent, the parent's 'parenting' ability, the child's temperament, the relative openness of communication within the family, especially about the illness, the stage of development of the child, and the stage of the illness were important across all age groups, and closely paralleled the findings from quantitative studies reviewed in Chapter 2.

Mourning

Listing mourning as a third component of the structural-dynamic-interactive dimension attends to the interactive processes that affect the child's grief experiences. As with the other two components, the model draws attention to the interaction with illness stage and age group. Mourning is defined as the (successful and unsuccessful) adaptive processes children experience following the death of a parent (Freud, 1958; Furman, 1974; Osterweis, et al., 1984; Worden, 1996).

Outcome Dimension

I was interested in identifying factors that were associated with timely and more compromised reconstitution in the children when last seen 8 to 14 months after the death of the parent. A board certified child psychiatrist and I assessed the full record of each child's reconstitution and made a judgment about the child's success in returning to a preterminal illness level when last seen. Our assessment was based on five emotional and behavioral domains: psychological state and behavior (e.g., mourning, self-esteem, internalizing and externalizing symptoms), family relationships (e.g., with parent, patient, siblings grandparents, care takers), school competence (e.g., grades) and behavior (e.g., relation to teacher and classmates), after-school activities (e.g., sports), and peer relationships. The child was assessed by comparing their functioning before the terminal illness (as noted during the initial evaluations that were done by the clinicians and the history supplied by the parents) with their reported functioning at the end of our contact.

Four outcome categories emerged: Timely reconstitution, delayed reconstitution, compromised reconstitution, and symptomatic reconstitution. Initially, we defined three child attributes that characterized different outcomes: Timely reconstitution (improved or improving reconstitution in all five emotional-behavioral domains), compromised reconstitution (ongoing problems in at least one of the five domains that were *not* improving), and symptomatic reconstitution (emergence of new behaviors or interactions after the death of the parent that were consonant with a DSM IV diagnosis). A complete re-review of the family files clarified that within the timely reconstitution, the structural-dynamic-interactive attributes that were linked with the improved (new timely reconstitution category) and the improving (new delayed reconstitution category) were different.

Timely reconstitution reflected children who had returned to their previously described level of functioning in all five emotional and behavioral domains. *Delayed reconstitution* was assigned to children who had returned to their previous level of functioning in all but one domain, and in that domain showed evidence of improvement. *Compromised reconstitution* reflected children whose functioning had not recovered in one or more domains and who showed no evidence of improvement in the domain(s) in which they were experiencing difficulty. *Symptomatic reconstitution* reflected children who developed new psychopathological symptoms following the death of the parent that had not previously been in evidence.

Overall, 84 children (37 girls and 47 boys) were judged to have a timely reconstitution; 32 (15 girls and 17 boys) a delayed reconstitution; 13 (12 girls and

1 boy) a compromised reconstitution; and 10 (4 girls and 6 boys) a symptomatic reconstitution. Since a terminal interview was not done with the preschool children, these 18 (11 girls and 7 boys) were not assigned an outcome rating.

My intent in defining these outcome categories was to determine whether there were interactive factors from the three dimensions listed above (illness, development, and structural-dynamic-interactive dimension) that might be associated with different outcomes. A summary of the factors that were associated with each outcome in each of the four age groups is provided in the subsequent chapters of this book. A summary of the outcomes is presented in Table 4.3. Although this dimension emphasizes the outcome when the child was last seen, Figure 4.1 shows a two-way interaction between the outcome and the other three dimensions. This is to draw attention to the reality that the outcome is a gradually emerging process, and that the child's evolving outcome strongly interacts with the other three dimensions.

METHODS

Narrative Selection Strategies

For each of the five age groups, two detailed family narratives appear in chapters separate from the response-variation analyses. Where the detailed family narratives provide a more comprehensive picture of the ecological system of which the child is a part, the thematic analyses provide a broader description of the way a number of children deal with an aspect important at that age.

Ten family stories were selected for elaboration, two from each of the five age groups. The transcription and analysis of each narrative required extensive

Table 4.3
Child Outcome by Gender of Child and Gender of Surviving Parent

		Surviving mothers (N = 51)	Surviving fathers (N = 37)
Daughters	Timely reconstitution	21	16
N = 68	Delayed reconstitution	7	8
	Compromised reconstitution	4	8
	Symptomatic reconstitution	3	1
Sons	Timely reconstitution	34	13
N = 71	Delayed reconstitution	8	9
	Compromised reconstitution	0	1
	Symptomatic reconstitution	2	4

condensation (Riessman, 1993) and great care was taken to remove details that could lead to family recognition. Family selection based on the parent's and child's gender was done first. All but the youngest age group had one mother and one father survivor and at least one boy and one girl in that age group. I also selected families that would include father-son, father-daughter, mother-son and mother-daughter pairs. In the preschool group, both surviving parents were mothers, and their preschool children were both girls.

Family selection was also done to exemplify other important attributes. I wanted to illustrate one or more of the factors that have been linked to outcome in previous studies (Raveis et al., 1999; Siegel et al.; 1996; Worden, 1996) and others that represented a contrast. These attributes included: families with one or several children; patients with short and long illness, patients with problematic symptoms (pain, shortness of breath, personality or behavior change from brain metastases); patients who did and did not communicate with children about their illness and imminent death; immigrant families with acculturation and economic issues; children with timely and compromised outcomes. Finally, the roles of the parents in relation to child care included some families with a very traditional role definition, while others had a much more egalitarian and flexible role definition.

Data Analysis

The qualitative, collective case study analysis (Cresswell, 1998; Stake, 1998) of each child's experience was guided by what Runyan (1982, p. 100) described as "**Stage-state** analysis of the life course." (To reduce confusion, when the words **stage** or **state** are used to refer to Runyan's **stage-state** analysis of the life course, they will be bolded.) He suggested that the temporal approach of a life-course orientation is more effective in analyzing situations that require one to consider the interaction of personal, behavioral, and situational variables over time. The life-course orientation is presented as an alternative to other orientations that focus primarily on how traits, psychodynamic processes, situational influences, or all of these impact on affects, symptoms, and behavior. The predictive limitations of these other approaches have been recognized (Mischel, 1968; Mischel, 1973). The **stage-state** analytic approach provides "a method for examining the movement of persons through a social structure over time; for investigating the alternative routes or sequences of processes through which initial person-situation configurations may be linked with an array of potential outcomes" (Runyan, 1982, p. 101). In this approach, **stage** is defined broadly to indicate periods in a process (e.g., stages of the illness, stages of development). **States** within a **stage** are designed to identify "specific kinds of persons behaving in particular ways in particular social and historical circumstances" (Runyan, 1982, p. 102).

A two- to four-page summary was developed for each child. Under the **stage** (age group and illness stage), themes and categories and the related behavior-person-situation determining processes that might contribute to the outcome were identified. There were three sources for identifying potential categories: significant variables from the quantitative analyses of our own and other published findings, clinical knowledge of the demands of the illness experience on patients, children and their families, and other factors and processes identified in the family data. The sequence of processes or interactions ("behavior-determining processes, . . . person-determining processes, . . . situation determining processes" [Runyan, 1982, p. 84]) that are described in the structural-dynamic-interactive dimension of the model that link the potential categories with the outcomes were sought. Potential categories that did not have such links were discarded. (An example of a discarded category often cited in the literature as linked to poor outcome was ongoing or intrusive images of the deteriorating state of the dead parent. This category was not evident in our data, possibly because we did not comingle traumatic deaths with anticipated deaths.)

A comparison of the categories and processes or interactions between children in each age group clarified within-group variations and patterns. A comparison between age groups was then done. For example, a few categories (e.g., mourning, parental relationship) remained important across all age groups, others (e.g., anticipatory grief, preparation for leaving home) were specific to one or more age groups, while still others (separation anxiety) were ubiquitous and typical at younger age groups but uncommon and linked to a less favorable outcome in older age groups. A return to the complete record to insure that important connections were not omitted, misrepresented, or altered by the data reduction methods was repeatedly done.

Transferability, Trustworthiness, and Dependability of the Findings

One can correctly argue that interventions alter the course of the parental death experience for families and that the responses of the parents and the children described in this book are influenced by this intervention. The information that was used in this book was an ongoing monthly to bi-monthly account that, including the psychologist assessments and the telephone contacts during and after the intervention, usually spanned about two years. We believed there was great value in obtaining and analyzing ongoing information about families' coping efforts (Christ, et al., 1991). It is difficult to sustain participation of parents and children in a study that includes more than two or three interviews and tests if it does not include some form of help for them as they undergo the stress of a spouse's severe terminal illness and then the bereavement and reconstitution processes.

An example of how the intervention may have altered the findings is the way information about the illness and death of a parent is relayed to children, and in turn the outcomes if more parents had not informed children in a timely way. This intervention emphasized the need of the children for information. These findings are not 'naturalistic' findings, but rather provide a more detailed description of the course of an experience over an 18- to 24-month time span. I see it as complementing the more naturalistic information that can be obtained with two or three test batteries and interviews done months apart (Silverman, et al., 1995; Silverman & Worden, 1992b; Worden, 1996).

Findings from this study may be more transferable to families of patients who seek treatment for cancer in major centers than to families who do not or are unable to move from their immediate community for such treatment. The few relatively financially disadvantaged families in this sample show how the impact of poverty alters the experience and may alter the outcome as well. The traumatic death experience also elicits reactions and responses that are quite different from those seen in this population (Eth & Pynoos, 1985a; Eth & Pynoos, 1985b; Eth & Pynoos, 1985c; Pynoos & Nader, 1990; Pynoos et al., 1991; Pynoos et al., 1995; Terr, 1983; Terr, 1990; Terr, 1995).

On the other hand, the availability of information that describes the gradual process of evolution in responses to the impact of such a family tragedy has value. Certainly, the descriptions shared by the families as they struggled with the terminal illness and then the reconstitution process are invaluable. They invite the reader to generalize from these to their own experiences (Stake, 1998). The availability of more detailed information obtained from families over a relatively long period of time enhanced our goal of achieving a "faithful understanding of human phenomena" (Fisher & Wertz, 1975).

5

Children 3–5 Years of Age

Themes

This chapter describes the impact of terminal cancer on the lives of 18 children—11 girls and 7 boys—aged 3 to 5 years. They came from 18 families, and their surviving parents were 15 mothers and 3 fathers. The narrative stories of 3 of the children are described in more detail: Rachel in Chapter 1, Katja in Chapter 6, and Amanda in Chapter 8.

DEVELOPMENTAL THEMES OF PRESCHOOL CHILDREN

Our understanding of the children's experience requires familiarity with the rules of pre-operational thinking. The most pertinent rules are summarized below and in Chapter 2. These children's lives are centered on the family—their social forays, even in preschool or kindergarten, do not yet provide another meaningful social center. The microsystem of the home is their meaningful ecological world (Bronfenbrenner, 1993). Their very sense of well-being depends on the presence of the parent, usually the mother, or a familiar parent surrogate.

Cognitive Development

Although language develops rapidly in 3- to 5-year-old children, as does the symbolic meaning attached to the words, nonverbal communication remains their 'lingua franca.' Communication through play, drawings, and symbolic play is more effective than words to connect with the child's thinking (Piaget, 1952). A 4-year-old boy drew a father sitting between a dog and a cat in the yard, while the other children and mother were inside the house looking sad. The family had no dog, but the boy always wanted one, and egocentrically assumed that his father also wanted one. The picture was the gift to his dead father he placed in his coffin. This was also a typical expression of grief from a 4-year-old child.

Pre-operational thinking is characteristic of children between the ages of 2 and 7 years (see Chapter 2) (Flavell, 1963; Ginsburg & Opper, 1979). Their thinking is egocentric to the point that they automatically assume that others know what they know and think like they do. Unless the listener has a good idea about the plot of a story the young child is telling, so many details will be left out that the listener will be thoroughly confused. More problematic is the child's magical thinking, which further confuses the unprepared adult who is unaware that the child "knows" that thinking or verbalizing a bad or angry thought causes illness and death.

Another attribute of pre-operational thinking is the inability to *reverse* a reasoning process. Recognizing this feature in 3- to 7-year-olds is crucially important when attempting to correct their erroneous self-blame. When children in the pre-operational stage try to retrace their thought process, they end up at a "starting" point that bears no resemblance to the original one. This cognitive feature contributed to parents' difficulty in relieving their children's guilt by changing their assumption that they had caused their parent's disease. However, in our sample, as in Kranzler's study of pre-school parentally bereaved children, 3–5 year olds generally did not feel responsible for the parent's death as was so frequently true in 6–8 year old children (Kranzler et al., 1989).

Emotional-Psychological Development

The demarcation between cognitive and emotional-psychological development is less clear in this age group than it is in older children. For example, the younger of these children initially could neither comprehend nor emotionally accept the permanence of the parent's death, which reflected both cognitive and emotional influences. Two reactions, both present in children this age, are more clearly emotional-psychological: their anxious reactions to separations from the primary caregiving parent and their inability to tolerate their parents' expressions of strong emotions, such as sadness and crying. Expressions of intense rage or sadness frightened them.

Social-Ecological Development

Social development outside the family is minimal in this age group. Although many of the children in our sample attended preschool, the main benefit was the establishment of a routine that could be maintained almost as a safe haven during the turmoil of the terminal illness and death. An exception was participation in bereavement play groups. The children benefited greatly by being able to talk about the dead parent at home after they participated in bereavement groups. One mother speculated that her child probably learned a vocabulary in the group that facilitated this expression. The children also learned to draw pictures that described their grief. Another exception was observed in some 5-year-olds whose social development was enhanced by participating in kindergarten. Their ecological world was *almost* exclusively centered in the home microsystem (Bronfenbrenner, 1979). Two experiences exemplified the impact of systems beyond the microsystem on the development of some of the children. First, those who participated in play bereavement groups enhanced their ability to communicate with the surviving parent about the death and enhanced their ability to mourn. Second, being teased by preschool peers about not having a two-parent family often prompted a request for a replacement parent.

Patterns of Responses in Preschool Children

The pattern of the young children's responses to the parent's terminal illness and death differed from the pattern observed in the older children. They usually were more disturbed after the parent's death, whereas older children were usually more disturbed during the parent's terminal illness. Most stressful during the terminal illness were the separations from the primary caregiving parent.

Terminal Illness

Understanding the Illness

Most distressing to 3- to 5-year-olds was the change in the caregiving parent, that parent's preoccupation, and the frequent separations, not the illness. The children's muted and unclear reactions during the parent's terminal illness were, in part, the result of their inability to understand the significance of events as they unfolded. They focused almost exclusively on the visible signs of illness, such as the ill parent's progressive loss of locomotion or inability to lift an arm or throw a ball. For example, one 5-year-old was vague about her father's illness, but she did know that he took medicine that made his hair fall out. What upset these children most was that the symptoms of cancer and its treatment changed how the ill parent interacted with them.

There were differences between the 3-, 4-, and 5-year-old children's comprehension of events during the parent's illness. Three-year-olds tended to be vague about what was happening, but they were often more aware of the patient's symptoms and altered ability to function than their parents realized. Careful choice of words, aided by the use of objects (like toy IV bottles and dolls, or a doll in a box to describe burial) was used to convey even fairly sophisticated information.

Four-year-olds began to understand that something serious was happening and that the adults were extremely upset. Their concerns were sometimes incorporated into their play. In the narrative in the next chapter, 4-year-old Katja developed a fantasy game in which fathers and sisters got sick and died and then were resurrected or replaced by new fathers and sisters.

Although 5-year-old children were more aware that the parent was ill, and some knew the name of the illness, they were unable to comprehend how it affected the body. If they knew the parent was likely to die, they might view the death as an exciting event.

Because children express their distress through play, drawings, or fantasies rather than through words, many parents underestimated their distress. Also, because they reacted more strongly to the separations from the parent who was their primary caregiver than to events related directly to the illness, parents sometimes concluded, mistakenly, that the child was not affected by the parent's illness.

Asking Few Questions

Although children tend to ask "Why?" incessantly, it was interesting to observe that even bright, inquisitive children did not ask questions about their parent's illness during the terminal stage.

Four-year-old John asked no questions about his mother's illness. However, he became withdrawn and seemed more timid and cautious at home after his mother's diagnosis. The fact that his father was in the process of separating from his wife when she became ill only complicated the situation. He had many friends in preschool and had no behavior problems there, but he said little about his mother except that he missed her a lot when she was in the hospital, and he seemed confused about why she had to be there. His father believed that John should be shielded from facts about his mother's cancer because he was so young, so John seldom visited her.

Young children do not ask questions for a variety of reasons. First, they often do not know what questions to ask. Second, in some cases, the child had never known the parent when he or she was healthy and, consequently, had little basis for comparison. A third reason is that younger children more readily accepted changes, such as the presence of a hospital bed, oxygen bottles, or intravenous tubes. They seemed to be more interested in how the paraphernalia worked and how they could play with it rather than in why it was there and what prognostic inferences they could draw from it. Obviously, parents who relied on the idea that "If he wants to know, he will ask" were making a serious mistake.

Reactions to the Primary Caregiver's Behavior

In marked contrast to their muted reactions to the illness, the children reacted strongly to separations and to their parents' intense emotions. Numerous frequent, unplanned, and sometimes lengthy separations caused by medical emergencies occurred during the patient's terminal illness. These emergencies were difficult for parents to manage without interfering seriously with the young child's schedule and care. As described in Chapter 1, at age 3 Rachel clearly showed how traumatic the separations from her mother were for her, although familiar family friends cared for her while her mother stayed at the hospital with Rachel's terminally ill father.

The mother of 4-year-old Cindy said that it was difficult for her to identify any grief reactions in her daughter after her husband died because Cindy was so relieved to have her mother home. Cindy's anxiety in response to the separations from her mother had eased greatly and, in fact, her mood had improved now that her mother was more available.

For most children, visits to the hospital were effective in easing their anxieties. Seeing the patient, no matter how ill he or she might be, seemed to reduce the frightening unease that often filled the void in the children's understanding.

Reactions to Parents' Intense Emotions

Preschool children were easily overwhelmed by their parents' intense emotional reactions to the illness. For example, at age 3 years, Rachel spoke about this in a direct way when she informed her mother after they had cried together that "Two people can't (aren't allowed to) cry at the same time, and I was crying first!" More dramatic was her refusal to enter her father's hospital room after he and her mother had tried to include her in their sadness. Among the other frightening parental emotions were depression, emotional withdrawal, anger, and impatience. The children's reactions to the ill parent's troubled emotions were often oblique and indirect. For instance, 4-year-old Katja's imaginary companions probably reflected her fear of her father's irritability, angry outbursts, and obvious physical deterioration (Chapter 6).

Some children exhibited severe symptoms and behaviors in response to a parent's extreme loss of control:

> Debbie developed severe phobic responses, initially fighting with children in nursery school and then refusing to attend school altogether. The 3-year-old also developed severe separation anxiety: first, she refused to ride in the school bus and then refused to stay with her baby-sitter. Her extreme reactions appeared to be provoked by her father's violent outbursts and threats against his young children. (Before his diagnosis, domestic violence had been reported in this family.) When his disease metastasized to his brain, his rages increased. Whenever the children misbehaved, he threatened to call the police, and, not surprisingly, Debbie became terrified of policemen.

Some young parents interpreted current notions concerning the value of more open communication to mean that they should share their most intense emotions even with their very young children. These parents needed to recognize the difference between communicating with their child about the illness, which was helpful, and sharing their intense emotions, which was not.

Each family had its own unique emotional climate to contend with that was based on pre-existing relationships within the family, the way individual family members responded to stress, the family's particular vulnerabilities and strengths, the challenges posed by the cancer, and the availability of other individuals to help the family. In most cases, the family's emotional climate tended to become worse as the patient's condition deteriorated.

> Brad had his father's name and was strongly identified with him. The 5-year-old and his 8- and 10-year-old sisters were glad their father was home more, even though he was sick. Brad proudly told the interviewer that he watched over his sisters when they rode their bikes in the neighborhood—he watched out for cars. Brad's mother was having difficulty being open with the children about their father's probable death even though his long hospital stays and advancing symptoms alerted them to the possible danger that lay ahead. Driving home after visiting their father in the hospital, all three children confronted their mother, asking her if their father would die soon. However, when she still could not acknowledge his terminal condition, Brad confronted her again, asking her whether his father would die by Brad's next birthday. When the father's symptoms of pain and shortness of breath became worse, all three children began to act out more. The girls became more aggressive, critical, and angry toward their mother, and Brad joined in. He also began engaging in provocative behavior, burping loudly at the table and acting 'fresh' with a man he met dur-

ing a hospital visit. Later, Brad asked his mother: "Why does God let people die? Can God save someone who is in a hospital room dying?" One month later, his father died.

Children's Symptoms and Behaviors

During a parent's terminal illness, preschool children demonstrated relatively few psychological symptoms or misbehaviors. Their symptoms were dependent on the adequacy of arrangements for their care, the frequency of separations, and the emotional climate in the home. Characteristically, their symptoms during the parent's terminal illness were transient. These symptoms included night terrors, difficulty sleeping, becoming more clingy or stubborn, having more temper tantrums, or complaining of physical symptoms that commonly were similar to the patient's symptoms. Some children's sleeping, eating, and toilet-training behaviors regressed. Others withdrew from siblings and peers or engaged in aggressive behaviors. Parents often found that they could alleviate these expressions of distress by providing more consistent caretaking arrangements, reducing the number of separations from the primary care taker, or improving the emotional climate and trying to understand and respond to the child's underlying anxieties.

> One mother of two daughters, aged 5 and 7 years, left her job as an accountant and vacationed with the girls during the final summer before she died. As a result, many of the girls' early symptoms of anxiety and depression improved. Their mother subsequently found a therapist for each daughter, and at the final follow-up interview, the girls were functioning at a level that was equal to or better than the level at which they had functioned before the mother's condition was terminal. This mother recognized her husband's limitations in providing consistent nurturing because he worked long hours and was a recovering alcoholic. Thus, she arranged for others to help with their emotional care when she was no longer there. Although these children expressed the sense of loss of the mother they had gotten to know so much better, they had important memories and experiences on which they could build over time.

Responses to the Death and Family Rituals

Preparatory Information

Parents who provided their children with ongoing information as treatment progressed avoided the need to burden the children with complex information in too brief a time. Furthermore, the children were able to connect what they were observing with the information they were receiving. This process also gave them the words that could be used to discuss the events.

Equally important was not providing the children with false reassurance because even at their young age, false reassurance was often what undermined their trust in the parent and further confused them. Three-year-olds could be told about the treatment, its purpose, and how effective it was (or was not).

Five-year-olds sometimes asked direct questions: For example, "Is Daddy going to die?" Children with older siblings were most likely to ask direct questions such as this. Letting children know that people had died from the disease their parent had but that the doctors were doing everything they could to try to help the parent live acknowledged the reality. When parents were more evasive, the children often felt helpless and expressed anger and mistrust toward the well parent, both during the terminal illness and after the patient died.

Although young children did not need as much advance notice as older children did, when it became clear the patient was likely to die within a couple of weeks, they could be informed of that probability. Even these young children wanted advance warning that the patient would die soon. As one 5-year-old said, "I cried (when my dad told me that my mother died), but I knew (she would die) because Dad told me (it could happen)." Combining information that the patient would probably die with reassurance about how the children would be cared for and how family life would continue was always helpful. The children's concerns were about who would provide basic care, who would be their primary care giver, and whether life would go on as planned. "Will we still go to Disney World?" one child asked.

Informing the Child of the Parent's Death

No matter how carefully children were prepared for a parent's death or how often they had elaborated the theme of death and dying in their fantasies or play, they did not actually expect the parent to die, could not readily comprehend the permanence and irreversibility of death and the sadness associated with that eventuality. An 8-year-old pointed out that her 5-years-old sister thought her mother would come back after she died. As elaborated in Chapter 6, Katja's 7-year-old sister, Lara, explained the preschool child's response to her father's death well: "My sister doesn't know what dead means. The night he died, she and Mummy came to my bed. Mummy said, 'Your father died,' and my sister was laughing because she thought something exciting had happened." Their mother explained that Katja observed her and Lara's reactions carefully and cried because she saw that was the appropriate thing to do. As young children began to realize that death was final and irreversible, feelings of sadness, disappointment, disbelief, and devastation emerged.

Funeral, Burial, and other Traditional Rites

Most young children participated in the funeral and burial rites, although they often did not remain as long as their older peers, and usually did not go to the cemetery. Most parents wisely asked a relative or friend to take charge of and be available to the child, to leave with the child should they need to do so. Although most of the children did not understand the symbolism of the rituals or seemed a little befuddled by them, they clearly gained from participating in the various rituals. The major gain was that the parent's death became more concrete. When children did not attend the funeral, it usually reflected the surviving parent's concern about their reactions and the belief that not attending would protect them. However, the reactions of the children who did attend the funeral did not appear to support this belief.

As was the case regarding many aspects of preschool-age children's understanding, no single episode or explanation resolved the finality of the parent's death. After the funeral or wake, they continued to ask: "When is Daddy (or Mommy) coming home?" But each concrete episode further clarified the dead parent's true state.

Children also can be frightened by certain aspects of the death and the burial. For example, 4-year-old Katja had numerous nightmares after her sister told her that her father had been cremated because she was afraid he had felt the flames.

Most of the children derived great pleasure and comfort immediately after the death with items such as clothing, jewelry, and photographs that provided links with their dead parent. One preschooler wore his dead father's underwear; another carried his father's wallet and told his family that he planned to buy a house for the family with his father's credit cards.

In the ensuing months, many children enjoyed going to the cemetery with their surviving parent. One mother described her 4-year-olds behavior at the gravesite as follows: "Jimmy talks about his father. Sometimes he says, 'Daddy's in heaven and he's not coming back.' He attends to the grave for a few minutes, then he plays around, and then he returns to the grave, makes the sign of the cross and, when we leave, says, 'Bye Daddy.'"

Remembering the Dead Parent

The young child's openness and lack of defensiveness was usually evidenced in the early period after the death by talking easily about the parent, which was difficult for the grieving parent. They enjoyed remembering what they used to do with the parent before the death. Katja was delighted when Lara made her father's special pancakes. Another 4-year-old recalled that his father had tickled him; another boy the same age talked about how his father had tossed him up in the air. Recapturing such experiences not only helped children remember the good times they had had with the lost parent but also seemed to comfort them.

As young children began to appreciate the reality of the parent's death, they not uncommonly became frightened and anxious, and their separation anxiety increased. The toll of the parent's frequent and, at times, unpredictable absences during the terminal stage contributed to symptoms of increased apprehension about separations, occasional refusal to go to preschool, and nightmares that required them to sleep with the surviving parent or an older sibling. Some children developed transient phobias or physical symptoms, some of which resembled those the dead parent had experienced, such as headaches and stomachaches. Most children expressed the fear that they might be seriously ill, might die like the parent, or that the surviving parent, friends, or others might die. Others responded by becoming withdrawn. Temporary regression of sleeping, eating, and toilet training habits was not uncommon.

Children fairly quickly began to seek out attention and care from adults who were the same gender as the dead parent, which at times embarrassed the surviving parent because of their directness. Older children also searched for a replacement parent, but their approach was usually more subtle.

Bereavement and Reconstitution

Most children of this age were more distressed after the parent's death than they were during the terminal illness. Katja's sadness deepened in the weeks after her father's death, as she began to realize that, contrary to her reassuring fantasies, he would not return. Whereas the return to school and other activities away from home helped older children reconstitute their lives, the process was more vague and gradual among the younger children. However, pressuring the surviving parent to find another mother or father seemed to indicate that the children were entering the reconstitution stage. Some were ashamed of being different, whereas others, such as Rachel (Chapter 1), responded to being teased by peers about not having a daddy by asking her mother to find a new husband. Another indication that the children were entering the reconstitution stage was a return to happily participating in activities such as visiting other children, playing with friends, and going to preschool.

Understanding the Death

Over time, the children's conversations about the lost parent changed as they gradually accepted the reality of the death and its irreversibility. At least they could say the words, whether or not they understood the concept entirely.

> Two weeks after her father died, Jennifer asked her mother if he would be coming home for Hanukkah. The 4-year-old talked about her father constantly and said she talked to him and told him she missed him, and he told her he missed her too. However, she was doing well in school and was clinging less to her mother. Then she began to correct herself in her conversation when she said, "I want him to come home. Oh, no, he's not coming home."

Jennifer's behavior represented the typical progression of the young children's process of accepting the reality of the parent's death. For example:

> Three-year-old Brett talked openly about his father for many months after he had died. Then, one day his mother overheard him telling his grandmother that he was going fishing with his father, but he corrected himself, saying, "Daddy not here, he's dead."

> Amanda became more whiny and clinging after her father died. The 4-year-old sat in his chair with many blankets wrapped around her. When she began complaining of stomachaches, her mother took her to the doctor, and Amanda promptly asked him when she could see her father again. Three months later, however, she was able to say, "Daddy died."

Children this age expressed confusion about death and their own vulnerability in ways that were sometimes difficult to understand. For instance:

> Amanda kept asking her mother, "Is that person dead? Did she die? Do you die if you're old?" Then she asserted that "Dad died because he was old." Finally,

she asked, "If you itched all over, do you die?" and complained of itching. (During his terminal illness, one of her father's symptoms was itching.)

One of the few more traditional oedipal reactions was illustrated by 5-year-old Brad, whose relationship with his father had been a good one. He was afraid that his father might come back and that he (Brad) might be hurt, so he slept several nights with his sisters for protection. He began to dream that his mother was murdered, but these dreams subsided over a period of several weeks. Then he demanded that his mother tell him who would be his father when he grew up. He asked this question repeatedly and was dissatisfied with the evasiveness of her answers.

Shortly after the parent died, the children were likely to ask the surviving parent to find a replacement. Most of the girls launched a campaign to have their mother find a new daddy and, like Rachel, wanted a daddy who would be fun. One 5-year-old thought she would like to have two daddies, so that if one died she would still have another one.

When the mother was the parent who had died, most children were fairly insistent that women in the household should take on a parenting role. Several children became angry with the family housekeeper, who they felt should pay more attention to them instead of just cleaning. Those who rejected nannies and baby-sitters appeared to be unwilling to accept as a mother replacement someone who was not assuming the role of a mother.

Children were intensely upset about the loss of the "whole family" that they had believed would always be theirs and that gave them a sense of security and well-being. They also were upset about being different from other children, and they missed the family climate that had existed before the parent's illness.

Grief Reactions

Children expressed sad, unhappy, and angry feelings for many days or months. They sometimes became withdrawn at preschool, were distracted, or appeared to daydream. Transient regression from current developmental achievements was not uncommon. Sleeping difficulties and anxiety related to separations from the surviving parent were common, as were complaints about mild physical symptoms such as stomachaches, headaches, and exaggerated reactions to normal cuts and bruises.

Most children were inclined to use the quiet moments the surviving parent had established to talk about the dead parent. They enjoyed focusing on memories such as "Daddy and I used to whistle" or "Daddy used to tickle me." At times, their conversations were so casual that the surviving parent misunderstood their behavior as indicating a lack of feeling. However, some children had more difficulty talking about the lost parent. For example, Amanda's mother found that her daughter's attendance in a bereavement play group facilitated her ability to talk about her memories of her father, and her angry moods subsequently decreased. Some children benefited from individual counseling. When children were able to talk about their dead parent during the reconstitution process, they obviously felt better and functioned better.

Most parents were extremely sensitive to their young child's need for emotional support and tried to be helpful, despite the pain of listening to the child's memories about the dead parent. Children appreciated it when the surviving parent instituted quiet times for conversation, telephoned them at school, and informed teachers and other adults who could provide knowledgeable care. Parents also tried to provide new, fun experiences so that their children would have pleasurable feelings about their new family life that would counteract their inevitable confrontations with the "loss" of the family.

Impact of the Surviving Parent's Grief

Although surviving parents were faced with adopting new roles and making numerous changes in their lives, their grief tended to make them proceed at a slow pace. The lack of synchrony between a parent's more constant, longer, and intense mourning and the preschool child's more episodic grief created problems for parents. Their problems were compounded by their need to distance themselves from their wrenching grief by thinking or doing something else during a period when the child needed to talk about the dead parent and surround him- or herself with reminders of the parent.

Reminders of Grief

Anniversaries and other marker events such as holidays, Father's Day, Mother's Day, and birthdays were important reminders for the children. Although surviving parents were reluctant to observe such holidays, they found that observing them and remembering the dead parent with the child was beneficial. Visiting the cemetery on such occasions also was valuable. Although reminders were painful to parents, most preschoolers found that reminders were pleasurable. As I alluded to earlier however, they were upset when peers reminded them that they were different because they did not have a mother or father.

Parental Dating

Parents often felt pressured when their young child urged them to "get another Daddy or Mommy" and were embarrassed when the child clung to and adored adults who were the same gender as their dead parent. However, because dating was complicated, many parents wisely decided that their child had undergone enough traumatic separations and did not want to subject the child to a series of separations while they searched for a suitable mate.

Young widows were especially devastated by their husband's unexpected death and not infrequently had difficulty developing new relationships. They often realized that they were afraid of making another commitment because they might be forced to re-experience the same trauma. As a result, the women tended to delay dating much longer than men. Generally, the men were more inclined to remarry relatively soon, especially if they had young children. However, the behavior of the surviving parents in our sample varied greatly, depending on such factors as their opportunity to date, their relationship with the spouse who had died, and the duration of the spouse's illness.

All the children in this sample discussed parental remarriage with the surviving parent, if not before the patient died, then shortly afterward. Many were reassured to know that their parent would look for a person who would be a good parent as well as a good husband or wife. A few even listed the attributes they wanted in a new parent.

Estrangement From the Extended Family

Conflicts between the surviving parent and the dead spouse's family were almost universal and often led to estrangement. Thus, the young child experienced an additional loss.

> The father of three children aged 9, 5, and 4 years became angry with his mother-in-law after his wife died. Although his mother-in-law had provided care for the children and had kept in consistent contact with them, he believed she had not done enough for her daughter and refused to speak to her. This distressed the children because their grandmother was the only member of the extended family who lived in the area, and they had spent a considerable amount of time with her. Although their father told them they could maintain contact with their grandmother, they were afraid of incurring his rage and retaliation by doing so, and he was their only remaining parent.

There were many reasons for the conflict. The grandparents' grief was profound, and reminders of their loss as well as their dead child's loss when they looked at the young surviving spouse and grandchildren were devastating. Young single-parent families have many needs—emotional, financial, and care taking—needs that were difficult for grandparents to acknowledge and meet as they struggled to survive themselves. As a result, most in-laws gradually drifted apart from the parent and children. The surviving parent's remarriage made maintaining the relationship between grandparents and grandchildren even more complicated. However, young children benefited when their grandparents put aside their understandable despair and affirmed the different needs of the surviving spouse.

> Jack's wife, Arlene, had been ill for three years before she died, and their two young children yearned for the nurturing care they had been missing for some time. About four months after Arlene died, Jack began to date a teacher from his children's school who the children liked very much. Arlene's mother and father, who had helped with the children's care throughout their daughter's long, difficult illness, were angry and critical of their son-in-law. After a couple of months and some careful reflection, however, they prepared a birthday dinner for their son-in-law's new girlfriend together with the children. Jack was very touched, and they all had a pleasurable evening together. The grandparents explained that they just wanted to be sure that the woman Jack became involved with was able to be as loving to the children as their daughter had been. But they could see that although this woman was different from their

daughter and expressed herself in different ways, the children liked her and she cared for them.

RECOMMENDATIONS FOR PROFESSIONALS AND CAREGIVERS

Terminal Illness

1. *Explain the changes caused by the cancer and its treatment in a consistent, on-going manner without being overly optimistic or pessimistic.* Information that explains what the child is seeing and hearing is most important.

2. *Establish a time when the child can ask the parent questions and share feelings and thoughts.* Many parents find that bedtime, when they can lie next to the child and talk about the illness, is a good time.

3. *Use play and art to illustrate and make concrete the complex events that are occurring in the family.*

4. *Realize that having "a good cry together" may be frightening rather than cathartic for the young child.* However, if the parent does express intense emotion, it should be explained. Because young children are so self-referential, a careful explanation is necessary: For example, "I'm crying because I'm sad that Daddy is very sick. I'm not crying because of anything you did."

5. *Honor the child's inability to experience or observe intense emotions more than briefly.* Changing the subject or going off to play are important safety valves. For example, although young children respond well to hospital visits, the visits are more satisfactory if they are brief and if some activity is planned.

6. *Arrange for the child to visit the parent in the hospital.* Hospitals are now much more amenable to having young children visit. It is important for the parent to bring a few toys, enlist a spare wheel chair for the child to play with, or arrange to have a meal together. The visit should not extend beyond the child's tolerance.

Death and Family Rituals

1. *Communicate with the child throughout the parent's advancing and then terminal illness, focusing on explanations for what the child sees and hears about the disease.* For example, explaining the illness, treatments, and the patient's progress is a way of developing a language that can be used to discuss illness, treatment, and ultimately death, as well as related emotions.

2. *Use concrete details to describe the fact that when a person dies, all bodily functions cease and the person will never come back.*

3. *Use other examples of death, such as the death of a pet or a grandparent, as understandable analogies.*

4. *Use play, drawing, and other expressive activities to enhance the child's understanding.*

5. *Suggest emotions that the child might feel so he or she can respond in ways others will understand.*

6. *Prepare the child for the rituals that will take place.* Describe what the child can expect to happen, what role the child can play, what roles other people will play, how others will feel and behave, and how the child may feel. Encourage the child to participate in these rituals.

7. *Assign a care taker to remove the child from the wake or funeral after a brief time if this seems necessary.* The usual hour devoted to such ceremonies is often too long for most preschoolers.

8. *Reinforce the child's continuation of positive activities.*

9. *Reassure the child about the surviving parent's ability and determination to provide care.*

10. *Shortly after the death, provide the child with transitional objects that seem important to the child.* These items may include some of the dead parent's possessions or photographs of the parent, especially photographs with the child.

11. *Prepare for a surge of separation anxiety, sleeping problems, the desire to sleep with the surviving parent, clinging behavior, and other temporarily regressive behaviors.* If the situation does not improve within a couple of months, set up a system of rewards for sleeping alone and returning to previous developmental functioning.

12. *Prepare for the child to talk frequently about the parent during the first few weeks after the death.*

Bereavement and Reconstitution

1. *Continue setting aside time to talk with the child about the parent who died.* Because most surviving parents are extremely busy, it is easy to overlook the importance of talking with the child. Substituting a quiet chat for a bedtime story can be helpful, as can bringing up pleasant memories of the dead parent or looking at a family album together. After awhile, the child may begin asking questions about or bring up incidents involving the dead parent.

2. *Be prepared for the child to misunderstand why the parent is experiencing strong emotions and correct these misunderstandings during quiet talks.* Another source of misunderstandings may be older siblings who freely share information that the child may not comprehend.

3. *Help the child remember pleasurable activities he or she participated in with the parent who died, although such discussions can be painful to the parent.*

4. *Give the child access to the dead parent's possessions that might be of interest and provide a sense of ongoing connection and identity.* It was best to give the child realistic choices. For example, valuable jewelry can be put in a safe place and looked at together.

5. *Share photographs of the dead parent with the child.* Although pictures can be a source of grief and pain for the surviving parent, they are usually a source of pleasure and comfort for the child. If the parent cannot do this, grandparents may be able to do it.

6. *Discuss the possibility of dating with the child, recognizing that the topic is complicated.* Although young children may clamor for a new parent, they can be upset and jealous when the new potential parent proves to be different from the lost parent. The children may believe that the new person will separate them

from the dead parent or dilute the surviving parent's affection. Another factor that must be considered is the potential for additional losses if the parent stops dating a person the child has become attached to. It is comforting to know, however, that most young children adapt quickly to a new parent if the new spouse honors the importance of the child's continued relationship to the parent who died.

7. *Prepare to celebrate anniversaries and holidays as good times that facilitate memorialization of the dead parent.* Although children usually enjoy the ritual of including the dead parent on such occasions by visiting the cemetery, they may change their mind suddenly and refuse to go. This behavior is not unusual during developmental transitions.

8. *Explore the availability of play group experiences.* Grouping children who are experiencing the loss of divorce or a parent's death is often successful. Children seem to enjoy these groups and benefit from realizing that they are not the only ones without one parent. They may enjoy hearing about other children's reactions and sharing memories.

9. *Keep in mind that the young child's mourning process differs radically from an adult's mourning.* Whereas the intensity and frequency of the adult's feelings of overwhelming sadness and loss gradually diminish over time, the child's mourning process has a different pace and can involve intense feelings that come and go for years.

10. *Seek a professional evaluation for the child if severe symptoms persist.* Examples of such symptoms include an inability to engage in carefree play after six weeks; persistent clinging, fear, and nightmares; irritability or acute sadness after two or three months; difficulty separating from the parent and functioning poorly in preschool; a prolonged preoccupation with dying and joining the dead parent; and, of course, persistent developmental regression in sleeping, eating, and toilet training habits.

11. *Consider counseling or therapy* for the surviving parent if the parent's symptoms of grief become symptoms of major clinical depression or if the symptoms prevent the parent from maintaining adequate emotional involvement with the young child. Depression in the surviving parent has been highly correlated with disturbance in 3–5 year old parentally bereaved children (Kranzler et al., 1989).

6

Children 3–5 Years of Age

Narrative

MOTHER AND 4- AND 7-YEAR-OLD DAUGHTER

"My Sister Makes Our Daddy's Famous Pancakes."

This is the story of Katja, who was 4 when her father died. Like so many of the 3- and 4-year-olds, she played rather than spoke her thoughts. It was her older sister and her mother who talked and told us a great deal about Katja. However, this story is also about how pre-operational children experience and think about the illness, death, and reconstitution of their family. So the story is also about Lara—who was 2 1/2 when her father was diagnosed, 5 when he became terminal, and 7 when he died. Her recollections, her understanding, and her reactions, which she shared generously, are those of a pre-operational child. Like so many of the 6- to 8-year-old girls, she was very garrulous—she loved the attention and the opportunity to talk to the interviewer. She loved being knowledgeable and opinionated, all attributes that made her an excellent raconteur. She had had a lot of practice in this. Her mother loved her chatty style and found in her a kindred spirit.

Background

Both Peter and Eva were born in Romania, geographically not too far apart, although their families did not know each other. When Peter was 16 and Eva was 15, both families fled to the United States following political unrest. A shy person, Eva recalled that her first three years in her adopted country were a nightmare, and she would have returned to Romania many times over if she had been able to. No one in her family spoke English, her high-school classmates made fun of her accent, and she became even more shy. "I turned off all emotion. I just ate to stay alive." Such depression is not uncommon in adolescent immigrants who struggle with the loss of place while beginning to develop an independent identity. When she went to college, she discovered a Slavic department, and life suddenly changed for her. She did well in school, made many friends, and met Peter when she was 20 years old. She earned an advanced degree, then worked in her profession for a number of years.

She and Peter married when they were in their late 20s. Two years later, Lara was born, and Eva left her job to take care of the family: "Peter was a mechanical genius. He started a manufacturing business of his own in a basement, and by the time we were married, it was a real business with a whole building and more than 20 full-time workers."

Diagnosis

Six years after Peter and Eva were married, his cancer was diagnosed, and he decided to sell his business and begin enjoying life: "Doing the things for which I never had time." He gradually rebuilt their house, which became a full-time avocation.

It is difficult to determine when the terminal stage of Peter's illness actually began. It was five years from his diagnosis to his death. After the diagnosis and three months of chemotherapy, Peter underwent a knee replacement procedure to remove the cancer but save the leg. One year later, his physicians discovered that the cancer had metastasized to his lung, and he underwent lung surgery and more chemotherapy. None of the standard chemotherapy regimens seemed to be effective: Within 12 months, his cancer had metastasized to his other lung and his spine and, a few months later, to his hip bones. At this point, he entered a clinical trial. Like many recipients of experimental drugs, he kept hoping either for a cure or for at least being able to live for many more years. His fighting spirit and his tolerance for pain were remarkable.

Terminal Stage

Lara was 5 years old and Katja was almost 3 when their father entered the terminal stage of disease, although it would be two more years before he died. He maintained his fighting spirit, despite the major problem of his bone pain. With each new trial of chemotherapy, he and Eva renewed their hopes, only to have them dashed when the treatment failed. As Eva said: "It is too much like an emotional roller coaster." She said that although he usually was in much better spirits than she was, his anger and irritability became severe at times. Unfortunately, Peter's mother, because of her own grief, added to their stress by blaming Eva for his illness. Eva was angry, but she understood that when men got sick in the "old country," their women were blamed for not taking care of them properly.

Eva believed that Lara's temperament was similar to her father's: "Sweet and nice, but then very stubborn, and then again extremely sensitive and loving and caring. She has no control over her emotions. She identifies with Peter; she even looks like him." Eva explained that Peter had a better relationship with Katja than with Lara because Lara was much more complicated for him to parent.

Because Lara unwittingly provoked Peter, she often became the focus of his outbursts. Typical of preschool children, her play reflected her awareness of and distress about her father's condition. She began to bang up her legs while play-ing, then complained that her knees hurt. She often complained of a stom-achache, but the physician could not find a cause. She became fearful, had diffi-culty sleeping, and climbed into her parent's bed at night. Because Peter's emotional control was poorest at night, he would become angry with Lara, shout, and bring her to tears on occasion. Eva said that she and Peter also had different attitudes about child rearing: He believed in being strict and punitive, whereas she was easygoing and encouraged her daughters to be outspoken and independent.

When Peter began receiving palliative treatment, Lara became even more upset by her father's emotional outbursts. By now she was 7 years old. She was afraid of shadows moving in her room at night and was even more frightened of being alone. She climbed into her parents' bed in the middle of the night more often. When an accident or theft occurred in the neighborhood, she exaggerated the threat. She was afraid of burglars, then of fire. Each attack of fear lasted a couple of weeks, then gradually subsided. Although Lara had not been told that her father had cancer, she asked the interviewer if her father was going to die, a directness typical of 6- to 8-year-old youngsters.

Surprisingly, Lara did extremely well in school during this period. Her teachers couldn't say enough good things about her, and Lara was proud of receiving a report card with all "Excellents" at the end of first grade. As a reward, Eva took her out for lunch—just the two of them.

Katja, on the other hand, did well at home during this period. She reflected the lack of apparent distress demonstrated by many preschool children—espe-cially those who had an easy temperament, whose routines were maintained, and who had a mother at home. As Eva reported: "Katja is very well adjusted, she is very laid back; she loves everyone and everyone loves her. She has a good relationship with her father and her sister."

Three months after Peter began palliative radiation, Eva's parents returned from Romania and moved into the Vicek household to help out. Although Eva initially welcomed this arrangement, it soon became clear that her parents dis-agreed with her and Peter about how to handle the children. For example, they were aghast that Lara would dare say "No!" to her grandfather—behavior that was unheard of in the old country.

Understanding the Illness

Lara's understanding of her father's illness demonstrates how earlier 'understanding' was maintained over time. She demonstrated the merging of unrelated events that is so common in children who are at the preoperational stage of thinking.

Lara told the interviewer she did not know the nature of her father's illness. Reflecting on memories of events that took place when she was 5 years of age, Lara, now 7, said that his illness began when he was repairing the house and dropped an electric drill on his foot. She explained, "It was bleeding a lot and my Mom wouldn't let me see it. Then they took him to the hospital and they put in a new knee, which then went into his back and he broke his leg and his back, and now he has to use a wheelchair sometimes." Lara was angry at her father because she thought he had dropped the drill on his foot on purpose. She was afraid he would go to the hospital for an operation, and then more and more blood would come out and he would lose his heart and die. "I would be very sad if Dad were to die. If Mom would die, then grandmother and grandfather would take care of us, and they live in Romania."

Eva explained that Lara was 4 years old when Peter's knee was replaced surgically and almost 5 when he accidentally dropped the drill on his foot. Peter was home alone without a car. Because he was bleeding profusely, he called 911. Eva and Lara were returning home in the car when they saw the ambulance. Lara wanted to run into the house to see what had happened, but Eva did not let her until the mess was cleaned up. Although she tried to correct Lara's misunderstanding about the cause of the accident, Lara insisted on believing her own interpretation of the event, thus merging two disparate events.

When the interviewer asked Lara if she felt responsible for her father's illness, she denied thinking it was her fault. However, she recalled that once, during a drive in the country, she was singing in a way that annoyed her mother. At the end of the trip, her mother was car sick and later said she had been sick because Lara had been singing so much. This made Lara wonder whether one person's behavior could make another person sick. Although she did not connect this insight directly to her father's illness, it seemed likely that it was the source of some of her anxiety.

Beginning Acceptance of the Parent's Terminal Condition

The tension in the family increased as Peter's disease advanced and the treatments proved to be less and less effective. Peter desperately tried to gain more control over his disease. He wanted to move to Romania because he had heard about a man who was able to heal people by placing his hands on them, but by the time they discovered the man's whereabouts, the man was no longer practicing his "art." Peter then focused his attention on obtaining treatment in Germany. Eva felt torn between her husband's wish to search for alternative treatments and maintaining constancy in her daughters' lives, which she believed was the best plan.

Five months before Peter died, he finished remodeling a bathroom, despite his pain. He told Eva he needed to do it to feel useful. When the pain in his chest increased, he coughed a lot and had severe night sweats. He began talking about death as a part of life but complained about the unfairness of dying so young.

Observing her father's increasing symptoms and debility caused Lara to worry even more about his possible death and she spoke openly about her concern to the interviewer. She felt nervous because she thought her father was going to die. "That makes me cry a lot and be real mean." However, she explained that she did well in school because "I don't worry about Dad in school because I concentrate on work." She wondered what would happen if her father died or if both parents died. She was not sure what the word "orphan" meant.

Eva was surprised by Lara's thoughtful suggestions about who should take care of her and her sister in the unlikely event that both parents died. When Lara entered second grade in the fall, the structure of school was helpful. But at times she was still emotionally volatile at home. After a fight with her mother, she threatened to run away and kill herself.

Katja, then almost 5 years of age, suddenly started a new game. She began talking about imaginary "sisters and fathers" who went to the hospital, where some died and some did not. Those who died reappeared again. Eva did not know where Katja's ideas came from, but they seemed to keep her happy and satisfied.

Later, Katja added new members to her imaginary family. She replaced her old imaginary father and sister with new ones and seemed content to have the new family get sick, go to the hospital, die, and then reappear. She announced to everyone that she was Babette, a teenage baby-sitter whom she idolized.

Preparation for the Death

Four months before Peter died, Eva began thinking about life without him and experienced anticipatory grief. Her feelings vacillated between fear that her daughters would get into trouble without a father and feeling that she could handle anything and would manage somehow. She also was concerned that the children might be scarred for life and wondered whether she could prevent such an outcome.

Peter expressed fear of going to sleep because he thought he might suffocate. Eva was heartbroken watching Peter, who could no longer walk, scoot around on the floor fixing the house. When she offered to help him, he angrily refused. When he began making a stained glass window, she tried to dissuade him because the job was obviously extraordinarily difficult for him. His response was, "It makes me feel alive and it distracts me. Let me enjoy my time." Eva was relieved when a member of a supportive care unit was assigned to come to the house to monitor Peter's pain medication.

When the Christmas holidays arrived, Eva did not feel like going through the customary decorating and celebrating. However, the girls asked her about it and she decided to do it for them, and she discovered that it lifted her spirits as well. However, one day during the Christmas holidays, she could not find her outdoor boots and suddenly began crying uncontrollably, overwhelmed by a feeling of "I'm not able to take it any more." Peter was furious with her. After two days, she regained her composure because "I realized that I really needed the numbness that I had been feeling." Later, Peter told her that she frightened him when she cried because he desperately needed her to be strong, not weak and out of control like his mother.

Two months before Peter's death, the tumor in his spine became worse and he was forced to use a wheelchair. It was difficult for him and Eva to adjust to each step in his decline. His hands were weaker and he could hardly hold a cup of coffee, not to mention the tools needed to finish the stained glass window. A number of different health care specialists came into the home at least once a week to provide massages, nursing care, pain monitoring, and exercises. Peter seemed to like these visits, but Eva believed they were not helpful. She said that at times she felt she could not even use the bathroom in peace without 10 people asking her a question about something.

At this point, Peter's pain was partially controlled by steroids and morphine. According to Eva, Peter was even more emotional than before: "The other day, he looked at Lara and started crying. He told her he is so happy that she is such a good daughter." When he told Lara that he might die, she became upset, went upstairs, and cried.

Lara was convinced that she was the cause of her father's recent paralysis, a typical feeling among early school-age children. She recalled that shortly before he became paralyzed, she spilled milk on the floor and her father slipped and fell as he was cleaning it up. She believed the fall was the reason why he was now unable to walk. Lara had suddenly become much better behaved and acted more mature, helping her mother take care of her father.

Katja maintained her imaginary family. Fathers and sisters kept dying and being resurrected. She had added a number of brothers who were much bigger than her father. She announced to Eva: "I can be in the street by myself because my brothers can take care of me." Eva explained to her that because these brothers were imaginary, they could not really take care of her. She needed a parent to be with her when she was on the street.

Death and Family Rituals

Four weeks before Peter died, palliative radiation to his back was completed and the steroids were reduced. Eva mobilized herself and began exploring possible jobs. It made her feel good to begin preparing for the future. She had not worked for seven years and was afraid she would not be able to find a suitable job. She was gratified when her former employer offered her a supervisory position, but she declined the offer because the job was full time. She also made plans to hire a girl 'from the old country' to take care of the house and help with the cooking so that she could work part time. Peter fantasized that the girl would make all sorts of wonderful baked goods and he would regain some of his weight.

Lara refused to go to school one day because Eva had forgotten to order a book she needed. She had more stomachaches and headaches and felt left out because Katja spent so much more time at home.

During the final week of his life, Peter began eating less, then stopped eating and drinking altogether. On the day he died, he told Eva he was ready to die. He died peacefully that night.

When Eva told Katja that her father was dead, she was curious: "I want to see him," she said, crying as if she thought she was supposed to. Eva took both girls into his bedroom to say good-bye to him. Lara recalled: "My sister doesn't know what dead means. The night he died, she and Mummy came to my bed. Mummy said: 'Your father died' and my sister was laughing because she thought something exciting had happened. It was very sad, Mummy cried until the priest came. We hugged each other." Eva then called the police, who came and were sweet to the girls, putting handcuffs on them and playing with them until the paperwork was signed.

Each girl made a birthday card, which went with their father when he was taken away. As Lara explained: "I drew a picture of me and my sister giving our dad flowers, the colors he likes, and wishing that he would have a happy life there. We put the picture in the coffin with him." Katja made a card of "our house", with friends inside the house, she and Daddy holding hands outside the house. From the girls' viewpoint, the house represented their father.

Eva had cards printed and Lara passed them out at the funeral. Both girls came to the funeral. More than 100 people came, including Lara's classmates, teachers, the principal, and many of the mothers of Lara's classmates and Katja's classmates in preschool.

Peter wanted to be cremated so his ashes could be taken back to Romania. Eva explained to Lara that Peter had been cremated in accordance with his wishes and his ashes would be brought home soon. Lara promptly told Katja, who immediately began waking up in the middle of the night. After that, both girls crawled into their mother's bed at night, and Katja's night terrors continued to wake her up.

Katja kept asking when Daddy would come back, and Lara reminded her, "He is never coming back, he's dead." Katja also kept asking where he was— whether he was still at the funeral home. Lara explained to her that "When someone dies, their body does not work any more. Their soul is not there. It's with God." Eva was surprised that although the family was not religious, Lara clung to religious ideas. Eva found herself thinking: "This is so final—there will never be happiness again. How do people get over it? But we are starting to have some good times even now."

Two days after the funeral, Lara went back to school. She was relieved to be back with things to do. The teacher gave her a large paper flower that was filled with many cards from the children and lovely notes from her friends. They all expressed sadness about her daddy.

Eva was more concerned about Katja than about Lara. A few days after the funeral, she recalled yelling at Katja about something, and Katja started crying—very hard. "Katja had a closer relationship to Peter than to me." Peter would have comforted Katja, now Eva had to do it. Eva gave Katja a hug and a kiss and said: "That was from Daddy." As Eva told the interviewer, "It's hard being both the good guy and the bad guy."

During the first few weeks after Peter's death, Katja cried more often and Lara seemed moodier. Both girls were already beginning to experience situations that were different because their father was gone. One night, Lara was struggling with her math homework and said math was much harder now because her father had always helped her with it. Eva acknowledged that math was hard and said it was good to keep talking together about Daddy because it kept his memory alive. Both girls talked openly about him. They liked to take care of the little tomato plants he had planted with them and to remember the good times they had had together.

Bereavement and Reconstitution

Five weeks after Peter's death, Eva found that his death had not completely "sunk in" yet. "A part of me still thinks he's there. I thought about going home and telling him about something funny that happened. I have a sense of his spirit and his presence, and it is very comforting."

During an interview, Lara remembered playing with her father—putting a magnet on his knee because it was metal. She also remembered that when a new hospital bed was delivered to the home, she knew her father was going to die. Lara explained that her mother was now working and she was proud of her, but she wanted her mother to quit working: "I don't get to see her that often. I got a new housekeeper, and my grandmother helps with my homework. Mom has to do bills that my Dad used to do."

Lara explained the cremation as follows: "Daddy wanted to be burned so that his ashes could go to Romania. It doesn't hurt because they can't feel anything. My cousins wanted to know about getting burned. When my mom first told me, I felt kind of spooked. I wonder how many ashes you have when you get burned." Lara received an excellent report card and a good grade on a report she had written about cancer and a book she had read on the body. She believed she was doing well in math because "our dad had already worked with me on these things."

At school, Lara talked to a social worker every Friday about how she felt and also went to a rap group every week. "When I go to sleep, I have scary times. The ghosts come—they make funny faces. Then I go to Mom and sleep with her. When I feel bad, I talk to my mom, but sometimes I'm afraid she is doing something very important and she might lose her job if I bother her, so I wait." Her advice to other children was "Don't worry, nothing that you did caused it (your parent's death)." Her main worry was that her new cat would die the same way her old one did a few weeks earlier. "I cried for two days when the cat died. We buried it on the side of the garden." When asked about her mother getting married again, Lara said, "I asked Mom once, 'Are you going to get married again?' She doesn't know. It would feel kind of strange. It would be hard if they got married and she had another child. I hope it wouldn't be a boy, they're wild, but if it was a boy, they should take it because that is better than nothing."

Unlike her chatterbox sister, Katja was quieter, and Eva reported that she seemed sadder. She also said that Katja used to be able to play alone, but now she wanted to interact all the time with Eva, reflecting her anxiety. Katja expressed her grief primarily by wanting to talk about positive experiences she had had with her father. When asked whom she talked to when she was sad, Katja said: "I talk to my mommy and my sister." Later she said: "Daddy tickled me a lot. I miss him, but I still have my mummy. . . . My Daddy could make good pancakes. Now my sister can make his famous pancakes."

Search for a Replacement

Eva planned to quit her job so that she could return to Romania with the girls over the summer vacation to bury Peter's ashes. She found that her loneliness was increasingly hard to take. She told the interviewer that Lara suggested Eva should marry Daddy's friend, the one who drew pictures with them.

Lara worried because the other children at school teased her, and she wondered what they were thinking about her. She was afraid they might laugh at her because, like her friend Janice, she did not have a "together family." The kids laughed at Janice because her parents got divorced and her mother remarried and then had another baby. They also laughed at Lara, "but I don't know why they are laughing."

Katja still had her imaginary friends, but less often now. Instead, she wanted to have more contact with her mother and the neighbors. Katja was temporarily afraid of bugs shortly after she was told that her father had been cremated, but Eva said Katja was getting better.

Eva met with the interviewer shortly after the family returned from Romania at the end of the summer. They had a second funeral for all of Peter's many relatives, which intensified Eva's feelings of loss. The children also went to that funeral; the three of them went to the grave several times, planted shrubs, and watered them. Eva said that after returning to the United States, she had the feeling that she did not know whether she belonged here or in Romania. She did not want her children to experience that feeling. She explained that everything had changed a lot in the old country since she was a girl. There was more crime and more unemployment. She said that Katja had adjusted easily in Romania and had adjusted well again after returning to the United States. Although she had become more talkative, she wanted her mother to watch her while she played rather than play alone, as she had done before. She was doing well in preschool and liked it.

Grieving and Building New Connections

Both girls talked about their father, remembering mostly positive things they did together or the way he would cheer them up. They often talked to each other and to Eva about the birdhouse he had made to protect the birds from the cats, how he had made each of them a bedroom, and especially how he had made the beautiful stained-glass window for them. Lara, like Peter, loved country music and Katja loved his famous pancakes. However, typical of children her age, Lara grieved for her father at times. Eva told the interviewer that several days earlier, she went into Lara's room in the afternoon and found Lara crying. When asked why she was crying, Lara said she was thinking about Daddy.

Katja voiced some of the worries typical of preschool children: She worried about becoming ill herself or about her sister or mother becoming ill the way her father had. Eva said that during supper with the girls a few days before, Lara did not want to eat her vegetables, and Katja said: "You want to be healthy, don't you? You don't want to be like Daddy, to die." Lara responded, "Why not? Then I wouldn't have anymore homework."

Eva said she wanted to return to Romania permanently but was torn because the girls preferred to stay in the United States. "If they move, they both want to take Peter's house and the dead cat." The children craved having a man in their lives: "It's almost embarrassing the way they respond to every man they come in contact with. They are almost overbearing!"

When last seen 14 months after Peter's death, Eva said she had decided the family would spend a year in Romania to see how life would go for them there. Katja talked about missing her father and wanting a new father. Although Eva and the girls experienced periods of mourning, they did so at different times and with different intensities. Eva was worried about some of Lara's fears. For example, Lara insisted on leaving the movie theater if the movie had a scary scene. Lara was both worried and excited about spending a year abroad. She continued to do very well with her friends and at school. She was no longer teased by them. She was learning to play the piano and proudly played two pieces that she had recently learned for the interviewer. Katja continued to do well in preschool.

Summary

Peter and Eva's story shows us how long, devastating, tiring, and sad the slow dance toward death can be. Peter's determination to live—or at least prolong his life—his fighting spirit despite excruciating pain was remarkable. Although his suffering took its toll on the family, he left an important legacy of commitment, caring, creativity, and refusal to give up. Another important legacy was his love and affection. His children also were fortunate because they had a loving, consistent, intelligent, understanding mother. Because she cared deeply for them, informed them, and encouraged them to participate in maintaining contact with him, and later in the funerals, she mitigated their anxiety to a great extent. However, her strong identity as a traditional wife who defers to her husband prevented her from filtering some aspects of her husband's loss of emotional control with his children.

Katja and Lara were doing well when last seen 14 months after their father died. Perhaps as a consequence of the momentum of their development, they had reconnected with friends, with school, and with their father. Although they will continue to mourn him, their memories are good ones. They loved the house he built for them, they enjoyed his pancakes, they tended the garden he had planted with them, and they shared pleasant memories about their interactions with him. But most important, they were enjoying their life. They did not want to move to Romania.

But after 14 months, Eva, Peter's widow, was still confused and searching. She was barely over the worst of her grief and was just beginning to figure out who she was and what she wanted to do with the rest of her life—a life without Peter. Like most of the surviving parents described in other chapters, she experienced a major identity crisis because of the transition of roles required after the death of a young spouse—a crisis that many young, single parents fail to resolve. Eva not only needed to finish mourning her husband, she also needed to deal again with the three-year-long depression she had suffered in adolescence because of her forced emigration from Romania. Her pre-adolescent paradise had ceased to exist, but she needed to search for it by returning to it. Although she desperately needed to connect to the rest of her life, she had just begun that process. The contrast between the length of Eva's mourning and the much shorter mourning of her daughters, between Eva's ongoing struggle with her search for a new identity as a widow and a single parent and her daughters' adjustment to their new life, is evident, and quite normal and expected.

7

❦

Children 6–8 Years of Age

Themes

This chapter describes the impact of terminal cancer on the lives of 33 children—16 girls and 17 boys—aged 6 to 8. They came from 30 families, and their surviving parents were 17 mothers and 13 fathers. (In this and the next chapter, when the word child is used, it refers to 6- to 8-year-old early elementary school children.) The important themes that are germane to children in this age group are surveyed in this chapter. Chapter 8 discusses the experiences of two families and ends with a summary of the characteristics of the children and families that constitute the different outcome categories when the families were last seen 8 to 14 months after the parent's death.

DEVELOPMENTAL THEMES OF EARLY SCHOOL-AGE CHILDREN

Children this age were extremely troubled by the unfolding tragedy of the parent's illness and death and they showed their distress. They often appeared to be sad and dejected, and they felt rejected. Sometimes they were angry, irritable, and disappointed. Whereas preschool children seldom comprehend the finality of death until after the funeral, 6- to 8-year-olds began to anticipate the death during the parent's terminal illness: they evidenced anticipatory anxiety rather than anticipatory grief, as did the older children. In addition, most of them understood that the parent who died would not return; however, precisely what the catastrophe meant for them and how much they worried about the family's survival can only be imagined. As one 8-year-old put it: "I began to think that Dad will die, and then maybe Mom will die, and the whole world will end!"

Four areas of development are important in understanding the responses of these children to the parent's terminal illness and death: (1) the transition between preoperational and concrete operational thinking, (2) the young child's emotionality, (3) the parent's central role as protector and enhancer of self-esteem, and (4) the child's expanding outside world.

Transition Between Pre-operational and Concrete Operational Thinking

Cognitively, this is a transitional age for children. Although some show concrete operational logical capabilities, like the older school-age children, their thought processes often reflect the illogical and magical thinking that is more characteristic of preschool children. Two common attributes of pre-operational thinking—magical thinking and nonreversibility—led to and maintained erroneous conclusions that were difficult to change by logical discussion. Combined with the desire of adults to protect them by withholding information about the death, children this age were often confused and clung to their own erroneous explanations of events.

> A 7-year-old girl prayed that God would take her mother so that she would not suffer so much. The next day her mother died and the child said, "I think I killed her!"

> An 8-year-old explained that she had not wanted to talk about her mother's impending death during the first interview. Her mother's illness was terminal at that time, and the child was afraid she would somehow bring her mother's death about if she talked about it. After the death, she talked about her much more easily.

It was difficult to change the children's ideas by using logic because of their inability to reverse their thinking process: that is, the children were unable to retrace an erroneous conclusion to its source. The 7-year-old who prayed that her mother's suffering would end believed she had (magically) caused the death. Later, she was unable to retrace how she had arrived at that conclusion. She just "knew" that she was responsible for her mother's death.

Early School-Age Child's Emotionality

These children expressed strong emotions: sadness, anger, anxiety, guilt. They not uncommonly and erroneously felt rejected, and they also experienced strong fears about the well-being of both parents. This characteristic emotionality distinguished them from older school-age children, who kept their emotions at bay by distracting themselves with activities and intellectual pursuits. Younger children could not distract themselves easily from the tragedy of the situation and therefore became overwhelmed. This is a characteristic that has been described in research on children's coping and self-regulation abilities (Mischel & Mischel, 1983; Mischel et al., 1989; Compas et al. 1988). Because their strong emotions promoted more illogical, primitive thinking, providing them with solace was more difficult. One troubling characteristic of these children was their tendency to personalize external events. For example, many viewed a parent's withdrawal as a rejection for something bad they had done.

> Seven-year-old Katy's father, who had a brain tumor, withdrew from her because he was afraid that if he continued to interact with her, she would remem-

ber him as he was in his deteriorated state. Katy cried throughout her initial session with the interviewer as she described the changes in everyone in the family since her father's terminal illness. "Mom has a bad temper because Dad is very close to dying." From this more logical statement, she promptly moved on to an illogical one: "Mom doesn't care for me anymore; no one listens to me. My daddy doesn't love me anymore because he won't let me sit on his lap." She felt rejected by her father's withdrawal and by her mother's anxiety and angry depression.

Although Katy understood her father's symptoms and the disease process and had repeatedly been told that he was too sick to play with her, she continued to experience his withdrawal as rejection. She understood her mother's extreme distress about her husband's impending death and the family's financial difficulties, but she also experienced her mother's behavior as a personal rejection. She felt devalued by these 'rejections.' The logical inconsistency is manifested in her answer to the question of what advice she would give to other children: "It's helpful to talk to your mom so you can understand how you feel."

Katy's reactions typified the experiences of many children her age, who automatically assumed that when either parent expressed any negative affect, they were to blame.

Parent's Central Role as Protector and Enhancer of Self-Esteem

Although these children were more independent than preschool children, they were not self-sufficient. They needed the parent's assistance, nurturing, reassurance, and encouragement to maintain a sense of security, well-being, and self-esteem. A great reduction in self-esteem was a major problem and a marker that these children were under severe stress. Thus, emotional responsiveness and reassurance from a parent was extremely important to them. They needed assurance that they were valued, loved, and would continue to be cared for and that the family would survive.

Before his father died, a 7-year-old gave the following advice for other children in his situation: "You have to fight (the disease) with (the patient), and just know that you are surrounded by love."

Child's Expanding Outside World

Although these children attended school and were interested in learning, the school experience was often more stressful than supportive. The pressure to perform and succeed was distressing to many, especially when they were trying to cope with so many stresses because of changes in the family climate and routine. They valued 'friends,' but friends were not the source of distraction or solace that they were to older children. Instead, their peers sometimes teased them about not having a mother or father, about the surviving parent's remarriage and about the possibilities that they would have a new stepbrother or stepsister. Being treated as "different" was often synonymous with being lonely and rejected. For these reasons, children responded well to bereavement groups, in which they met other children who shared their concerns and who had some of the same feelings. They were no longer the only one who had lost a parent. For these children, the home microsystem remained central, but the school microsystem was beginning to gain in importance. At this age, teachers and the teacher's reactions were more important than peers. However, a paper with a good grade did not really raise self-esteem until it was praised by the parent. Like their younger siblings, their development was affected by the peer rejection they felt regarding their not having a "together family"; about having a family with only one parent. Their hesitation about their surviving parent remarrying was countered by their desire to be like their peers—they not infrequently began to request a replacement, perhaps in part due to this peer pressure.

PATTERNS OF RESPONSES IN EARLY SCHOOL-AGE CHILDREN

The children's responses varied according to the stage of the illness or bereavement, and depended on the information they were given. Their preparation for the death was complex, but they generally recuperated relatively quickly after the death, although some residual symptoms were not uncommon.

Terminal Illness

The children's awareness of their parent's impending death varied. Many of them spoke openly about being afraid their parent would die. Others, though aware of the illness, were unaware of the terminal nature of the current episode. A few were even unclear about the diagnosis and therefore were confused about what was happening to the parent. For most, the terminal illness was the time of highest anxiety and stress. Important issues during this stage included communication of preparatory information and managing separation experiences.

Communication of Preparatory Information

Because most of the children were reluctant to reveal their fears about the patient's possible death, especially to either parent, parents could not be guided by the children's questions when trying to decide when and what type of information they needed to provide. Including the children in family discussions about changes in the patient's illness and treatment was often helpful. Regular updates were also important to them.

> Dan proudly told the interviewer that he participated with his older brothers in family meetings about his dad's illness. It gave this 7-year old a sense of value, importance, and inclusion in a family that was becoming closer and more cohesive to deal with this stress.

Conversely, 7-year-old Daria said: "There are secrets in this family. Families shouldn't have secrets. I don't feel like I am part of this family anymore."

Need for Information

Three types of information were helpful to children during the parent's terminal illness: (1) the name of the disease, its progress, symptoms, treatments, and causes, (2) the relationship between the patient's behavior and appearance and the symptoms and treatment of the disease, and (3) the prognosis, including when death was probable and when it was imminent.

The name of the disease, its progress, symptoms, treatments, and causes, involved concepts that were generally beyond those the children could comprehend. On the other hand, when first interviewed, even if children had not been told directly that the parent had cancer, most were aware of that fact because of conversations they had overheard. However, if a parent informed them directly, they seemed to feel they had permission to ask more questions.

The relationship between the patient's behavior and appearance and the symptoms and treatment of the disease were often confusing to the children. They were especially distressed by changes in the patient's abilities and spoke poignantly about the patient's inability to engage in sports, to play games, and to have fun with them. Some were angry about these changes, attributing them to the patient's willful neglect or rejection of them or to malingering. They also were upset, and often angry, about the patient's reduced mobility and altered appearance and mood, and at times blamed the physicians and the hospital for these effects.

One boy believed that his father's irritability after chemotherapy, coupled with the fact that his mother remained in the city two nights a week to stay with her husband while he was undergoing chemotherapy, was because his parents no longer loved him. Children were angry about changes in the parent's functioning even if they understood that the changes were caused by the disease.

> Eight-year-old Robert and 6-year-old Ann were very upset with their mother's inability to wheel her chair into their room at night to talk with them, read to them, or mediate their conflicts. She had been ill for more than two years, and her loss of mobility interfered with her parenting abilities. This was especially difficult because she insisted on trying to parent them without outside assistance, although she was physically incapable of doing so. As a consequence, she needed to keep them in the house most of the time, and her children were extremely angry about this loss of independence. After their mother died, Robert and Ann told the interviewer that they wanted to have fun for a change and asked her to play games with them.

The prognosis, including when death was probable and when it was imminent, were difficult areas to communicate to the children. In contrast to their reluctance to ask parents, these children were likely to be quite blunt with the interviewer: "Do you think my daddy is going to die?" or "I'm afraid my mommy is going to die." Even when they had not been told that death was imminent, some inferred this from the patient's symptoms, the parents' anxieties, or the reactions of others.

Because parents had the most difficulty providing their young children with information about the pending death, some waited until it was too late. When told that the parent's death was imminent, most of the children cried briefly, asked a few questions, and returned to their usual activities. Later, they were likely to begin asking questions about plans for the future and who would take care of them. Some began to worry about the well parent's health, a worry that became acute and more common after the patient's death. Some asked what would happen if both parents died. Most of the children worried about this. Whether they asked this question or not, clarifying what would happen in the unlikely event that both parents died reassured them unless the parent named someone the children didn't like.

Special disease-related situations made it difficult for children to understand the progression of the illness. One parent had been chronically ill for many years. His transition to terminal illness was gradual. The child had difficulty understanding that the disease was now acute and terminal. Another parent had an acute reaction to the treatment of the disease and died unexpectedly. A third parent died suddenly when he developed acute leukemia while being treated for osteosarcoma. Situations such as these posed special communication problems with these children.

Unhelpful Communication

Some parents communicated with their children in ways that were not helpful. For example, some misunderstood "open communication" to mean they should share the full range and intensity of their adult emotions with the child. As with younger children, their expressions of severe anxiety, panic, despair, or rage increased the child's anxiety and fear. On the other hand, expressing moderated feelings, such as concern, gave children permission not only to share their own feelings but modeled how emotions could be expressed as well. Just how difficult it was for young parents facing the death of a spouse to discuss the illness and its prognosis with their children cannot be overestimated. This difficulty was compounded when the patient denied the terminal nature of the illness.

> Elaine was the 38-year-old mother of two daughters, aged 6 and 8 years. Her sister died when Elaine was just 3 years old, and no one had ever discussed the circumstances of her sister's death with her. Consequently, she was determined to communicate openly with her daughters about her progressive brain tumor. She was distraught about leaving the children, although she had made careful alternative plans for their parenting after she died. When she talked with them about her death, she emphasized her belief in reincarnation. Some day, she said, they would be together again. Because this thought was comforting for all three of them, she discussed it often and in great detail.
>
> The 8-year-old clearly understood that death was permanent and that many years would pass before she would see her mother again. She did not want to

talk about her mother's death ahead of time. On the other hand, the 6-year-old enjoyed these discussions. Her father said she talked about death as if it were an exciting event that was about to occur. After her mother died, however, she became angry and dejected and was preoccupied with the wish to die so that she could see her mother sooner. Her understanding of reincarnation was that her mother would return soon—as her mother. It required several months of clarification and reassurance before her mood improved and she began functioning normally at school.

This example reflects the pre-operational thinking of a child in the early elementary grades in a highly emotional situation in which a parent inadvertently reinforced a belief that death could be reversed.

Although some parents intended to be protective by delaying giving bad news, it often created more stress in children after the death because the death was experienced as more sudden, unexpected, and traumatic. For a few, withholding information led to a more distressing reaction after the death.

A 7-year-old girl expressed rage and distrust of her mother, the doctors, and the hospital for several months after her father died suddenly of a brain hemorrhage after going to the hospital in an ambulance. Because her mother had not forewarned her about his probable death, the child believed the hospital was responsible for his death. She reproached her mother by saying, "They killed my father. Why did you take him there?" Mistrust was not a previous characteristic of the mother-daughter relationship, and it was not relieved until several months of repeated discussions, counseling for the mother, and individual counseling and a bereavement play group for the child.

Symptoms and Behaviors

These children reacted to the stress of the parent's terminal illness with anger, anxiety, sadness, and fear. Conflicts with siblings and peers often increased. Regressive behaviors such as being childishly demanding, stubborn, and clinging were common. Other behaviors, such as bed wetting, were less frequent. There were very few instances of soiling.

Children's reactions were closely tied to what was happening around them: They reacted to separations and to changes in their own activities. Some became upset and angered by tighter restrictions on their activities imposed by temporary caregivers such as grandparents. They also reacted to the changed family environment, to the increased tension, anger, and depression, and to the lack of happiness, joy, and celebrations in the home. At times, they objected to the fact that the patient was receiving so much attention.

Because Dan's father was discharged from the hospital on the day of an important baseball game, his mother was unable to attend. As the 8-year-old asserted: "It's always Dad. His needs always come first!"

Because a temporary drop in a child's grades commonly occurred during the parent's terminal illness, parents were encouraged to communicate with teachers and other school personnel about the illness so they could support the child and not make unrealistic demands or become unnecessarily critical. Many children functioned better at school than they did at home, especially if previously they had been successful at school. However, they also were afraid of being disapproved of at school and being teased by peers because they were different. As one 7-year-old girl said, "It's not as special having just a mother." Peers can be insensitive and even cruel to each other at this age.

> Eight-year-old Ron sadly told his mother that when he told the class his father had cancer, one boy asked when his father was going to die. This made his mother realize that giving her children more information would protect them and prepare them better to deal with what lay ahead.

Reactions to Separations

Although the 6- to 8-year-olds did not need the parent's constant presence, they did need the parent to be as consistent as possible with them: for example, letting them know about the possibility of unexpected trips to the hospital and preparing them for how the situation would be handled and who would take care of them. If properly prepared, they usually responded well to temporary caregivers and baby-sitters, but they resented overly restrictive caregivers such as frightened grandparents. If separations were not prolonged and they were aware of the parents' whereabouts, they tended to be tolerant. However, if the separations were prolonged, they had problems, especially if they were not permitted to visit the hospital.

A planned visit to the hospital with children of this age often reduced their anxiety dramatically and led to improved behavior at home. For a variety of reasons, some patients did not want their children to visit them during their terminal illness. Some believed they were protecting their children from the trauma of their altered appearance. In reality, however, the children in this age group talked only briefly about their parent's appearance after the death. They were more likely to feel rejected by their ill parent's not wanting to have them visit. If adequately prepared, most children were not distressed by visits to the hospital, enjoyed them, and felt less anxious afterward. Their propensity to fill an information vacuum with erroneous explanations and notions seemed much more likely without this direct contact and communication. If parents could not understand the benefit of such visits, they could help the children by telephone communication and the exchange of letters, drawings, and gifts. However, seeing and hearing the patient and his or her caregivers in the hospital not only provided the child with an important confrontation with reality but also with reassurance that was difficult to accomplish in other ways.

> The mother of 7-year-old Dana had been at the hospital daily with her terminally ill husband for several weeks. With her 4-year-old sister nearby, Dana told her mother on the phone: "The doctors and nurses are at the hospital to take care of Daddy; you need to be at home with us."

Sam, age 6 years, and his 4-year-old brother were fighting more than usual. Their father could not understand why they were so difficult, since they had a housekeeper during the day while his wife was in the hospital. When the interviewer asked how they were feeling about their mother being in the hospital, they responded angrily that she had been there for 62 days; they knew that because they had been crossing off the days on a calendar they showed the interviewer.

Many ill parents came to believe that a good use of their remaining time was to stop working, if possible, or to work at home so they could spend more time with their children. A few parents expended tremendous effort to keep working until shortly before they died. This seemed to reflect an inability to come to terms with their terminal condition. This pattern was not usually tied to the need for money; it reflected the patients' terror at confronting their own death and losing the children they loved. Unfortunately, their lack of energy when they were home tended to limit the time and the quality of their interactions with their children. In addition, the other family members worried about them because of their exhaustion.

Preparation for Death and Family Rituals

Telling the Children

Many parents found that telling the children that their parent had died was the most difficult task they had ever faced, especially if the mother died. The children's responses ranged widely, from screaming or sobbing uncontrollably to quiet crying. Some of the children had no immediate response at all. Even when they were well prepared, some expressed surprise and acute distress. The acute distress of these children generally lasted no longer than a few minutes to an hour. They then returned to whatever they had been doing before the news, such as watching television, playing with siblings or peers, or going back to their room, or they remained with their surviving parent.

It was unusual for patients to talk with their children this age about their own imminent death. However, when an ill parent did so, the child often reminisced with pleasure about having said final good-byes to the patient. An 8-year-old remembered his father saying, "I love you" to him. One 7-year-old remembered how she had hugged her mother. Another 7-year-old was comforted by remembering how her mother had squeezed her hand; for months, she put herself to sleep with this tactile memory.

Many children were disconcerted by the patient's appearance or angered by the patient's inability to remember their name, but once the reason was explained to them, the situation seemed to have no lasting effect. Even if children did not say good-bye to the patient directly, they were comforted by writing their thoughts down and placing them in the coffin. The mother of one 8-year-old boy placed his letter in her husband's hand. A 6-year-old who had been unable to have a final visit with her mother said, "I wanted to be with her before she died when she said that word 'I love you'."

Attending the Funeral and Burial Rituals

Parents were advised to encourage their children to attend the funeral but not to insist if they were adamantly opposed. However, almost all the children this age agreed to attend the funeral. What was universally helpful to them was to observe the large number of people in attendance who cared for their family and for the parent who had died. Even if they found certain aspects 'scary,' they were glad they had participated. Many later reminisced about the funeral and wake with pleasure.

Concerns about the parent's appearance before death did not seem to have a lasting effect. The "bad" last memories seemed to relate more to a poor antecedent relationship or to a psychological trauma, not to physical appearance. The patient's appearance in the coffin was sometimes disappointing. One boy complained that "they" had sewn his father's lips together because his father looked different, not the way the boy remembered him: "(My father) looked like The Joker!" he complained. Others were pleased if the parent had been made up in a way that made the parent look better than he or she had looked shortly before the death. These responses seemed to reflect the children's desire to create a positive image of the parent.

Parents were inventive in encouraging children to place treasured objects in the casket. One 7-year-old son of a fireman placed his favorite toy fire truck in the casket. Some children placed teddy bears, pillows for comfort, letters of last thoughts and good-byes, family pictures, pictures they had drawn, poetry, favorite stones from the beach, or a treasured baseball card. One funeral director called the father of 6- and 8-year-old siblings to say the father would have to buy a second coffin if the children kept bringing gifts for their late mother! Clearly these gifts comforted the children. Parents found other ways to involve children in the funeral, such as having them hand out memorial cards. Some children enjoyed greeting people; others preferred to remain quiet. One mother even permitted her 7-year-old to join his three older brothers as a pallbearer, which made him extremely proud.

The children were always glad to see friends and classmates at the funeral, even if they did not interact with them as much as older children did. Whereas older children were helped and supported by peers, children in early elementary school seemed more relieved by not being ostracized by peers.

> Two sisters aged 8 and 10 years were highly ambivalent about their father, who had been an angry and unhappy man, and were reluctant to attend his funeral. When they heard that their friends would be there, however, they decided they would be embarrassed not to be there. In fact, they found that the funeral was a relieving and positive experience.

The positive outpouring of cards and gifts and the attendance at the funeral of extended family, neighbors, friends and classmates, teachers, principals, and other people in the community were sometimes surprising to children—they loved it. To have their parent celebrated in this way gave them a feeling of pride and pleasure, and they listened intently to what people said. Although they did not give eulogies themselves, as the older children did, they were glad when a speaker reflected their thoughts. Memorializing the parent began with this event.

Children's Responses

The responses of the 6- to 8-year-olds were often unnerving, leaving parents in a quandry as to how best to deal with them. The children said and acted what they felt. Unlike their older peers, they had not quite reached the ability to inhibit their expressions based on what they would predict to be other people's responses. Under stress they were still predominantly pre-operational and pre-latency in their cognitive and emotional organization.

Many children were relieved after the parent died, especially if the illness had been long and the parent had obviously suffered. One 8-year-old explained that she liked to talk about her mother now because the worst had already happened, and she no longer had to be afraid about causing something bad to happen by discussing it. Children were relieved that the parent was no longer in pain. However, one 7-year-old girl reflected what most seemed to experience: "I know she is O.K. in heaven, but I need a Mommy now."

Most children thought the parent watched them from heaven. One 8-year-old said it felt like his mother had gone on a long vacation and not taken him with her. Another boy said he thought his father was in heaven walking on golden streets. The children spoke openly about the fact that they talked with their dead parent. For the most part, these were comforting experiences.

Parents were often surprised that the children were more outspoken and asked more direct questions than did their older siblings. For example, after learning that one of their parents would soon die or had died, many of them asked the prospective survivor: "Are you going to marry again?" Some quickly let their surviving parent know that they did not want him or her to do so—a position that usually changed within a few months. Other comments and questions included, "Will you be sad for the rest of your life?" "I know your heart is broken because Mommy died." An 8-year-old said it was unfair that his mother died and his grandmother, who had cancer for a number of years, was still alive.

Soon after the death, many children spoke openly and explicitly about wanting to die so they could be with the parent. Eight-year-old Tim said, "I want to die to be with Mom." His 6-year-old sister was more dramatic: "I want to kill myself to be in heaven and visit Mom." Like other children her age, she thought a lot about what her mother was doing up there. Although such comments were expressions of distress and longing and were not accompanied by an intent to inflict harm on themselves, the progression of this thought content needed to be monitored. If these thoughts did not gradually subside, if they seemed to become fixed and inflexible, and if they were accompanied by other symptoms, a referral for therapy was recommended.

Some children said they did not like themselves and wanted to change; others exhibited severe aggressive behaviors. Those who exhibited these types of responses later proved to have a more compromised outcome than other children did. Some who exhibited negative thoughts about themselves soon after the death were able to recover from their despair by the time of the final evaluation.

An increase in separation anxiety was quickly apparent after the death. The children very often wanted to sleep with the surviving parent. Most parents permitted their children of this age to sleep with them for several weeks before trying to wean them from this form of comfort and reassurance. Some parents, who believed it was best not to allow their child to sleep with them stayed with the child until he or she fell asleep instead. Children became afraid that something terrible would happen to the surviving parent; if the parent smoked, they worried about the parent's health and wanted the parent to stop smoking. Some followed the parent around. One father of two young daughters said he felt like they were 'glued' to him. Children often spoke of nighttime being the hardest because they had trouble going to sleep and were awakened from dreams. They also had nightmares about 'monsters.'

In addition to sleep disturbances, children expressed their distress during the early period after the death by crying, having more temper tantrums, increasing their oppositional behavior, or having more conflicts and aggressive behaviors with siblings and peers. Some had problems with enuresis, whereas others had somatic complaints such as stomachaches, headaches, or eating problems. Those who believed they had not been prepared for the death were likely to be fearful or angry at the surviving parent, and most expressed a sense of betrayal and mistrust.

Bereavement and Reconstitution

The children's expressions of grief were generally more overt than those of older children. Although they did not maintain a continuous dialogue about the parent, as could occur among preschool children, they were eager to look at pictures and to talk about the parent and their own thoughts and emotions. Most often their mourning was characterized by joyous remembrance of the parent who died. Their sadness and longing could also be intense and profound. They often felt family life had lost security and normalcy.

> Shortly after his father died, 8-year-old Dan reported: "If mother cries, I cry too. Then I think about Dad. Will we be safe? Will we have a regular family?"

The bereavement and reconstitution of the 6- to 8-year-old children were almost exclusively shaped by the surviving parent. In this sample, the outside world could not begin to provide the distraction, the boost in self-esteem, or the solace that older children and adolescents gained from school, peers, and other significant adults. The surviving parent immediately needed to take over the caregiving tasks of the parent who died to provide empathic nurturance, patient understanding and clarification, a consistent structure, and discipline. This was more difficult for surviving fathers, but in situations where the father had been both the patient and the child's primary nurturer, it posed special challenges for the mother.

The reconstitution experience of the child was shaped by four factors:

understanding of the death, emotional reactions to the death, grieving, and the reconstitution of the family.

Understanding the Death

As Dan indicated, children felt the loss of their security, both individually and as a family, as a consequence of the death. When the mother was the parent who died, they felt the loss of essential caregiving as well. Children this age also understood the universality of death more clearly than did their younger peers.

> Cindy was concerned that, with her mother's death, she might not have anyone to take care of her. This 7-year-old also had a sense that life was more fragile than she had realized: "I might die tomorrow," she said. She felt that she would be better off if her mother was alive because now she had baby-sitters "who won't teach me the way my mother did or won't know how to take care of me when I get sick."

Children worried about their personal health and the vulnerability of the surviving parent. Such fears were especially acute if there were multiple cancers in the extended family. In several families, the parent's death was preceded or followed by the death of grandparents.

> In one family, the grandmother lived with the family after the mother died and her cancer became terminal within six months of her daughter's death. This was traumatic to the daughter. The 8-year-old began to worry about her own susceptibility to cancer.

> In another family, a grandfather died two months after the father. The 7-year-old girl became enuretic shortly after the second event.

In these situations, parents were encouraged to acknowledge the shocking nature of what had happened, explore the child's views of the events, and provide information that might help to provide the child with a realistic perspective. Children also needed reassurance that they would continue to be cared for.

The tendency of children in this age group to use illogical and magical thinking in such an emotionally charged area contributed to their vulnerability after the death. More than any other age group, these children struggled with a sense of guilt and personal responsibility for the parent's death.

> Melissa retained the belief that her dreams of her mother's death caused the death to happen. As a consequence, this 6-year-old became preoccupied with suicidal thoughts as a punishment for her crime.

Emotional Reactions

Separation fears continued to be important. Children clung to their surviving parent, and sometimes became overwhelmed with sadness and fear when at school, day camp, or with friends. Phone calls from the parent were often sufficient to reassure them. At other times, they could not be consoled and had to return home. One father placed loving and reassuring notes in his daughter's lunch box. Most parents called their children often if they were in camp or with friends. One mother observed insightfully that it was easier for her child if the child left her than if she left the child. It was difficult for children to have their surviving parent away overnight during the first six months after the other parent's death, but some parents were able to take brief vacations that their children did not find unduly stressful. Staying with familiar family or friends and receiving daily telephone calls from the parent was especially helpful. Nevertheless, parents were generally counseled against extended separations from the child during the first year.

> Eight-year-old Daria came from an immigrant family that had experienced a number of traumatic losses before her father died of cancer. Most recently, her 5-year-old cousin had been killed in a car accident. Since Daria's father had been home because of his cancer for a number of years, he had become her primary caregiver. Daria was an excellent student, and he helped her with her homework. She was extremely distraught when he died. Her older cousin described her as nervous, touching her hair, putting her hands in her mouth, and wringing her hands at the funeral. Daria's mother had difficultly empathizing with Daria's needs. After the wake, the mother visited her family without Daria, intending to remain there for a month, but she returned sooner on the urging of the cousin who was caring for Daria, because she was demonstrating unusual regressive behaviors.

Some children also experienced vague fears about their own vulnerability. They suddenly became afraid when they were in a dark theater. They worried about their bodies and had headaches and stomachaches that sometimes kept them out of school. School phobia, although rare, also occurred. Some of their physical symptoms bore a striking resemblance to the symptoms that their parent had experienced during the terminal illness.

Although the children had strong emotions, they needed the parent's permission and encouragement to share them. They were not as uninhibited as preschool children, who could talk constantly about the parent who died. Instead, these children tended to do what they had done before the death: hold back questions and worries for fear of upsetting the parent or eliciting the parent's disapproval. When given permission, however, many children readily expressed their thoughts and feelings.

Grief and Mourning

The expressions of grief and mourning by the 6- to 8-year old children were more evident and complex than that of their younger peers, but also more confusing to the parents than that of the older children. These children grieved the loss of the person unlike preschool children who grieved mostly for a special function the parent had provided. The person they mourned was their protector, their care-taker. Their affect and behavior evidenced their vulnerable self-esteem. At this age the parents are almost exclusively the source and suppliers of self-esteem. Where the dead parent had been the one that praised and encouraged, this became an important task the surviving parent had to learn.

What was confusing to the parent was the way they mourned their dead parent. The children sporadically talked about missing the parent, mixed with sad and angry feelings; more often, however, they wanted to talk about the parent in a happy way. They enjoyed recalling things they and their parent had done together, such as going fishing, playing baseball, doing homework, shopping, going on vacations, planting vegetables, cooking, or making "Daddy's famous pancakes" (see Chapter 6).

> In the days after David was told about his father's death, he said he thought about the good times they had had together. The 8-year-old missed his father. He thought his father's body was cold because his spirit had left it, and it was the spirit that kept the body warm. He thought he would feel closer to his father when his family vacationed in Florida because that was where he and his father had had such a good time.

The children enjoyed 'talking to' the deceased parent at bedtime, in church, or in the cemetery. They also were comforted by the thought that the dead parent was watching over them—an almost universal image that children described and turned to when they were stressed.

> After receiving coins for her lost tooth, one 7-year-old girl said: "I know where Mom is: She's the tooth fairy." Her father said, "Well, if anybody would want that job, it is your mom. She would make a great tooth fairy!"

Many children in the early elementary grades were less reluctant to go to the cemetery to visit the grave than were older children. Although they did not spend a great deal of time at the grave, they enjoyed bringing gifts and decorations. For example, a 7-year-old girl brought stones from the beach to form a heart because "I think Mommy will like that." The children enjoyed looking at pictures and watching videotapes of the parent who had died, but surviving parents often avoided these experiences because they feared losing control of their emotions and frightening their children. Thus, children sometimes found it easier to involve grandparents or other relatives in their grief.

Parents were encouraged to model the expression of feelings but not to overwhelm their child with the full intensity of adult grief. Children were often attentive to the parent's grief and tried poignantly to help them feel better.

> One 7-year-old had expanded her mealtime prayer to include a special prayer for her dead mother. This caused her father to become teary-eyed. Before dinner, the girl said to him, "I'm going to pray for Mom tonight. Are you going to be sad?" When he said he would be, she brought a large box of tissues to the table and told him that she had noticed that "You always feel better after you cry."

Children also derived consolation by having the dead parent's possessions, such as photographs, jewelry, clothing, books, cards, and a broad range of other objects that had special meaning and importance in their relationship with the missing parent. These objects were especially important in the early postdeath period; most children put them aside as time went on. For daughters who had lost their mother, the favorite objects included photographs, jewelry, clothing, and toys from the mother's youth. For sons who had lost their father, the favorite objects were books, knives, baseball cards, fishing equipment, and clothing.

Waking up in the night crying, complaining about dreams or nightmares, and talking about missing the dead parent were common during the first few months after the death. Most parents accepted these episodes as a transient need for solace.

They also had sad and bitter thoughts that made them feel discouraged and fearful about their ability to survive and to measure up. Although they were less preoccupied than were older children with the injustice of the situation, they were angry that God would allow their parent to get sick and leave them.

> Eight-year-old Kara said she was worried about growing up without her mother, although she understood that her teachers and family were all trying to help her. Her grandmother was also dying. She said bitterly that she no longer believed in the tooth fairy, Santa Claus, or the Easter Bunny: "I don't know why they come up with such silly things as the tooth fairy."

The children worried about who would comb their hair, take care of them when they were sick, help them with homework, and help them become competitive with peers. Some asked if they would still have vacations and fun times together. They felt especially low when there were conflicts with the surviving parent or their grief was not appreciated or understood. As one 8-year-old said, "Dad made me feel special."

Anger was expressed by children in this age group, which Mark's story in Chapter 9 illustrates. However, it was not until children reached the ages of 9 to 14 that anger became a more dominant emotion in their grief experience.

Children's anxiety and anger about the lack of understanding and care they received from the surviving parent and other adults was often mixed with and compounded by their grief for the parent who had died. Conversely, children who felt more comfortable with their care arrangements often experienced less severe and less complex grief.

Reconstitution of the Family

Because of their central role in the lives of 6- to 8-year-olds, the well parents had to assume a broad range of new roles and functions during the spouse's terminal illness and after the death. The children were helped most by the surviving parent's responsiveness to their grief and by the careful development of a new but predictable environment.

Because surviving parents were aware of the special relationship that their spouse had had with the child, they worried about their ability to substitute appropriately for the missing parent. Changing these imbalances was quite effective.

> John, a busy investment banker, had been very involved in the rearing and care of his young children. However, after his wife's brain tumor was diagnosed, he realized that he had not been especially comfortable with their 8-year-old daughter, Carrie, and therefore had left much of her care to his wife. After the diagnosis, he realized that he needed to develop more rapport with Carrie. With focused effort, which included therapy for her, he was able to accomplish this goal over the next two years so that after his wife died, Carrie said, "I can talk with my daddy now, and he makes me feel better. He used to work a lot before, but now we can talk. Sometimes he is tired so we have to shout so he can hear us."

The difficulty of changing roles and functions within a family should not be underestimated. John expressed it well when he told the interviewer, "I can't imagine how people do this without money. I have enough money to hire all the help I need and it's (still) overwhelming." Most surviving mothers struggled with how to discipline their sons, which was a far greater challenge when their sons were in an older age group. Fathers could be sensitive about finding ways to understand and relate to their young children.

> In a family session, 8-year-old Jim told his father, Henry, that he missed his mother most when Henry yelled at him. Jim explained that this was so because his mother would tell his dad not to yell at the kids so much when they got in trouble. Henry later told the interviewer that he had learned something in that session and was controlling his temper better because he did not want to make the same mistakes his father had made with him. On the anniversary of his wife's death and at times when they felt especially lonely, he allowed Jim and his 6-year-old daughter to sleep in his bed with him. They slept on their mother's side of his king-size bed. Henry said he did this "because everybody just felt bad." Jim later told the interviewer that his father hugged them and made them feel better.

During discussions with the interviewer, other fathers and mothers reflected honestly on their abilities, energy, and the tasks that needed doing. They thought about other adults who might be better able to provide certain aspects of their young children's care and who would be acceptable to the children. These adults included members of the extended family, housekeepers, baby-sitters, and counselors. Parents also enlisted the help of informed teachers, coaches, guidance counselors, school nurses, pediatricians, and others who could help their children during the grief process. Children talked openly about using these resources to help them with difficult moments that occurred throughout the day. The fact that children used these resources did not contradict the surviving parent's central role.

Most parents used bereavement groups, individual counseling for themselves or their children, or individual and group therapy as aids in the grieving and reconstitution process. These professional services were often effective. Parents noticed that their early school age children's ability to talk about the parent who died increased and their behavior improved after participating in a bereavement group.

However, at times children found that their groups were too confronting. They could be upset by hearing the extreme experiences of other children. For example, a girl from an inner-city school was especially upset by a boy in her group because both of his parents had been killed. Another boy complained about the group, but his mother noticed that he participated fully when he attended and seemed to be more open when discussing his late father.

Constructing a predictable family life after a parent's death was an important way of helping children regain their previous level of functioning. There were often new caregivers and new rules to adjust to. Although other people could help with homework and sports, it took time before children believed that these people were adequate. As one boy said, "My grandfather plays baseball with me, but he's not as good as Dad." A 7-year-old dissolved in tears when he discovered in school that he had left his spelling book at home because his mother had been the one who always made sure that his book bag contained what he needed before he left in the morning.

Many children yearned for a 'regular family' again, but their early questions about whether the surviving parent would remarry were sometimes misunderstood as a lack of love for the parent who died rather than a reflection of the urgency of wanting life to return to the way it had been. Although initially the children were likely to ask the parent not to remarry, most of them were inclined to say that they needed more help with the household chores within a few months after the parent died. They wanted to feel safe, secure, and valued as they had been. It also reflected their grieving the loss of the parent who died and their search for a new one.

> John's father was able to stay home from work for several months after his wife died. Three months after the death, John told his father he wanted him to go back to work so that the family would return to normal. Six months after the death, John began encouraging his father to date, saying that he wanted a new mother so that life could become like it used to be.

When the parent actually began to date, however, some children became ambivalent again because they were afraid of losing the parent's love to the new person or to another child that might be born. One 7-year-old, the youngest of four brothers, told his mother before she had begun to date that he wanted a baby sister. Another 7-year-old announced to her mother that she thought boys were too messy; she would rather have another sister.

To surviving fathers, the challenge of taking care of and nurturing children in this age group was usually overwhelming. Finding adequate substitute care was not easy or even possible for some. This was an added impetus to find a replacement by dating soon after the death of their spouse. But some women also dated early, explaining that they had been preoccupied with the care of an ill spouse for several years and wanted male companionship. Both fathers and mothers were deeply moved by their children's obvious yearning for attention from adults of the same sex as the dead parent and wanted to give them a replacement.

RECOMMENDATIONS FOR PROFESSIONALS AND CAREGIVERS

Terminal Illness

1. *Inform early elementary school children about the parent's illness on a timely basis.* This information should include the name of the disease and its process, symptoms, treatments, and prognosis.

2. *Model expressions of emotion.* Children in early elementary school can be overcome with strong parental emotions of anger or sadness. Sharing more controlled emotions when discussing certain events, especially emotions the child also may be experiencing, is effective.

3. *Communicate with the child's teachers and other significant adults in their lives about the parent's illness.* Teachers need to be aware that a drop in grades is not unusual, especially during the terminal illness.

4. *Establish consistent primary caregiving with one or two people who communicate well with the children.* Inconsistent caretaking has a negative impact on younger children's behavior and sense of well-being. Caregiving arrangements should be explained to young children so they can predict and prepare for separations and changes. Inform caregivers of the children's need for reassurance and support in addition to attention to their physical needs.

5. *Prepare the child for medical emergencies that require the parents to leave the house unexpectedly.* The first time an emergency occurs, the parent needs to explain the situation to the child afterward and point out that it will probably happen again. Parents should be concrete: for example, explain where the child will find the baby-sitter if the parents are not in their bed. It is preferable for children to be cared for in their own home whenever possible.

6. *Do not rely on children to ask questions about the parent's illness.* Children this age need permission to ask questions and express emotions about important family problems. Many refrain from doing so because they are afraid the parent will be upset, the answers will be too scary, or the parent's illness will become worse in some magical way if they talk about it.

7. *Encourage children to maintain developmentally appropriate activities to the degree possible.* Emphasis should be placed on what is not "lost" and what has not changed; however, changes that have occurred should be acknowledged.

8. *Keep in mind the parent's central role in providing children with support and ways of maintaining their self-esteem.* Parents need to reflect carefully on their ability to spend adequate time with these children because of job or other caretaking responsibilities. The parent who has difficulty understanding and relating empathetically with children this age needs to identify a substitute (a relative, a therapist, or a counselor). Parents should remember to praise children for achievements in school and efforts to help.

9. *Evaluation and counseling should be considered for children this age* if they are experiencing severe anxiety, especially separation anxiety, school phobia, preoccupation with self-blame or evidence low self-esteem. When the mother is the patient, this area is more likely to be a problem for the children.

Death and Family Rituals

1. *Inform even young children about the parent's worsening condition and probable death.* Providing time for final good-byes helps the child grieve after the death. The Catholic ritual of the last rites demonstrates that it is not that impossible to judge when a parent is close to death or to get help from experienced doctors and nurses in the hospital in making that judgment.

2. *Provide empathic support for the child's initial responses to the parent's death.* Encourage the child to express him- or herself and demonstrate warm, loving, and caring concern for the child.

3. *Encourage the child to attend traditional rituals.* Occasionally, a child will not want to attend these rituals. However, inviting a few of the child's friends, eliciting the aid of a favorite adult to be available to the child during the parts of the rituals that are most troubling is usually enough to overcome the child's initial reluctance and fear.

4. *Include the child as an active participant in the ceremonies whenever possible and whenever the child shows an interest or willingness to participate actively.* Placing objects in the coffin, contributing to the content of the eulogies, or distributing memorial cards are all ways a child can participate.

5. *Be prepared for blunt questions from the children this age around the time of the death.* Questions about remarriage and having more children are not unusual.

6. *Do not be surprised by the brevity and episodic nature of the child's expressions of grief.* Surviving parents of children in the early elementary grades need to be prepared for the child's eagerness to return to normal activities—school, playing, being with friends, and having fun—after what appears to be a brief period of mourning.

Bereavement and Reconstitution

1. *Continue the dialogue with young children about their thoughts, feelings, and reactions to the many changes that are taking place in their lives.* By doing this, the parent is more likely to have the opportunity to correct erroneous information and reframe events in ways that support the young child's self-esteem.

2. *Communicate with school personnel and others who have contact with these children.* These individuals can ease the child's transition back into developmentally appropriate activities and assist with potentially hurtful peer interactions. Remind teachers that peers may tease because they themselves are anxious about such an event.

3. *Maintain as much consistency and predictability as possible in the child's caregiving and living arrangements.* If possible, this planning should begin before the patient dies. Especially when the mother is the patient, consideration needs to be given to how this will be managed.

4. *Separations from the parent lasting more than a day or so can be quite difficult for children this age during the first six months after the parent's death.*

5. *Encourage the children to talk about, remember, and participate in memorializing activities.* If the parent finds that these activities are too painful, other people such as grandparents may be able to assume this role. The crucial point is that these children need someone with whom they can share their grief.

6. *Be prepared for children's affect to be more positive.* Children's mourning includes remembering the parent with pleasure rather than being sad and mournful when talking about the parent who died.

7. *Help the children cope with the many changes that take place because of the parent's death.* Remember to praise the child's efforts to adapt in order to maintain the child's self-esteem.

8. *Understand that children in this age group express intense feelings of grief only fleetingly.* These moments may be followed by a desire to play and have fun.

9. *Use outside help.* Parent bereavement counseling, individual or group, can be very helpful. Children's bereavement groups were also helpful and may be available in the school.

10. *Consider evaluation and therapy for children this age if their anxiety, depression, guilt, poor self-esteem, or thoughts of killing themselves persist for more than several months after the death.*

11. *Parents should consider obtaining counseling for themselves if they have prolonged symptoms of depression or anxiety, a problem with alcohol or other substances, or exacerbations of previous emotional or mental health problems.* Such problems can impact negatively on parenting ability.

8

Children 6–8 Years of Age

Narratives

These stories concern the responses of two families to the onset of terminal cancer. Seven-year-old Mark Stone, the boy in the first story concerned the interventionist more than did 8-year-old Coleen O'Leary, the girl in the second story. Already during kindergarten Mark was a bit immature, and worried professionals about a potential problem with hyperactivity. However for Coleen, a cascade of secondary stressors—the loss of all nurturing supports—had a powerful effect. The things she had control over, she did well: she was an excellent student, was liked and respected by classmates and teachers, and she behaved well and responsibly at home. Yet her outcome was more troubled than Mark's.

MOTHER, 7-YEAR-OLD SON AND 4-YEAR-OLD DAUGHTER

"Daddy Was an Awesome Coach!"

Background

Mark's father, Maxwell Stone, was an attorney who started his own firm a year before his diagnosis. Helene, Mark's mother, was on the editorial staff of a fashion magazine. She enjoyed her work and did not leave her job until Amanda was born and Mark was 3 years old.

Helene found that Amanda was much easier to handle, to understand, and to like than Mark was. Amanda was neat and easygoing, whereas Mark was intense and turned a room into a shambles just by walking into it. Helene told the interviewer that Maxwell could relate much better to Mark than she could. Mark and his father played and rough housed, and both loved baseball. Maxwell was teaching Mark to catch and hit the ball, although Mark was not a natural athlete. But neither was Maxwell.

Illness

Maxwell's cancer did not produce overt signs of disease at first. Fatigue, a cough, night sweats, swollen lymph nodes on his neck, and some vague chest pains were his early symptoms. When the symptoms did not improve, he finally went to a physician about a year after his symptoms began. A biopsy established that he had leukemia. Both parents kept the children informed about their father's treatment procedures in a matter-of-fact way. For example, they explained that because the doctors gave him medicine, he would feel sicker for a while. The children seemed to accept Maxwell's gradually reduced activity. Neither one asked any pointed questions nor showed any overt reactions to their father's illness.

Terminal Stage

When Maxwell failed to respond to the third course of chemotherapy, he and Helene had to confront the possibility that his disease was now terminal. That was only two years after his initial diagnosis. A bone marrow transplant was the last hope. Maxwell had to remain in the hospital for eight weeks, during which time Helene visited him every day. An au pair who had lived with the family for many years cared for the children. The parents now informed the children that their father had cancer and that it was extremely serious. Maxwell changed his work situation drastically so he could stay home. Although his stamina improved over the next six months, his disease did not.

Mark's life changed gradually after his father came home. His only reaction was that his anger was a bit less controlled. He loved his Ninja Turtles, but he loved his Wrestler Boys even more. "I want to be tough like the Wrestler Boys so I can beat up a boy at school because he punched me in the stomach."

Mark felt that his teacher gave too much homework, but his grades were As and Bs, and, as he told the interviewer, he did not get into trouble at school: "Other kids get me in trouble because they tell the teacher sometimes that I did something wrong, but I didn't. Amanda gets me into trouble at home, and Daddy is the one who makes me stay in my room for a long time. Then I get angry and mess up my room. I sneak out and visit my friend without anyone knowing. I leave a note saying 'I'm running away.'" Mark, in common with many children his age, was prone to dramatize and exaggerate.

When Maxwell was hospitalized again, Mark visited him a couple of times. After the first visit, Mark told the interviewer: "He looked like a wiener because he didn't have any hair." After the second visit, when Maxwell's disease was more advanced, Mark said, "Daddy looked funny—puffy and all white."

When Maxwell returned home, Mark at times was annoyed with his father's limitations and his need for care:

> He hogs the good TV downstairs, and I have to go upstairs, and that TV takes a long time to come on. He asks me to do things for him when he watches TV, like get the *TV Guide* upstairs or scratch his back and his head. But I don't like it. He should pay me $10. I'm like a slave. I think he has to go to the hospital because he complains too much.

Experiences such as the following sharpened Mark's separation concerns. Mark woke up during the night to get a glass of water. His parents were gone. They had to rush to the hospital because Maxwell started bleeding, and they decided not to awaken Mark. Mark explained, "It's a good thing Doreen (the au pair) was there. I thought someone stole my parents." Following this event, Helene carefully prepared Mark for the possibility of such sudden departures and instructed him about what to do.

Mark also reached wrong, although interesting, conclusions that were commensurate with his stage of development:

> I know that I can't catch Dad's cancer. It's not like AIDS; you get that from sex and from drugs. Doreen smokes, so she might get AIDS from smoking. I learned that at school.

> I'm scared that Daddy will die, but I know that he won't because Mommy said so. The one good thing about getting sick is you get to stay home and watch TV all the time.

> I got real mad when they wouldn't let me have the Nike sneakers, and they made me go to my room and I messed it up. Then I wanted to kill myself. Then Mommy and Daddy would kill themselves to be with me, and then I would be an angel. (Then Mark changed his mind:) I didn't want to kill myself. Angels don't wear clothes and I couldn't wear my new clothes. (Mark was a serious clothes-horse.)

Helene gradually took over more control of the home. She found that she was always threatening Mark and hating herself for doing it. So she tried a different approach—using more positive reinforcers—which seemed to work.

Mark had a good year in first grade: He had friends and received good grades, and the teacher was pleased with him. However, Mark was becoming slightly obese. When Helene's parents moved in to help, the au pair left. Mark began asking more questions about his father's illness, and Helene answered them after exploring how much he understood. This seemed to make Mark feel better.

Preparation for Death and Family Rituals

Dying is difficult for everyone, but it is especially difficult for a young parent. Five months after his bone marrow transplant, Maxwell had another relapse, which indicated a serious prognostic change in the disease. Maxwell reacted to this change with depression, which cut him off from his children. This consequence was not acceptable to Maxwell, who said: "I decided to get off my butt." He spent more time with Mark and, when his energy level allowed, took Mark to a ball game or to the movies, "men's movies" about Ninja Turtles and wrestling. Maxwell also coached Little League for as long as he could.

This sequence of events—the change in disease state, the emotional reaction to the change, and the altered life course—took place a number of times in the lives of all patients during their terminal illness. Maxwell, in common with so many patients in this sample, chose a course that would be helpful to his children.

A week or so before Maxwell died, Helene told both children: "Daddy is so sick now that there is nothing left for the doctors and nurses to do to make him better. He will not get better, and he's going to die." Mark cried when she told him, and Amanda had trouble going to sleep that night. Later, Mark told Helene: "I made Daddy get sick because I broke his heart. I didn't scratch his head and back when he wanted me to." Only gradually was Helene able to dissuade Mark from this erroneous conclusion.

Helene made plans to involve Mark and Amanda in the funeral and burial and in sitting Shiva and began reviewing ways to discuss the Jewish rituals with them. Before she could carry out this plan, however, Maxwell died. When Helene told the children, both of them cried, but Mark's reactions included anger: "How could he do that without telling me?"

The children's teachers and many of their classmates attended the services, which was helpful to the children. Amanda showed more regressive behavior than Mark did, becoming whiny and clinging. Mark said, "She sits in Daddy's chair with lots of blankets. She was sick to her stomach and needed to see a doctor." He added that he developed chest pains and had hot ears. Helene explained to the interviewer that his father had had these symptoms. He also had a facial tick that was similar to his father's. These symptoms diminished rapidly.

Bereavement and Reconstitution

Helene set aside a special time each night to talk with the children about their father. Amanda often used the word "dead" and then asked when she could see him again. Mark was more resigned; he was sad because he could not do things with his father anymore: "Daddy coached me in soccer, and that is how we got to be the championship team. He was an awesome coach! That's why I'm the best player on the team. We never lost a game! Well, I kind of made that up."

During the first week after Maxwell died, both children slept in bed with Helene. Later, only Amanda slept with her, once a week.

Mark informed Helene that "I'm the man in the house now, and I'll take Daddy's place." Helene thanked him but said that was not necessary.

Mark mourned his father in ways not unlike other 6- to 8-year-olds: briefly and sporadically. The episodes were usually triggered by an event, a dream, or a special time for talking. Mementos of the dead parent, which are especially comforting for children this age, also played a significant role for Mark. For weeks after the death, Mark carried his father's favorite baseball card and wore his father's neck chain, ring, and watch every day. He had a recurrent dream in which people thought his father was dead, "but he wasn't; he was alive."

> Home is not as much fun now. Daddy was fun—lots of laughs. He could draw. He could understand me.

Both children joined an art bereavement group at a local hospital. Mark's facial tick subsided, and his teacher said he remembered to do his homework pretty well. Forgetting to do his homework had been a major problem during Maxwell's illness.

Both Mark and Amanda began talking more openly about their father. Helene believed that this was a good sign and encouraged them to do so whenever possible. "This may be because of the art bereavement group. The other night, Mark and I were looking at Maxwell's picture in the obituary column, and we both had a good cry. Mark talked about how much he missed his father."

Mark's bereavement gradually changed. During the first few weeks after Maxwell died, Mark often complained to the school nurse about chest pains, but physically he was all right. Chest pains were among Maxwell's early symptoms. About four months later, Mark was less preoccupied with physical ills. For example, Helene recalled that when Mark twisted his ankle at school, she took him to the doctor, who found Mark's ankle uninjured. Mark then insisted on going back to school. A similar change took place in the importance of his father's mementos. At first, Mark wore some of his father's clothes, his shorts and ties as he pretended to be a warrior and a wrestler. Three months later, Mark began keeping his father's underwear, jewelry, and ties in a box in his room rather than carrying or wearing them. He kept his father's favorite baseball card with his other cards, but he no longer felt that he needed to keep the other items near him.

An important part of the reconstitution experience for the surviving parent is learning to take over some roles of the dead parent and experimenting with other ways to handle situations that emerge. In Helene's case, setting limits and dealing with the children's fighting was a concern. For example, if one of them received gifts, the other wanted the same number of gifts, and they argued over who had the most. This made Helene lose her temper.

A while later, Helene decided that she had to be tougher with both children "to reestablish them. Maxwell was the disciplinarian, and now I have to take on that role. But I'm not too clear about how to discipline Mark."

When the children became excessively demanding, Helene initially lost her patience but then explored other ways to encourage them to be more independent. "Mark kept asking me to do things for him that he should be able to do himself, such as tying his shoelaces. This annoyed me, so I put a stop to it".

"The other day, I found myself yelling at Mark about all the things he was doing wrong, and he ran to his room and slammed the door. So I caught myself, went in and apologized to him, and gave him a hug and a kiss. He was so happy! I realized that I needed to do more of that—to be more positive with him about himself, to make him shine."

Helene weighed many factors concerning the children, such as their need for school and friends. She described several self-correcting experiences: For example, she asked Mark to come home from playing with his friends by a certain time. When he was late, however, she realized that the time she had set gave him too little time to play. She also found that some of her expectations were unrealistic and was pleased that she was learning to correct them.

The process of mourning and its pace differs for parents and children. Five or six months after the death, most 6- to 8-year-olds remember the dead parent mainly on special occasions. The surviving parent, on the other hand, may only be getting over the initial numbness and may suddenly become wracked by more powerful mourning experiences. As is so often the case, five months after the death, Helene found that her grief became more intense and harder to bear. She was now grieving for her well husband rather than the sick one.

The evidence of children's greater ease in dealing with the facts of the death or their part in it, is usually apparent only in specific situations. For example, Mark no longer wanted to talk as much about people dying. When a friend of Helene's asked Mark what had happened to his father, Mark said: "He is gone, caput, he's dead." On another occasion, Mark volunteered: "I don't think Daddy died because of me anymore; it was God's fault. God is stupid. He kills everybody. He doesn't know anything."

When Helene gave the children the choice of going to the cemetery or visiting her parents on Father's Day, they chose to visit their grandparents and gave the flowers intended for the grave to their grandfather.

For the surviving parent, reconstitution involves many aspects that affect the welfare of the children directly or indirectly. Finances, work, and parent replacement are some of the larger issues the surviving parent must tackle.

Five months after Maxwell's death, Helene bought a smaller, less expensive house nearby, and she thought long and hard about how the move might affect the children. "The kids will go to the same public school, so that part should be O.K. We'll move during summer vacation so it will be less disruptive. The kids have seen the new house, and they seem to like it."

Helene also began thinking about her work future. "Maxwell left us enough money to survive, and his business is doing well. I want to prepare myself for a different career than I had before, so I'm working 12 hours a week to pay for a business course." She subsequently began attending night school once a week. When Mark announced that he didn't need a baby-sitter anymore, she reframed the situation by saying that the baby-sitter was for Amanda, and he could be the sitter's assistant.

A child's search for a replacement for the dead parent can take many forms. For example, when Maxwell's cousin visited shortly after Maxwell's death, he and Mark wrestled, and Helene's father attended a Boy Scout dinner with Mark. Wrestling and the Boy Scouts were Mark's favorite father-son activities.

Both children began pressuring Helene to get a new daddy. Although she knew she would eventually be interested in marrying again, she did not feel she was ready. She was able to laugh when Amanda's 5-year-old friend asked her one day: "When are you going to get a new daddy for Amanda?"

Several months after Maxwell's death, Helene began dating a family friend. She felt embarrassed because "People are going to say, 'So soon after his death?' but they don't understand that for two years, physical intimacy was no longer possible. I don't view this relationship as a permanent one. What concerns me is that the children will become attached to him and then be hurt again."

The children teased Helene about the fact that her boyfriend gave her a birthday present. Mark, who was competitive with him, again announced to Helene that he wanted to assume some of his father's roles around the home.

When the interviewer saw Mark 14 months after the death, he seemed much easier to talk to: He was more open and more willing to share information about himself, but he was worried about getting cancer. Maxwell had a brother who had also died of cancer some years before. Mark was beginning to think about this. More recently, an aunt was diagnosed with severe mental illness, these occurences increased Mark's worries. Helene had decided he might benefit from some therapy, so he had started seeing someone once a week. He told the interviewer he liked seeing a counselor much better than participating in the art bereavement group. He obviously was in touch with his feelings about his father and continued to mourn him, but he was also able to talk feelingly about many everyday things, and he continued to do well in school.

Summary

The story of the Stone family exemplifies many points summarized in the previous chapter. Both parents contributed to ameliorating what could easily have been a difficult outcome, certainly for 7-year-old Mark. Maxwell's decision "to get off my butt" and spend quality time with Mark was important, and left a great legacy—an image of a loving father who was well pleased with his children. Helene informed her 4- and 7-year-old children about Maxwell's illness, its progression, its prognosis, and, finally, his death, in a stepwise, incremental fashion. They felt informed, and each subsequent step in the progression was less difficult for her to manage. Finally, keeping life regular and predictable so that Mark knew no one had "stolen" his parents, all contributed to reducing Mark's and Amanda's anxiety. As a result, Mark even had a good school year.

Helene's grief was powerful, she suffered the loneliness and the resentment of isolation as a single parent. Helene learned to be a good single parent by taking over Maxwell's role as disciplinarian. She also learned what is one of the hardest things to do with a hyperactive, messy, unruly 7-year-old boy: to set limits without lowering his self-esteem. Like so many successful parents, she used all available resources well. She sent both children to an art bereavement group and then obtained a therapist for Mark because his symptoms had not completely subsided.

FATHER WITH 7- AND 20-YEAR-OLD DAUGHTERS

"I Like the Little Girl in the Grave Next to Mom's"

Coleen O'Leary had a more troubled outcome than did most children her age. There were no villains in her story to account for it. Certainly not Coleen, a dark-haired, blue-eyed Irish beauty who 'was the spit and image of her mother', Barbara. When Coleen was 7 years old, Barbara became terminally ill with ovarian cancer. Although Coleen tried hard to please everyone, she never found a constant, parenting adult who could provide her with motherly comfort, encouragement, and praise. Although she became an excellent student, she found solace only at her mother's grave. There she befriended and almost envied the child whose grave was close to Barbara's—a girl who was 2 years old when she died "and now is almost 12."

Coleen's 20-year-old sister, Mara, was not a villain either. She had struggled to achieve independence from her close-knit family as a young adolescent, and her mother's illness renewed that struggle. Mara felt pulled back into the family to help care for her mother and Coleen, but she was afraid she would not be able to reestablish her independence. To her former fears concerning independence was now added the specter of developing the cancer that affected so many women in the family and that might take her mother's life. These fears made her unable to provide the consistent mothering that Coleen needed.

What about Joseph O'Leary, Coleen's father? Eighteen months after his wife's death, he remained deeply depressed. He was mourning not only for Barbara but also for his father, who had died before Joseph was in his teens.

And Barbara? Like all terminally ill cancer patients, she suffered the ravages of cancer and its treatments before she died. Her severe anxiety attacks, which occurred when her terminal illness was first discussed, revealed the degree of her fear. Her need to continue working until her last hospitalization further emphasized her difficulty in facing her own death or the pain that her illness was inflicting on her daughters.

Avoidance was a communication strategy that the entire family tried to implement. For some family members, this strategy seemed to work well because it protected them from anxiety and permitted them to continue leading productive lives. For Coleen and Mara, however, the strategy did not work well because it deprived them of the kind of continuous direct communication, information, and interaction they needed to understand and master their feelings about their mother's illness and death and the subsequent changes in family life.

Finally, what about Barbara's younger sisters? They tried to help, but Coleen was a painful reminder that they had lost their eldest sister and also a reminder that two of them had been treated for the same cancer. Although Barbara and her sisters had teased each other about who would be next, they implicitly assumed that no family member of their generation would die of the family curse. Dying was for the older generation, and Barbara had broken the rules by dying.

Although it is difficult to make something as impersonal as a genetic quirk the villain, it is the best we can do. All the family members were victims of that quirk. The fears of the female members of the family concerning their vulnerability to cancer and an early death imposed a threat that was extremely difficult to master, as all observed its tragic consequences for the beloved eldest sister, mother, and wife.

Background

As children, Barbara and Joseph met shortly after his father died. In high school, they began going steady and were known to their peers as "Barb-and-Joe," almost as if they were one person. Joseph was wild as an adolescent, and drank too much: "beer—never hard liquor." Although people in their working-class neighborhood did not view his behavior as desirable, they thought it was understandable because he had lost his father. "He's a good kid. He will settle down once he gets married." His mother's judgment was harsher; she threatened to send him to an orphanage if he didn't straighten himself out. He managed to graduate from high school and even attended college for a while before enlisting in the Army.

Barbara went to work as a seamstress after graduating from high school. She and Joseph corresponded, she proposed two years later, he accepted, and they were married when he was discharged from the service. This sequence of events set the tenor for their relationship: She took care of the family and had the final say on all decisions. Joseph became a policeman. He had close relationships with all his police buddies, drinking a bit more than most, "but never on duty!" Barbara always drove home from social events because he usually drank too much, but he was never rowdy or belligerent.

Barbara remained extremely close to her sisters, and all of them lived within a couple of miles of each other. She often said, "It's as good as large families can get." The only cloud was the family history of cancer.

Terminal Stage

Barbara was hospitalized many times: three times for surgery and numerous times for courses of chemotherapy. She lost her hair, was violently sick to her stomach, and lost a lot of weight. Unlike her sisters, who were both in remission, she didn't seem to respond to the treatments. She insisted that Coleen should not be told about the illness because she didn't want her to worry. Joseph's attitude was, "It's female cancer—I don't know anything about it. I expect Coleen's aunts to talk to her about it." Joseph then described Coleen's reaction to her mother's illness: "Coleen wants someone around all the time. She misses her mother a lot at night when she is in the hospital. She calls me at the precinct when that happens. She's a good kid, does very well in school, helps around the house."

Coleen was 7 years old when the family was first interviewed. She seemed sad and was initially apprehensive when her father stepped out of the interviewer's office. However, she settled down quickly when she learned that he was in the waiting room. When asked about her mother's illness, Coleen said, "I think Mom has cancer." Later she confided: "I'm scared Mom is going to die." She also revealed that she sometimes sat up with her mother all night after she received her treatment, wondering if she would ever wake up from the deep sleep that followed. These were nights when her father worked the night shift.

The interviewer was somewhat puzzled about the communication in this obviously caring and close-knit family. Providing Coleen with information about the usual side effects of chemotherapy (about the deep sleep, for example) would have reassured her. In addition, other family members could easily have been available to help care for Coleen when her mother was too ill to stay awake. They certainly seemed willing to do so. Regular visits to the hospital also would have alleviated her separation anxiety.

To clarify the situation, the interviewer decided to talk with Coleen's 20-year-old sister, Mara. Mara had a complicated background. She had struggled to achieve independence from her close-knit family as a young adolescent, and her mother's illness renewed that struggle. Mara felt pulled back into the family to help care for her mother and Coleen, but she was afraid she would be unable to reestablish her independence later. To her former fears concerning independence was now added the specter of developing the cancer that affected so many women in the family and that might take her mother's life. Mara explained the family's way of communicating: "We never get any information. If I want to know what's happening to Mom, I ask Coleen. She acts like she's asleep when Mom or Dad talk on the phone, and that's how we get our information."

This pattern of communication was established early during the mother's illness and continued when the chemotherapy began to fail and new symptoms emerged. Mara said that on the way back from a family trip to visit old friends, she had asked her mother about her continuing symptoms and what she thought was going to happen. When Barbara tried to respond, she had a severe anxiety attack. Because of her difficulty breathing, they took her to a local hospital. "She almost died right then." After that episode, the family was reluctant to raise the subject of cancer openly with her. As a consequence, communication became fragmented and indirect—a situation that was most difficult for a child who was almost 8 years old and was hungry for information and clarification, but instead was full of misunderstandings and erroneous information.

Joseph worked a rotating shift. He explained that Coleen stayed with one or another of her aunts at night when he worked the night shift and her mother was in the hospital. Mara was supposed to help out as well. But Coleen described the limits of that plan to the interviewer: "Mara tells me she is coming home after work. I wait up for her, then fall asleep about midnight. I look for her in the morning, but she isn't there. Sometimes she stays with her boyfriend. I worry that she got in another car accident, she has already had one, and she fell down the stairs and broke her leg."

Barbara was hospitalized five times in the three months before her death. Although deteriorating physically, she worked nine hours a day at the checkout counter in a grocery store, cutting back to five hours just before she died. When she came home, she fell into bed exhausted and slept until it was time to go to work or to the hospital for chemotherapy. Maintaining this level of activity despite her exhaustion reflected the denial of her terminal condition and her underlying fear and sadness. It also resulted in a severe withdrawal from her family. Mara came home less and less until the very end of her mother's life.

Because Joseph felt depressed at home, he went out more often with his friends. When he was home, he worked on the house with one of his buddies. Barbara had asked him to fix up a room with its own bathroom for Mara. She thought that if Mara had her own room and bath, she would come home more. Joseph complied and explained to the interviewer: "Mara will do what she wants to do. There is nothing I can do about it. When she is tired of her boyfriend, she'll come home."

As her symptoms worsened, Barbara began having more contact with Mara, who visited her regularly in the hospital. Both Barbara and Joseph were irritable with Coleen because her clinging and fear of being alone threatened their denial. As Joseph explained: "Coleen has stomachaches and headaches. Last night, she didn't want me to go to work. She calls me at work two or three times a night." Joseph worried that Coleen was becoming more like Mara because she didn't want to go to school. It was less threatening to view this behavior as rebelliousness than as a response to her mother's obvious deterioration.

Coleen had trouble sleeping alone when Barbara was in the hospital and told her father, "I want to sleep with you. I'm lonely, Dad." She was frightened by some of her mother's new symptoms, such as her difficulty breathing. When Barbara returned home after chemotherapy treatments, she occasionally had anxiety attacks and cold sweats, and Coleen seemed to be the only one who could soothe her and calm her down.

Death and the Family Rituals

As Barbara's chest pain grew worse and she had trouble breathing because of lung metastases, her denial began to crumble, but it was hard for the family to mobilize. Instead, everyone seemed more confused. Barbara had always been the family organizer, and neither Joseph nor her sisters thought of assuming this role.

A few days after Barbara was readmitted to the hospital, the family held a meeting with the hospital social worker. Coleen still had not been told that her mother was now dying. Finally, Coleen was permitted to ask specific questions about her mother's illness and treatment: "What is her cancer? Why does Mom have all those tubes in her?" However, she never asked whether her mother would die.

Joseph, now clearly depressed, withdrew from all discussions about immediate plans. "The doctor said she would die in a week or two," Joseph said, repeating over and over like a mantra, "When it's over, it's over. Can't do nothing about it. I don't want to cry. I wish it were over, and then I wish it had never happened."

Coleen's aunt worried that if Coleen visited Barbara, she might ask if her mother were going to die. The aunt perceived the ability of children this age to be "truth-tellers," but she was unable to respond to the underlying anxiety that evoked such direct questions. She said that the doctor had told Mara that her mother would probably die within a few days, and that seemed to have made Mara more upset. Mara even began worrying that she would develop the family cancer. Barbara had asked her sister how much time she had left, and the sister and Joseph discussed who should tell Barbara she was dying. They decided that Mara should tell her mother if the doctor did not tell her first. The sister told Joseph that Barbara wanted some help in writing letters to Mara and Coleen, but they could not decide who would help her write them. The sister also reported that Barbara wanted to know how Coleen was doing in school. She did not know what to say, because Coleen's grades had dropped. It was difficult to alter the established pattern of avoidance when circumstances changed and clearly demanded confrontation.

The day before Barbara died, Coleen went to the hospital. Her mother talked with her and asked her to bring some pictures she had drawn. The next day the entire family went to the hospital to say good-bye to Barbara. Although Barbara was nearly comatose, she nodded a few times and squeezed Coleen's hand. Coleen thought her mother was very sick because of all the oxygen bottles and all the tubes going into her, and she was afraid that her mother had found out about her poor grades. Because Coleen was anxious and uncertain about how to act, she turned to Mara to see if it was all right to cry. When Mara said that Mom was turning blue, Coleen was scared and burst into tears, and her aunt comforted her.

Hundreds of people came to the wake and the funeral. The family was not only well known in the community but also well liked. The family's private life was the painful one. Mara said that at the wake, Coleen ran around talking with friends and family members. "It was almost as if she didn't understand what was going on."

At night, Coleen remained anxious and clinging and wanted her father to stay with her until she fell sleep. After retiring, she talked to her father, almost two hours every night, and told him how much she missed her mother. Joseph tried to comfort her by telling her that he cried, too. He told her that when he felt very sad at work, he went to the bathroom at the police station and let himself cry.

One night, after visiting the cemetery, Coleen asked her father how deep her mother was buried. She seemed relieved when Joseph explained that it was very deep—six feet. Coleen was consoled because she had stepped on the mound and was worried that she had stepped on her mother.

Joseph expressed concern about Coleen's increasing separation anxiety, her wish to stay home from school, and her dependency on him. The first day she agreed to return to school, a week after Barbara's death, she was afraid to get on the bus, then ran home crying. She was worried about her father's health. She also felt that her father yelled at her too much, that he was taking his anger out on her. Coleen wanted to get away from him and stay with Mara and Mara's boyfriend. Joseph said he drank very little out of respect for his wife, but that not drinking made him more irritable.

During the first month after Barbara's death, Mara worked in the morning so she could be home when Coleen returned from school. Barbara's sisters also had Coleen stay with them after school. At times, Coleen could express her anger at her mother: "She promised she would come home, and she never did!" Coleen didn't want to tell her father how much she missed her mother because she was afraid she might hurt him. She felt comforted by the doll Barbara had made for her during a hospital stay, by photographs of her mother and the family, and by her mother's wedding ring: "When I'm older, Mom will miss my prom, and if Mara gets married, Mom won't be there. I'm in a wedding in four months: a junior bridesmaid for my cousin. Mom won't be there, but I'll pretend she is watching me from heaven." Coleen also was sad because she had only one grandparent "and he has cancer. My other grandfather died in an accident, and my mother's mother died of cancer, like my two great aunts and my mother."

Coleen was seeing a guidance counselor at school every two weeks and liked to talk to her. She often had stomachaches and headaches and didn't want to go to school on those days. She was extremely worried about her father's increased drinking and grouchiness and was afraid he and her sister would fall apart: "They just fight all the time. Mother used to make it better and stop them, but she isn't here anymore."

Bereavement and Reconstitution

By the sixth week after Barbara's death, Coleen began attending school regularly. "I was afraid of going back to school. I hadn't seen my friends for a long time, and I was afraid they would ask me about my mother. But they sent me lots of cards and letters, and that made going back much easier. We are going to have a show in school. I dance in it. I have sold 22 tickets. Mother was there last year and was very proud."

Coleen developed several ways to experience her grief and comfort herself: "At the funeral, Mom had all this jewelry on. I never knew she had that much. Her wedding ring is in my jewelry box. I can't wear it, but I can look at it. Mara gets mad about that."

"I love the book (*How to Say Good-bye*) my counselor gave me. She talks to me with my best friend Lisa. Her parents were divorced."

"When I feel sad at school, I go to the bathroom and remember how Mom squeezed my hand the day before she died. I never really got to say good-bye to her. I want to get good grades at school for her, so I study a lot.

"I like to go to the cemetery and think about heaven, that it is like clouds. I think Mother watches over me and Mara. In a grave close to Mom's is a little girl who died when she was 2. She would be about 12 years old now. I bring flowers to Mom's grave and then put some with the little girl.

"I like to remember the last time Mom hugged me because it makes me feel better."

At home there were secondary stressors that followed Barbara's death. Coleen had no one with whom she could mourn safely. Joseph's mourning, his conflict with Mara and sometimes with Coleen, and his intermittent drinking were a source of concern to Coleen. "I talk to Dad and Mara because I don't like to cry alone. But I'm scared when Dad cries because maybe he will never stop. Sometimes I wake up at night and hear Dad crying, listening to old songs. His eyes are all red. Then he comes in my room and gives me a hug."

Coleen developed more overt symptoms. Family members struggled so with their own grief and fear that it was difficult for them to respond to her muted cries for help. The avoidant communication style seemed to have limited the ability of all family members to prepare themselves for the death. Four months after Barbara's death, Coleen still had difficulty going to school in the morning, especially when her father worked the night shift and was home days. Her grades, however, were now excellent.

Six months after the death, Coleen continued to mourn alone: "When I go to the cemetery, I stand in front of Mom's grave and tell her I love her. I think she would say that to me, too. Then I go stand in front of the little girl's grave. I feel sad for her because I have a life and she doesn't. I wonder what it's like to be dead." Coleen felt happy at the cemetery, where she felt her mother's presence.

During the summer Coleen stayed with her aunts when her father worked nights. No one seemed to recognize how disruptive his schedule or her staying with different aunts was to her. Mara came home less and less, and Coleen began expressing her anger about Mara's abandoning her. As Coleen told the interviewer: "I wish Mara would stay home. She is like my mother; she takes care of my hair and things. But she and Dad always fight. Then Mara goes and stays with her boyfriend."

Mara dreaded coming home. "Dad always yells at me. If I forget to put something away, he gets mad. Mom used to put things away so he wouldn't yell at me." According to Coleen, her father was becoming more extreme about things being put away. Coleen said: "When he caught me putting some of Mara's things away, he yelled at me for doing that."

Joseph's deep mourning continued to preoccupy him. He said he had become angry with Coleen and threatened to send her to an orphanage. He knew this was wrong, but he was unaware that his mother had made that exact threat to him shortly after his father died. He did not remember describing this episode some months earlier (see page 99). At this point, the heaviness in the air at home was palpable. Coleen's open grieving was difficult for him. She placed pictures of Barbara and him all over the house so that she could see them in every room. He asked her to please put them in her own room because he found it too upsetting. Joseph was also experiencing complicated bereavement related to his father's death when he was 12 years old. He said he often thought about his father's death now, and he felt that his dying was very unfair. "It comes back to me. I wish I had my father here now." Joseph said he liked going back to work. It was less depressing than being at home. However, out of his desire to help Coleen, he made a decision that inadvertently made parenting even harder for him. He changed to a desk job in the police department eight months after Barbara's death so that he could be more available to his daughter. As a result, he lost all ongoing contact with his buddies, who had been a major source of support. He seemed even more depressed.

When the new school year began, Coleen again did not want to go to school. She was afraid she was going to be separated from all her friends in the new grade. Coleen still had trouble going to school in the morning and had headaches and stomachaches in school. She worried that something might happen to her father when she was in school. Joseph said that Coleen woke up in the middle of the night screaming, saying she was not going to school the next day. She would not talk about what she had dreamed about. She refused to go to bed unless her father sat next to her and talked until she fell asleep.

The intensity of Coleen's preoccupation with her mother had not diminished 14 months after the death. Joseph described the following episode to the interviewer: Coleen went to the cemetery with one of her aunts, but when it began to rain, she was not allowed to go to the grave. Coleen screamed and cried and became hysterical, then refused to go to school the next day. According to Joseph and his sister-in-law, "Coleen is trying to put one over on us so she won't have to go to school." Coleen's separation anxiety increased markedly after that episode. She frequently got up in the middle of the night and climbed into bed with her father. She and her sister also worried more openly about getting cancer "like all the women in the family."

Summary

Fourteen months after Barbara's death, Coleen had returned to her previous high level of functioning in school and with peers, but uncharacteristic of children her age, she became more and more anxious and depressed over time. Her father also was more depressed and his drinking problem had increased. His isolation after changing jobs and losing his buddies so that he would be available to his daughter removed him from a significant support group. And his unfulfilled dependency needs, which Barbara had met, added to his longing and craving and compounded his grief. Some aspects of his increasing preoccupation with his own father's death seemed to be part of his pathological mourning reaction.

Mara, too, was having problems. She had to deal not only with her own mourning but also with her mounting recognition and terror that she might develop cancer and die as painfully as her mother had. Because Mara was often the focus of her father's rage, she came home less and less often.

Coleen continued to mourn her mother as acutely as she did during the first few weeks after the death. Although she did well academically, socially with her friends, and in after-school activities, she could not master her fears about separation. She was terrified that something would happen to her father when she wasn't home; thus, the dynamics of her school phobia were apparent. But her separation anxiety was compounded by the lack of emotional nurturance and support. Coleen's aunts tried to reach out, but they, like Mara, were unable to provide Coleen with the parenting she so desperately needed. She reminded them of their eldest sister and of the reality that they already had the family cancer or might soon develop it. Coleen's very presence was a reminder that it was only a matter of time before it might be their turn to die.

Coleen found solace by visiting the cemetery and seemed to identify with the little girl who was buried close to Barbara's grave. Like one of her mother's sisters, Coleen also felt Barbara's presence. Barbara was constant. She was a mother who was always there, a mother who smiled down on and watched over Coleen. She was a mother who even in death provided Coleen with what no one else in her life could manage to provide.

OUTCOMES

By the final assessment, 8 to 14 months after the parent's death, 19 of the 33 children in this age category had achieved their previous levels of functioning in all of the major areas: psychological state, relationships at home, academics, athletics and after-school activities, and developmentally appropriate peer relationships. Seven had a delayed reconstitution, five a compromised reconstitution and two a symptomatic reconstitution.

Characteristics of Timely Reconstitution

There were 33 early school aged children, of whom 19 had a timely reconstitution. Five had suffered the loss of a mother; 14 of a father. For these children, the loss of a mother presented more difficulty for effective reconstitution than the loss of a father. Fathers found it difficult to comprehend the illogical and erroneous conclusions and the emotionality of these children, and they found it difficult to respond to the children's realistic dependence on them for care and for the maintenance of their self-esteem. Children openly expressed their distress about the loss of normalcy and the complete change in the emotional climate of the family. They missed the parent as a person and most talked about wanting to join the parent in heaven. Their open, sometimes dramatic expressions of distress; the nightmares, sadness, the stomachaches and headaches, tearfulness, temper tantrums, stubbornness, and disappointment were testimony to their grief, grief that gradually lessened.

What characterized these families was that the surviving parents were active problem-solvers, but also realistic about what they were able to do and in what ways others could be enlisted to help. They effectively filtered their child's stressors and learned to understand the child's sometimes illogical reactions. This group of parents did not hesitate to use the help of others if they thought their child might be able to function on a higher level as a consequence.

Characteristics of Delayed Reconstitution

What was different about the seven children with a delayed reconstitution was their struggle with maintaining self-esteem. These seven families encountered multiple stresses or family situations that presented unusual difficulties for surviving parents. This included families with more than four young children and limited income, in which needs of the children this age were at times overlooked. In one family, the father who died was regarded as abusive by all but the 8-year-old boy, who felt alone and isolated with his grief. In another family, the material grandmother, who had terminal cancer, was living in the home and died six months after the mother died. Another included a boy whose learning disability was undiagnosed until some months after the patient's death. These complex and demanding situations presented unusual challenges to the surviving parent—a challenge to understand and respond effectively to the young child's need for empathy and understanding.

Characteristics of Compromised Reconstitution

The five children with a compromised reconstitution experienced not only low self-esteem, but depression and regressive symptoms as well. In these situations, not only were the stresses numerous, but the surviving parent was overwhelmed and unable to function effectively. Either the parents were markedly depressed or they demonstrated a severe lack of empathy or inability bordering on unwillingness to understand and respond to the dependency needs of such young children. Either condition created serious empathic or competence failures.

Characteristics of Symptomatic Reconstitution

Finally, one child with symptomatic reconstitution had symptoms that were severe enough to warrant a psychiatric diagnosis. These were new symptoms that developed after the parent's death. In this situation the child's reaction seemed a response to the serious mental illness of the surviving parent who was denying his own condition and therefore was unable to obtain adequate treatment to prevent his illness from influencing his parenting. The mother who died had been a major protector of the child from the father's disturbing behavior.

DISCUSSION

The 33 young, school-age children described in these two chapters are developmentally in transition. Socially, they are starting to move out, but the home microsystem is still the predominant one. They have entered school where new rules, responsibilities, and demands enter their lives. Teachers and peers can be a positive resource, but they cannot substitute as providers of the very basic emotional needs only the parent can provide at this age. With these children the parent or parent substitute is still the primary source of self-esteem. The teacher, coach, other adults, by their approbation, are an important source of self-esteem to the older, school-age child. Peers are a resource for solace and support, but to the adolescent, not to these children. Really, only the parent or parent substitute can do that.

The thinking and understanding abilities of these children are also in transition. They are starting to think more rationally and logically, they are more certain about cause and effect, but inconsistently, as when it deals with important and emotional issues. Events require explanations—unfortunately, being quite self-involved and magical-correlational in their logic, they are frequently self-referential in attributing cause to the illness and death.

Perhaps most significant is the important role the parent or parent substitute plays in the life of these children. The children are vocal in expressing their feelings, but they are often unclear and confusing as they express the thoughts that give rise to these feelings. In short, the child needs someone who can clarify what the child is thinking and feeling, can reframe events to make them more understandable, can reassure and build self-esteem by praising the child's accomplishments and by emphasizing the child's importance.

Most parents did this, and much more, to help these children cope with the family tragedy. But for some, there were additional stressors that further compounded the problems of survivors.

9

Children 9–11 Years of Age

Themes

This chapter describes the impact of terminal cancer on the lives of 37 children— 19 girls and 18 boys—aged 9 to 11. They came from 33 families, and their surviving parents were 20 fathers and 13 mothers. (In this and the next chapter, 'children' refers to 9- to 11-year-old children.) This chapter summarizes the developmental attributes that were important in understanding these children. The summary is followed by descriptions of how the the children coped with the family tragedy, how they and their families responded to the terminal illness, how the surviving parents prepared the children for the death and family rituals, and how parents helped them cope with their bereavement and reconstitution. Chapter 10 discusses the experiences of two families and ends with a summary of the characteristics of the children and families that constitute the different outcome categories.

Developmental Themes of Later School-Age Children

Nine- to 11-year-old children are at a relatively tranquil age. Although important changes in their cognitive and emotional development are taking place, the changes are quantitative rather than qualitative. Quantitative changes, such as increased sophistication in the use of concrete operational thinking, lead to emotional equilibrium. Qualitative changes in both the emotional and cognitive domains, which will be illustrated in the chapters on adolescence, are generally accompanied by emotional disequilibrium.

Three developmental characteristics were especially important in the ability of these children to cope with the stress of the family tragedy: the emergence of logical thinking (concrete operational), more effective use of defenses against disquieting emotions, and an active engagement in the home, school, sports, and friend microsystems (Bronfenbrenner, 1979; Bronfenbrenner, 1993), as evidenced in their more meaningful participation in their own expanding world. Two experiences exemplify the way these systems affected their development, specifically in relation to their mourning: they chose homework themes related to the illness, which enhanced their intellectual defenses, and they became involved in after-school activities with peers, who also did not value emotional expression (this was an important respite from painful mourning).

Capacity for Logical Thinking

The capacity for logical thinking develops rapidly in these children. It becomes a powerful tool they can use to help them manage the turmoil caused by a parent's illness and death. Like younger children, they tend to feel guilty and responsible for their parent's condition. Unlike younger children, however, they are able to reverse their thinking and use information more logically to alleviate their distress. For example, one child said: "My father told me about cancer and explained that my mother's cancer is not my fault, but it's hard not to feel that way sometimes." Although the children may want the dead parent to return, they understand more clearly the difference between wish and reality. Another child in the study said: "I wish that my father would come back to life. I know it's not going to happen, so I try not to play around with that fact in my head. I won't have my dad, but I'll have other people."

The parents of the children described in this chapter did not always provide information in a consistent manner. Unlike their younger colleagues, however, some of the children were able to demand information. Some were bitter and deeply resentful when they believed that information had been withheld. For example, one 9-year-old bitterly complained to the interviewer that he wasn't told about his mother's cancer for a long time because he was the youngest child in his family. "I should have been told because I'm part of the family and I should know!"

They also could become hypervigilant and mistrustful when insufficiently informed.

> The mother of 10-year-old Byron had not told him how seriously ill his father was until shortly before he died. Toward the end, she tried to share more information with her children; by then, however, it was difficult for Byron to integrate all the complex facts. When his father died, he said, "Why didn't you tell me he was so sick?" Angry, rebellious testing characterized his early bereavement. When he listened on an extension telephone as his mother was talking, Byron realized that she was talking with his father's oncologist and screamed, "You've got cancer too. I know it!"

Before the initial interview with a child, some parents warned the interviewer that the child would probably not participate because he or she did not want to talk about the illness. They were pleasantly surprised when the child welcomed the opportunity to talk about the patient's condition. In contrast to the 12- to 14-year-olds, rarely did these children *not* want to talk about the facts of their parent's illness and treatment.

Also characteristic of these children was that they rarely shared their emotional reactions with anyone. After the parent's death, they were usually eager to review their successes and the specifics about their continuing growth with the interviewer. At times, they even described their disappointments regarding how family life was being reorganized. The few who were willing to talk about their grief did so, but only briefly and sparingly.

Child's Expanding World

These children were involved in many more activities outside the home than were their younger peers. This provided them with opportunities to distract themselves and to avoid the tragedy of the parent's illness and death. Gaining competence in sports and other after-school activities also provided them with opportunities to build their confidence and self-esteem. When these activities involved the ill parent, remembering the parent's praise and pride in them provided a positive focus for their mourning.

> Michael's experience was a common one. This 11-year-old described how sad he felt when he played tennis or participated in a swim meet. When he automatically looked up at the bleachers, he expected his father to be watching him, as he had done so often: "But then I realize he's gone."

Leaving home to participate in activities does not reflect *going away from* parental relationships but *going toward* new experiences. The process of "leaving parents" is emphasized to a greater degree during adolescence. The children engaged in activities with other children. They talked with them about games, activities, and social experiences; however, they usually did not confide in peers about emotionally charged issues such as the parent's illness or death. For these discussions, they remained dependent on parents and other adults.

Because other adults, such as teachers, coaches, guidance counselors, and school nurses, were important to children this age, and their approval was a source of self-esteem, their comfort and understanding was a critical source of solace for children who were grieving the loss of a parent. The children in our sample often felt more comfortable relating to these adults because they were concerned about upsetting the parent. When informed and encouraged by parents, these adults were able to support the child effectively. This was especially helpful when the parent was unavailable or away from home, which often occurred during the terminal illness.

Many parents supported the participation of their sons and daughters in a broad range of activities. Contrary to the stereotype, the fathers in the sample often coached their daughters or became outspoken advocates for their daughters' developing athletic prowess.

> Nine-year-old Diana described her father as "a great person—a lot of fun to be with." He took her to the park, went bike riding and roller skating with her, and liked to wrestle with her and her brother. She described how her father had taught her to ride a bike and recalled how frightened she had been because the

first time her older brother had ridden his bike, he crashed into a pole. Her father encouraged her to overcome her fear, so Diane said: "I just did it!"

Effective Defenses

Children this age have developed more mature, effective defenses. Consequently, they were able to contain their anxiety and focus on developing their competence. The success of these defenses confused parents in our sample, who interpreted the child's lack of visible anguish as callousness and indifference to the tragedy. At times, this view prevented them from understanding and empathizing with the child's underlying emotional pain and from providing the kind of guidance and support the child needed.

Because the children not only defended themselves against the event that initiated their turmoil but against the connection between the turmoil and the behaviors that emerged as well, they and their parents had difficulty understanding the reason for their behaviors.

> Ten-year-old Rosa's father had nurtured her and helped her develop competence in school during the five years he was ill. During this time she developed a more strained relationship with her mother. Although Rosa managed the many stresses of immigrant life well, she became overwhelmed by feelings of helplessness and hopelessness shortly after her father died and lost interest in school and peers. Instead, she watched television and sucked her thumb. Because she didn't understand her behavior, she felt even more hopeless and was afraid she was going crazy.
>
> Rosa's mother agreed to obtain counseling for Rosa. She told the interviewer that she thought Rosa's problem might be a delayed reaction to her father's punitive behavior during the month before he died because he had brain metastases and was in great pain. Because Rosa had not reacted to his uncharacteristic behavior at the time, her mother had not discussed the reasons for her father's behavior with her. Rosa was subsequently referred for counseling to help her understand her sudden, severe regression.

PATTERNS OF RESPONSES IN LATER SCHOOL-AGE CHILDREN

Patterns of Responses to the Terminal Illness

Many children in the sample showed a crucial need for carefully sequenced information about the parent's illness, treatment, and impending death. They tried to master the enormous stresses and showed a remarkable capacity to help care for the ill parent. Some experienced anticipatory grief.

> Nine-year-old Kristine said she worried that her father would die and she would not have him anymore: "Dad's my pal and my buddy. If he dies, we won't be able to go out to dinner or to the hardware store anymore."

Integration of Information

The children were able to integrate relatively detailed information about the illness without becoming overwhelmed and confused. When the information was insufficient, however, they listened at doorways or on telephone extensions, which led them to jump to inaccurate conclusions because, lacking the adolescent's cognitive abilities, they were unable to comprehend the context in the absence of more comprehensive detail.

> Brian, age 9, complained that he overheard conversations but couldn't make any sense of the bits and pieces he heard. Thus, he became extremely anxious when "my Mother was talking funny when she took her medicine. Dad was giving her a needle, and she told me to 'go away.'" Brian thought the needle must hurt her and felt that his father did not feel good giving it to her. Brian said that he often asked his mother if she had taken her medicine when she looked sicker than usual: "Sometimes when people look under-the-weather, it is like they didn't take their medicine." He was trying to understand her declining condition and erroneously assumed that she was not taking her medicine rather than that her disease was progressing and she was having expected medication side effects. Adolescents would not have made this mistake, given the same information.

Why did parents fail to understand their child's need for updated information? Four reasons stand out. First, many parents struggled with their own denial, their inability to accept that their young spouse was as close to death as the physicians suggested. Second, they were often so distracted by the illness that they lost track of the child's maturation. Third, the child's maturity and competence tended to be more evident outside the home, away from the stresses of the parent's illness, whereas they behaved in a more immature and regressive manner at home. Fourth, the child often tended to avoid emotions and kept personal feelings hidden.

Some parents exhibited a remarkable ability to provide their children with a regular flow of facts about how the disease was progressing, and were able to do so even when the disease was spiraling out of control. Mastering these facts gave their children a sense of control and a feeling of cohesiveness with other family members. The children were eager to learn about how treatments worked and how the disease and treatment affected the ill parent. This information often corrected misunderstandings that had emerged in their thinking:

> As 11-year-old Sean said: "Last year, Dad went to the hospital, but they didn't tell me it was cancer. A year later he had a tumor, and I finally figured out he had cancer. For a long time, I thought it was not cancer, just a tumor. My mom finally put it straight to me. I had to go up to her and ask. I thought he was sick, but he would beat it because he was strong. But you can see him now: He acts weird, says weird things, forgets things. He forgot where my room was. My mom explained that the tumor was affecting his brain. Sometimes he does things that are nonsense. Now that I know what's going on, I understand. Dad used to be

grouchy and I didn't understand; I thought he was mad about something. Now it doesn't seem that he is mad at me."

Some children wanted information about the hospital and the health care system. Two children updated their classmates regularly about how their parent was doing. Some functioned as the family informant, cutting out articles about new cancer treatments, giving them to the family, and presenting them as school assignments. Some wrote papers on cancer treatment; others, on euthanasia. One mother suggested that her son keep a journal of his thoughts, reactions, and questions. He found this activity helpful, especially when he talked over the entries with her.

The children especially valued formal talks with physicians and nurses about their parent's condition. They wanted to visit the parent in the hospital, not only because they missed the parent, but also because they learned so much by seeing and experiencing the hospital setting.

> When the hospital ambulance came for his father during a crisis, Michael's mother reassured him that the ambulance was well equipped. She said he could visit Dad in the hospital shortly. Michael called his father and visited him in the hospital as often as he could. He was proud that he had learned his way around the hospital: He knew where to find the cafeteria, the family room, and the gift shop.

During the parent's terminal illness, many of the children began to wonder whether they could catch the disease. They also wondered whether they might have caused it in some way, could have prevented it, or might have exacerbated it. Discussions about these concerns continued in various forms throughout the period of bereavement and reconstitution.

> Nine-year-old Diana described the difference between her and her 6-year-old sister's understanding of the illness: "(My sister is) much younger, and she doesn't take things as well as me; she doesn't understand. Since I'm three years older than my sister, I can put it in different words. She thinks that if she does something wrong, it's going to hurt (Mom). She worries a lot that she's going to catch it."
>
> When the interviewer asked Diana, "Do you worry about that?" she answered: "No, cause I talked to my mom about it and she said 'Well, I talked to the doctor and you can't catch it.' She's asked a lot of doctors, she's asked them all—that's the first thing she asks them, whether her children can get it."
>
> Diana then explained that when her parents clarified the fact that she was not responsible for her mother's illness, she believed them, but her sister was not so sure. When the interviewer asked Diana, "Do *you* ever worry that something that you did caused it, even if your dad made it clear to you that nothing caused it?" she said, "Not really, no, because I know it's not my fault and I couldn't have done nothing to prevent it. It wasn't our fault."

Involvement in Patient Care

Some children became involved in the patient's care. Their careful and thoughtful ministrations were moving demonstrations of their love for and desire to protect the patient and their need to be helpful.

> Michael adored his father, who shared his love of swimming and tennis. He cried while describing how his father would sometimes hold his hand when they sat together in the front seat of the car. "Now *I* hold *his* hand when he's in the hospital." Michael often volunteered to sleep in the den with his father, waking up every three or four hours to give him medication. He said he liked to help.

> Eleven-year-old Sean described how he worked hard to master the stresses of taking care of his father, whose brain metastasis affected his behavior: "His legs don't work. Sometimes he gets things in(to) his head and he gets up and we can't stop him. We have to put his pants on and his (colostomy) bag because he has forgotten how to do that. Sometimes it gets annoying. I don't think he even knows how old I am. I try to keep strong like my mom, but sometimes I feel sad. Sometimes my dad is so weird, I just take a deep breath, get up, go back, and do what I have to do. I think I'm doing my part."

Anticipatory Grief

The 9- to 11-year-olds were the first age group to consistently anticipate a parent's death and feel sad about the future loss. Michael and Sean's statements illustrate this anticipatory process, as do the remarks of 10-year-old Bob:

> Bob talked about how he missed playing baseball and basketball with his father. After his mother told him that his father's current treatment was ineffective, he wanted to look at photographs of his father as he had been before the illness. Bob said he thought about his father a lot and worried about him. He also wondered, "Who will play basketball with me? Who will fix my bike?" He thought he would want to be with his father when he died.

Reactions, Behavior, and Symptoms

The children in the sample experienced a broader range of reactions to their parent's terminal illness than did children in the earlier grades. Some exhibited few reactions, and their school performance actually improved. Others became angry and defiant and adamantly denied the impending death despite information to the contrary. These children expressed their anger through stubbornness, forgetfulness, messiness, conflict with siblings and peers, and talking back to teachers. In most cases, however, the anger was muted and bore no resemblance to the outbursts of anger observed among the adolescents and among children of divorce.

Although most of the children tended to avoid showing sadness, apprehension, and fear, some even avoided showing anger. A few became enuretic, especially when the patient was in the hospital and the well parent stayed at the hospital for extended periods.

Depressive reactions were less common, and they were less likely to have thoughts about suicide than did the 6- to 8-year-olds. When they did have such thoughts, it was easier to discuss them and reduce the guilt or rage that led to them.

Most children had some problems concentrating at school, and a temporary drop in their grades was not unusual. However, the grades of a few improved, presumably as a gift for the patient. These children were likely to have been successful in school from the beginning, and success had been an important source of their self-esteem. Occasionally, boys misbehaved enough to warrant a note from the teacher, but their behavior was mild compared with that observed in other age groups.

Children this age were more distressed than younger children by the parent's changing appearance and ability to function, the reduction in family activities and trips, and the prospect of a future without the parent's assistance, support, and love. But unlike the younger school children, they were less distressed by the chaos in the family caused by the demands of a terminal illness. When the patient was the same sex as the child, the child often expressed fears about catching the disease because of his or her strong identification with the patient. These children were helped by having an opportunity to learn what caused the disease and how it develops and progresses as a way of combating their unrealistic fears.

The children experienced fear of separation when the patient was in the hospital for a long time and the well parent also spent a great deal of time there. Under these circumstances, the children were more likely to express anger than anxiety or sadness. Although some had headaches or stomachaches that required them to stay home when the parent was discharged from the hospital, school phobia was not observed in this age group. Some children wanted to sleep with the well parent, especially during the last weeks of the patient's life, but they reported few nightmares.

Preparation for Death and Family Rituals

Need for Time to Prepare

Older school-aged children need more time to prepare for the parent's death than do younger school-aged children. Regularly updated information and the opportunity for final hospital visits seem to provide them with the most helpful context. When one boy received such updates and opportunities to visit the parent in the hospital, he obviously was proud: "I was surprised, but I knew it (the death) was going to happen because my mother kept me informed." Like younger children, these children found that hospital visits were meaningful, even when little communication with the patient was possible. The youngsters valued the visits at this state of the illness because they provided concrete evidence of the reality that the patient was dying and gave them an opportunity to say good-bye. Unfortunately, surviving parents often waited until it was too late for such visits.

It was easier for parents to tell these children the parent had died than it was to tell younger ones. One mother did an especially impressive job of communicating with her four sons as a group, which encouraged them to be supportive of each other.

Michael's mother had told her four sons several weeks before their father's death that he was likely to die. Two days before his death, she brought the boys to the hospital and told them he was dying. They all cried together and then went in one at a time to say good-bye. When her husband slipped into a coma and died, she was relieved to be alone with him when he died in her arms. Afterward, she drove to her in-laws' beach house, where her sons were staying, gathered them together under a big tree in the yard (their father's favorite place), and told them that their father had died. Michael's brother Tom recalled that it was the place where their father had told them just seven months before his death that he had cancer. They all cried and comforted each other. Then they drove down to the beach and, although it was cold, walked and talked and began their grieving.

This mother and father's use of a particular place—a favorite tree symbolizing shelter and protection—was a sensitive and empathic choice. The boys' decision to go to the beach continued the use of place and symbolism to provide solace and aid grief. One advantage of a well-functioning sibling group is that the children can help each other. The older children can help younger children with the facts, and younger children can help their older siblings by expressing emotion.

Need to Manage Intense Reactions

Managing the intense emotions they felt when told that their parent had died was difficult for many children this age. Some had unusual immediate reactions, which they later disavowed. One 11-year-old locked himself in his room when his mother came home from the hospital because he didn't want to hear the news until he was ready. Later, he was embarrassed about this behavior. However, wanting to be alone for a while was not unusual. Some children cried or screamed and one boy laughed, an expression of acute anxiety. Most parents recognized their children's struggle to cope with such emotional intensity and gave them time to collect themselves before exploring their feelings.

Need for Active Participation

The children wanted to play a role in the rituals and resented being constrained from participating. Although they appreciated their friends' attendance at the funeral, they tended to be more focused on and pleased about their own participation. Some served as a pallbearer, gave a reading from the Bible, presented a eulogy, handed out memorial cards, or served as an altar boy. "I threw some dirt on the grave," Sean said proudly, but he admitted that he had felt sad at the cemetery.

Brian was angry because his 13-year-old cousin was allowed to attend the first day of his father's wake and he wasn't. He and his brother were only allowed to attend the second and third days. His uncle explained that people would be crying and "carrying on" on the first day. Brian said he didn't care if people cried a lot and, even if he was afraid, he wanted to be there! On the second day of the wake, he was a little scared, but he was proud that he could stay.

Two children did not attend their parent's funeral. Their decision seemed consonant with their surviving parent's style of coping—avoiding painful feelings—rather than an expression of their own wishes. Immediately after the death, many children were afraid that the surviving parent might be more vulnerable. As a consequence, they tried to protect and please the parent.

Need to Put on a Brave Front

One difficulty in responding helpfully to children this age was their strong desire to cover sad feelings and "be brave." Some did not cry at the funeral for that reason and usually were reluctant to express the depth of their feelings and fears.

A month after his father died, Michael told the interviewer that he was especially sad at lunchtime at school. He had sad thoughts about his father, and he missed his mother, who, because of her busy schedule, had arranged for him to eat lunch at school. When the interviewer told Michael's mother about her son's loneliness, she arranged for him to eat lunch at home for a few more months. Michael worried about his mother and was reluctant to ask her to accommodate him in this way.

Fears of Other Losses

Because children this age often worried about the surviving parent's health, they watched any signs that the parent might be ill. They seemed to feel that since disaster had struck once, it might strike again! The children were often superstitious. One 9-year-old recalled that after watching a television program in which a parent died, she felt good that everyone in her family was fine, but she was concerned that she might have "jinxed" the family with her optimism.

Many of the children wanted to sleep with the surviving parent for a few days after the funeral because they were sensitive to separations from the parent immediately after the death. Many did not acknowledge their anxiety and instead were likely to become angry rather than sad. Two parents (a father and a mother) considered accompanying the patient's body for burial in their home country. In one family, the father decided against leaving when his two daughters strongly objected to being separated from him, and he arranged for his wife's brother to accompany the body. In the other family, the mother did go, but returned early, after her 10-year-old daughter phoned and expressed her sadness. Her daughter experienced severe stress after the death of her father, and the early separation from her mother exacerbated her distress. One father, who owned his own business and spent long hours away from home, complained that his daughters "shadowed" him after their mother died.

Bereavement and Reconstitution

Older school-aged children's expressions of grief continued to be quite subdued. School and activities provided helpful distractions as they mourned the parent and found their place within the new family structure. The fear of the surviving parent's vulnerability and the children's protectiveness of them made them easier to manage. Although the children challenged, tested limits, and were demanding, their expressions of anger did not reach the intensity of the adolescent's anger, and their sadness did not have the overwhelming and helpless characteristics of younger children. They continued to be helpful, positive, and pragmatic. They seemed able to move ahead after the first few months following the death.

> Eleven-year-old Sean maintained a positive attitude and a strong investment in school despite his mother's continuing problems with her diabetes after his father's death. He was able to admit that he was angry with God: "First he took Dad away, and now you are sick. That's not fair." However, he also stated firmly: "You have to move ahead."

> Ten-year-old Matthew said he would advise another child in his situation that, "It won't get better, but after a while your mind goes on to other things."

The bereavement and reconstitution period is shaped by a number of factors, including the children's school experience, their cognitive understanding of the death and the meaning it came to have for them, their emotional reactions to the death, their capacity and opportunity to mourn, and their adaptation to how the family was reconstituted. The emotional reserve of these children and their advanced defensive capacities continued to make parents question whether their mourning was progressing appropriately.

School

The acquisition of knowledge and skills continued to be a central developmental task for these children. Some of the children in the sample had updated their classmates regularly about the facts of their parent's illness, and some informed their classmates about the death, often in blunt terms.

> Sean said he was very direct with his classmates: "I told them my father died and I'm O.K. They were all asking if I was O.K. I don't mind when people ask me. My teacher told me that he was sorry, he knew my father was sick. It was really like any other day. (When) my uncle told me Dad was dying, I was a little sad but not surprised."

Some classmates wrote sympathy cards. More often they signed one card purchased by the teacher.

Erin's teacher sent a card that his classmates signed. He noticed that some of his friends did not say anything, just signed their names. He thought they probably did not know what to say. Erin said that was O.K. It was O.K. for them to "just be what they are."

Although their school performance declined temporarily during the terminal illness and immediate bereavement period, the children generally recovered within the first few months after the parent's death. It was unusual for a child's school performance to continue to decline more than six months after the parent's death.

Sean described his performance at school shortly after his father died: "When I'm in school, I have to keep my mind on my studies. I passed my (private school) test. My Mom was so happy. I'm not going to be modest on this one. I knew that I passed. It was so easy, so simple."

Meaning of the Death

Most children were concerned about the injustice done to them by their parent's death.

Diana said she felt sad and missed her father, especially when she saw other kids with their fathers. The 9-year-old felt that it was unfair that "Dad's in heaven, flying around and doing anything he wants, and I have to work." When she skipped a grade shortly after her father's death, adjusting to a new group of classmates was difficult. She missed her father's help and encouragement.

The children missed the encouragement they had received from the lost parent, the parent's appreciation of their successes, and the parent's observations of them as they ventured out on their own, played sports, danced, and succeeded at school.

Matthew said he tried to hit a home run for his father a couple of months after his father's death and was disappointed that he couldn't do it. He dreamed he was outside playing football, running fast, and his brother kicked him. "It's the only way he can stop me—I'm so fast." His father was watching him in the dream.

In addition to worrying about their surviving parent's health, the children also worried about their own vulnerability to disease. Most had symptoms that concerned them during the first year after the death. Some symptoms strongly resembled the parent's symptoms. Although some children continued to think they might be responsible for the parent's illness and death, they also were able to accept logical explanations and reassurance more easily then were younger children.

Ten-year-old Jessica thought that fighting with her brothers and being bad made her mother sick. Once the interviewer clarified the situation for her, she asked for the "real" reason for her mother's death.

Eleven-year-old Maya said, "I know I didn't cause her to get sicker, but sometimes I feel like I did. I made her yell too much and made her get a headache."

Children were curious about the particular circumstances of the actual death. Bob asked: "Did he die of suffocation?" Some of the children asked questions that the parent regarded as gruesome and inappropriate: For example, "Are the worms eating Dad's body yet?"

The children generally showed evidence of identifying with the dead parent, especially if parent and child were the same gender. This became apparent in the children's interests and activities. Boys focused on the sports their father had liked best. Some spent hours on the computer as their father had done. They excelled in subjects the father preferred. They believed they should protect their mother as their father had done. Girls struggled with feelings of responsibility for taking care of the family in the way their mother had done—they became more thoughtful, cared for, and were more parental with their younger siblings. For some children, identification with the dead parent was problematic. For example, Bob, the favorite son of an abusive, hostile father, became abusive and combative with his siblings, peers, and mother.

Emotional Reactions

One distinguishing characteristic of children this age that remained apparent during bereavement was their muted emotional reactions. They talked about the importance of being strong, brave, protective of the surviving parent, and going about their lives in the way the dead parent would have wanted them to. They expressed emotions only sporadically. Occasional headaches or stomachaches seemed to be an expression of their distress. Because of their emotional restraint, parents sometimes wondered if they were having any emotional reactions to the death at all. They misunderstood their child's effort to contain sad and lonely feelings and to invest in school and friends, regarding the child's demeanor as coldness and a lack of caring.

Parents also were upset by the angry reactions that some children exhibited during the year after the parent's death, especially when the surviving parent was a mother with sons and the father had been the principal disciplinarian. These mothers were challenged to find new ways of setting appropriate limits. Boys sometimes expressed their anger by being messy in their personal appearance and in their rooms, fighting with siblings and peers, provoking teachers and parents, and demanding and testing limits. Their anger often subsided when the surviving parent elicited the sad feelings hidden by the anger and was able to respond to their dependency needs.

Steve's father told the interviewer that his son had become angry and aggressive at school. In one week, the 11-year-old had had three fights because he had been teased about not having a mother. When his father talked with Steve, "the flood gates opened and he cried and cried. I cried too and we hugged and I reassured him." The father subsequently reported that after that conversation, he felt closer to Steve, and Steve brought up memories about his mother more often and spoke comfortably about her. The number of fights at school also declined significantly. The father also decided to create a family time on Friday nights, when he would have dinner alone with his two sons.

Girls were more likely to express sad and depressed feelings, and they also experienced reduced self-esteem. Some were shyer about making friends. Girls were more likely to feel some responsibility for the parent's death. Like the boys, they also expressed anger, usually through increased conflict with siblings and peers, by being more demanding and critical.

Although the children in this sample were fearful, their expressions of fear were usually not only more tempered than those of younger children but also more specific. Because they were afraid the surviving parent would become ill and die, they became protective of them. They also were afraid the family would not have enough money for the basics of life, and feared they would be unable to engage in many of the recreational activities they had engaged in before. And they were afraid they might fail in school or sports without the dead parent's guidance and support.

Grieving Process

The challenge for parents of children this age was to find a balance between supporting their age-appropriate avoidance of intense feelings and fostering the children's reminiscences and active grieving. Because most children were reluctant to initiate discussions about the parent who had died, surviving parents found that it was useful to celebrate marker events and use existing family rituals to help the children grieve. Birthdays, anniversaries, and holidays were opportunities to be together and share memories about the dead parent. Although at first some children were hesitant to visit the cemetery, in time many found that such visits were an important memorial experience. At that point, they began to feel more comfortable about mentioning the parent's name and talking about the parent. The grieving experience seemed to promote their fuller investment in school, sports, and friends.

The content of their grief reflected the change in the children's relationship with the parent. In these two-parent families, the father had more often taken the role of, and was remembered as, mentor and facilitator of competence, but also as friend and buddy by both girls and boys. Both also grieved the mother as organizer, stabilizer, care taker, love giver, cheer leader, protector, and someone to chat with.

When surviving parents reflected with their child on situations that were likely to be reminders of the lost parent, this also encouraged the child's grieving.

One mother of 8- and 11-year-old boys observed a father playing baseball with his sons on the beach. She mentioned how this reminded her of their father, who had been an avid baseball fan and played ball with them on this very beach. Then they all cried quietly together.

The children dreamed about the lost parent relatively often. Usually, these dreams were comforting. The dreams often involved the parent's continuing to watch over them, reassuring them, or supporting them. Grieving also was evident in their memories of activities they and the parent had engaged in together and in their use of objects that had belonged to the parent.

Eleven-year-old Sean said he thought about his father sometimes at night and sometimes he didn't. He had a dream about going to Florida's Epcot Center. In the dream, he and his father didn't go to places where they had gone when his father was alive; they went to an underwater place where Sean had always wanted to go. They also went to the top of a Japanese exhibit he also wanted to visit. "I dream about the places I wanted to go with my father when he was alive, and in my head I went there."

Ten-year-old Matthew had a dream about the first anniversary of his father's death. His father told him something good would happen to him during that month. Matthew felt comforted by this dream.

Ten-year-old Robyn described daydreams about her father looking down on her and protecting her.

When the children talked about and thought about the fun things they had done with the parent, their affect during these reminiscences was usually pleasurable. Some children were freer to discuss their feelings about the parent in writing. One 11-year-old girl wrote a paper for school on current cancer treatments. Another won a prize for an essay titled "What I would do if I were president." Her mother was surprised because most of the paper consisted of an autobiographical account of her relationship with her father.

Children enjoyed seeing photographs of themselves with the parent and wanted to remember the parent before he or she was ill and when they could do things together. They also treasured clothing and other items that had belonged to the parent because these items provided comfort and opportunities to reminisce about the parent during the first year after death. Gradually, however, these items were set aside.

Children showed a progressive ability to reframe positively their experience.

During the summer, Ann's mother took her children to visit relatives, who were scattered all over the United States. The 9-year-old comforted herself about the loss of her father by noting that her family was an extremely large one, and her relatives were very nice. Thus, she said, "Once a few years have gone past, some of the sadness will go out."

When the child's relationship with the lost parent had been conflicted or hostile, reframing the relationship simplified the child's mourning.

Because 9-year-old Cindy's father had been abusive to his wife and children, her older siblings seemed relieved after his death, but Cindy seemed conflicted and unsettled. When her mother gave her a photograph of her father beaming at her when she was 5 years old, Cindy fixed on the picture, put it on her night stand and often talked about how much her father had loved her.

The grieving of children who had a more highly conflicted relationship with the parent than the other children evidenced more relief, sometimes more anger and fear. The surviving parent's ability to affirm the validity of their negative but realistic feelings provoked by the deceased parent was extremely helpful to these children because it facilitated their grief process and allowed memorialization of the dead parent to proceed. In the following situation, the mother did not acknowledge her dead husband's drinking problem.

When dining with his mother in a restaurant, Jason sometimes angrily pushed wine glasses away from the table. When his mother began to date, the 9-year-old told her he was afraid she would marry someone who would drink and hit him (as his father had done).

Most of the children in late elementary school were also aware of preferences and coalitions within the family, but they could not discuss them easily. If a child had been a special favorite of the dead parent and the surviving parent and the child's siblings were relieved that the parent was no longer around, the child felt isolated with his or her grief because there was no one in the family with whom to share it. This was a potential problem for children whose parents had initiated a divorce or separation before the death and whose surviving parent harbored extremely angry, unresolved feelings toward the dead spouse.

Reconstitution of the Family

Reconstitution of the family with children of this age required the surviving parent to revise family roles and mutual responsibilities, devise new approaches to setting limits, and focus on issues regarding dating and remarriage. Parents found that it was helpful to frame these changes in family functioning as changes faced by all families in their situation. They should be viewed as ubiquitous problems of transition rather than an unfair imposition of change. There were inevitably many issues of rules and procedure about how the family would operate that needed to be addressed, and children this age often asked about them shortly before the parent died and immediately afterward.

Shortly after his mother's death, 10-year-old Tom asked his father: "Will we still use Mommy's rules?" In his family, the mother had been an effective organizer and limit setter. His father assured Tom that his mother's rules were good rules, so they would keep her rules unless they needed to be changed as the times and circumstances changed.

Many surviving mothers found that assuming the roles of disciplinarian and breadwinner was most daunting, whereas many surviving fathers had the most difficulty taking on the roles of nurturer and family organizer. Parents of both genders were confronted with the need to add these tasks to an already full plate of responsibilities.

The children also were faced with adopting new tasks. They had to take on more chores around the house, be more careful with money, and complete more homework on their own. Rather than resent the lack of a constant parental presence, many children were proud that they could help and enjoyed their increased independence. As long as the demands placed on them were not excessive and didn't interfere with their age-appropriate activities, they may have complained and dallied, but they did not refuse to help.

Learning to set limits as a single parent—especially for mothers with boys and fathers with girls, were among the most difficult changes. Surviving parents who were inexperienced in this area were confronted directly, having lost the huge contribution the spouse had made to family life through activities such as providing structure and limit setting. The absence of the parent who had set limits also confronted children with the reality of the loss of the parent, and their grief at the loss often explained some of the anger they felt with regard to limit setting. When the surviving parent made extreme changes in limits, the child tended to respond with even greater anger and acting out. Children this age tended to equate stricter limits with losing their independence and lack of limits as neglect. Different experiences with limit-setting problems are described throughout the narratives in the two stories in Chapter 10. The most important tasks for surviving parents were to assess their strengths and limitations, supplement their weak parenting skills by identifying another person who would handle the situation better, or seek out information that would enable them to handle the situation better themselves.

The children also were concerned about the person the surviving parent might choose as a new partner. When the subject of the parent's remarriage was raised initially, they tended to react negatively and watch the parent carefully in an attempt to determine whether the new relationship was serious. As time passed, however, they became less resistant to the idea of the parent's remarriage. If the person the parent chose demonstrated an ability to fill some of the roles left vacant by the dead parent, while honoring their continued importance to the children, many began to feel positive about the situation. For example:

> Eleven-year-old Ronald tried to persuade his 6-year-old sister, Debbie, to change her mind about her father's possible remarriage. In her opinion, their father was giving up his love for their mother too soon. Ronald wondered why she couldn't understand that their father "would continue to love mother in his memory bank," and pragmatically pointed out that because he and Debbie had too much work to do now, they really needed a mother around the house!

By the end of the first year after the death, most children regained their previous level of functioning in school and at home. Although they missed the lost parent, they believed they would survive.

RECOMMENDATIONS FOR PROFESSIONALS AND CAREGIVERS

Terminal Illness

1. *Begin giving the child fairly detailed information when the parent's diagnosis is verified.* The information should include the name of the disease, specifics about the disease, and the known causes, and it should be provided regularly. Enlisting the aid of nurses and physicians in discussing the disease is always helpful. Children should be informed about treatments, including possible side effects. If the disease progresses, this and the types of progression or metastases should be discussed. It also is important to clarify that changes in the parent's behavior are related to the disease or its treatment. If the disease becomes terminal, the child needs to be informed.

2. *Understand that anticipatory mourning is important for children in this age group.* Adequate information supports such mourning. Support them in expressing thoughts and feelings about the current and anticipated loss of the patient's involvement with them. Be prepared for a child to ask what will happen if both parents die.

3. *Enlist the aid of support networks.* Communicating with teachers and other adults who are involved with the child is especially important because children this age are unlikely to initiate communication about the patient, with parents but instead often turn to other adults for support. Teachers need to be informed that a temporary drop in grades, especially during the patient's terminal illness, is not uncommon.

4. *Encourage the child to visit the patient in the hospital.* These visits are crucially important because they enhance the child's ability to understand more clearly what is happening to the patient. The visits do not need to be frequent or prolonged. Children often enjoy going to the hospital gift shop or other public areas during the visits.

5. *Encourage the child to remain involved in after-school activities and sports and in ongoing contact with friends.* Grandparents may need to be reminded that this involvement is important.

6. *Encourage the child's interest in helping to care for the patient.* Parents need to exercise adult judgment to ensure such caregiving activities are appropriate for the child's age and realistic competence. No matter how competent the child appears to be, he or she should never be left in sole charge of the patient who is extremely ill.

7. *Be aware of any coalitions and special relationships within the family.* Does the ill parent have any special meaning to the child? How will losing the parent affect the child in relation to the surviving parent? Children of this age are aware of conflict and preferences within the family, and may be strongly affected by them but not feel free to discuss them unless the parent initiates such a discussion.

Death and Family Rituals

1. *Inform the child when the parent's disease progresses and when death is probable.* This will encourage the child to make final visits to say good-bye. When possible, the patient should tell the child directly. Although this seldom occurred in these families, the children were appreciative when it did. Inform the child either alone or with siblings that the parent has died. Discuss how the memorial and burial will be conducted. Inform the school about the ceremonies and invite students and teachers to attend.

2. *Encourage the child to participate in the ceremonies.* Discuss possible roles the child can play in them. Encourage the child to invite special friends.

3. *Follow the child's lead about returning to school after the death.* Keep in mind, however, staying out of school beyond the final ritual is usually not helpful.

4. *Help the child choose appropriate mementos belonging to the patient.*

5. *Reestablish family routines.* Children need instruction as soon as possible about necessary changes in family routines. Establishing a regular time to hold family meetings, possibly at dinner, is an effective forum for discussing changing responsibilities because it gives the parent the opportunity to explain why certain rules have to be changed, rather than putting the child in the position of breaking a rule that he or she did not know existed.

6. *Teach and encourage mourning.* Going through family pictures and discussing good times, trips, and so forth is a useful way to help the child mourn. Discussions about what happened, who did what, and so on is much more successful than talking about sadness. If the child expresses feelings, listen and facilitate them. Such expressions may not happen often.

Bereavement and Reconstitution

1. *Inform the child that the family may have to change its former routines.* These changes may include sharing more chores, establishing car pools that will take the child to after-school activities, and the like. Discussing such matters during dinner once a week can be helpful.

2. *Keep in mind that many children this age need to be taught how to mourn.* Spontaneous, controlled mourning by the parent, perhaps tearing or even crying quietly, can teach the child that sad feelings are normal and can be controlled. Although children this age may delay trips to the cemetery, these visits can be useful when the child is ready. Parents often need to visit the cemetery far more often than the children do. Most children this age usually can tolerate only brief visits. Planning an activity such as taking flowers, cleaning the burial site, placing and later releasing a special holiday balloon also can be helpful for some children.

3. *Reconstitute the family routines as soon as possible.* Encourage the child to participate in sports and other after-school activities, and maintain contact with friends. Expect the child to be happy and ebullient soon after the death; this is not a sign that the child has forgotten the parent. Adults need much more time before they can regain some or all of their happier feelings.

4. *Take on the roles formerly done by the patient.* Learning to be the disciplinarian or the supporter is not easy. Parents often liken this to learning how to be both the good guy and the bad guy. Sudden increases or decreases in limit setting usually resulted in rebellion or acting out. When parents discuss the reason for changes in limit setting and encourage feedback from the child, the transition is likely to occur more smoothly. It is difficult to remember that the child's anger concerning the change may be a way of mourning for the absent parent.

5. *Recognize that children in late elementary school experience separation anxiety in a different way than do younger children.* For example, although these older children may want to sleep with the surviving parent for a few days or weeks after the death, their need to do this is usually brief. Although some parents need this feeling of closeness much longer than the child does, allowing the child to sleep with them for prolonged periods is not a good idea. Children this age also need the surviving parent or parent substitute to be home because it is difficult for them to return to an empty home when they return from school, after-school activities, or visits with friends. For this reason, the parent should remain at home for the first few months after the death if at all possible, despite the fact that, superficially, it may appear that his or her presence is not important because the child is away from home so often after school.

6. *Do not despair if children, especially boys, are at their worst at home.* The messiness, the sulks, the anger, and rebellion often, but not always, are related to feelings about the loss of the parent. It may be helpful to seek objective feedback from others (e.g., teachers, coaches, parents of the child's friends) who can provide a more complete picture about how the child is doing in the outside world.

7. *Keep dating fairly private until there is a possibility that the relationship will become a longer term relationship.* Once informed about the relationship, the child is likely to have numerous thoughts and feelings about it. Thus, helping the child put those thoughts and feelings into words can be helpful.

8. *Seek individual or group grief counseling if needed.* Many surviving parents found that counseling helped them improve their mood and their ability to solve the complex problems they faced after the spouse's death. Although 9- to 11-year-olds are able to turn to other adults for help with their grief, the surviving parent remains a central figure in their support network. Children this age may also respond well to group counseling, which is available in some schools and hospices.

9. *Parents who exhibit prolonged symptoms of depression or anxiety, who have problems with alcohol or other substances, or who experience exacerbations of previous emotional or mental health problems should be engaged in therapy.* The possibility that grief reactions are complicated by earlier losses, by severe problems with single parenthood, by an inability to organize and solve problems adequately, or by a delay in forming constructive new relationships are additional reasons for therapy. These problems can seriously affect their parenting ability.

10. *Child therapy referral:* Consider referring children for therapy if they do not demonstrate a return to previous levels of competence in school, in after-school activities, and in involvement with their peers. Refer if the child's sadness persists without large blocks of pleasure or joy or if there is no indication of occasional and sporadic moments of sadness coupled with expressed thoughts about missing the dead parent.

10

Children 9–11 Years of Age

Narratives

As we saw in the previous chapter, older elementary school-aged children are doers. They are involved in school, after-school activities, and sports. They shy away from expressing their own feelings and from being around other people who express theirs. Although parents remain important to them, their self-esteem is not as dependent on parental approval as it is for younger children. Significant adults such as coaches and teachers also can provide solace, approbation, and self-esteem. Peers of the same gender are friends—people to do things with.

The two families described in this chapter provide important contrasts. The first family consists of a surviving father and his 10-year-old daughter. The second family includes a surviving mother, two daughters, and a son. Both parents learned the roles of becoming a single parent, and both mourned the loss of a spouse. In the first story, the father stayed home from work for seven months to care for his daughter. He is one of five fathers in the total sample who elected this option, and it was a good choice for them as well as their children.

In the second narrative, the mother faced a cascade of stressors that initially staggered her. She helps us understand the pain of grief, which is complicated by the need to develop a new, independent identity. Both she and her husband were devoted to his career as a rising young executive at a multinational corporation, which required the family to move almost yearly to a new geographic area of the United States. His was a two-person career, one where only one member was paid, a choice that both spouses willingly embraced. His death forced her to forge a new identity, no longer as the wife of an executive or as a protected member of a corporation. The lack of all support from both her own and her husband's parents left her to cope alone as an independent single mother.

FATHER AND 10-YEAR-OLD DAUGHTER

"My Daughter Is a Patient Teacher."

This is the story of Phil, a surviving father who moved from having a distant relationship with his 10-year-old daughter, Jennifer, to forming a close supportive relationship with her by immersing himself in her world after her mother's death. He devoted seven months to this process. Here is how it evolved.

Background

Susan was 30 years old when she met Phil, a divorced father with a teen-aged daughter. He owned a consulting firm and met Susan, a successful personnel officer in a major corporation, during a consultation. The marriage was a good one. They shared many work and social interests, Susan liked his daughter and the daughter liked her. However, Susan also wanted a child of her own. Both parents were pleased when Jennifer was born four years after they were married. Excluding a three-month leave of absence when Jennifer was born, Susan continued to work.

Illness

Jennifer was 3 years old when Susan's breast cancer was initially diagnosed. The disease had already spread to several lymph nodes. Susan remained busy, and she coped by focusing on the treatment, her job, and caring for Jennifer. When she was receiving chemotherapy, Phil's recently married daughter and his brother's wife often cared for Jennifer. Jennifer was almost 5 when Susan completed her treatment, and her disease went into remission. The family believed that Susan was cured. Phil was not one to talk about his feelings, certainly not feelings of fear and uncertainty.

Terminal Stage

Three years after her treatment ended, Susan began to experience pain in her hip and back, and a series of tests revealed that her cancer had metastasized to several bones. This major blow was alleviated only slightly by discussions with her oncologists about the next series of treatments with experimental drugs. Unfortunately, treatments over the next 18 months were ineffective, and the disease also metastasized to Susan's liver.

By the time Susan and Phil met the interviewer, the terminal nature of the disease was no longer in doubt. Susan was anxious and tearful. Jennifer, now 10 years old, had been unaware of her mother's illness until a few weeks before the interview, when she inadvertently saw Susan's mastectomy scar while her mother was trying on a bathing suit. Susan told Jennifer that she had been operated on several years earlier for breast cancer. Jennifer's response was "Oh." Susan did not tell Jennifer that her illness was now terminal.

Susan desired guidance concerning how to tell Jennifer that she expected to die soon. She wanted to know how to initiate an ongoing conversation about the matter and how to gauge the timing of conversations correctly. She didn't want to burden Jennifer, she also didn't want to wait until it was too late. "I want to know what Jennifer is thinking about without being intrusive."

Susan cried quietly as she thought about how Jennifer would fare after she died. She firmly believed it was important for Jennifer to have a strong support system. It was this conviction that prompted the family to plan to move at the end of the school year so that they would be closer to Jennifer's favorite people: Phil's married daughter and new granddaughter and his brother's family. Although this meant that Jennifer would have to attend a new school, both Phil and Susan agreed that living close to two women who dearly loved Jennifer and to whom Jennifer felt close was more important than the temporary disruptions she would experience because of the move.

Phil said that in addition to moving, he was planning to change jobs because his current job required too much travel. He would look for a job in a corporation where the hours were more regular and where he could be more available to his wife and daughter. He would also need medical insurance for himself and Jennifer when Susan's health benefits stopped after her death. He felt overwhelmed by all the changes he faced.

The interviewer met Jennifer a few days later. When asked, Jennifer said she was doing well in school, receiving mostly As, then proudly volunteered that she was the fastest runner in her class. She said that she and her dad ran some mornings before she went to school. In talking about the planned move, she said that her friends were all sad that she was leaving. She, too, felt sad about leaving her friends, but she was excited about being close to her baby niece, her half-sister, and her aunt. She was pleased that her mother would be home with her because she was taking medical leave. She liked taking on more responsibility at home because it made her feel that she was helping out.

When the interviewer invited her to do so, Jennifer asked many specific questions about her mother's disease: "How does liver cancer start?" "Can it spread?" "What exactly is cancer?" "What do cells and tumors have to do with cancer?" She had heard these terms but didn't know what they actually meant. She said she could not figure out why her mother got cancer because they all ate healthy food, and it didn't seem right or fair that this would happen in her family. She liked the "girl dates" she had with her mother, when they could talk. She emphasized how much she needed to know about what was happening and that she felt better when situations were clear.

Preparation for Death and Family Rituals

During the last meeting with both Susan and Phil, which took place four weeks before Susan died, many topics were covered. Susan was pleased when the interviewer gave her feedback about the interview with Jennifer, and she glowed when the interviewer described Jennifer's common sense, openness, curiosity, and excellent questions about cancer. When Susan learned that Jennifer was worried she might develop liver cancer because she had been hit in the stomach with a soccer ball, Susan explained that Jennifer had been uncomfortable when she was hit, but only for an instant. Jennifer developed mononucleosis a few weeks later, and her pediatrician suggested that she not play soccer for a while.

At the time of this interview, Susan was bedridden, and she knew that Jennifer was disappointed because they could no longer go out together; both had enjoyed shopping. Consequently, Susan substituted other activities. For example, she and Jennifer joined a video club because Susan knew there were many movies Jennifer wanted to see. Susan sadly added a long litany about her disappointments and how guilty she felt about what she could not do with and for Jennifer. At this point, Phil exploded, saying "Jennifer gets almost anything she wants anyway; I mean, right from the beginning!"

Because Susan's role in their relationship was to help Phil be sensitive to his daughter's needs, she disagreed: "No! Friends her age have their own TV, their own phone, their own little gadgets in their rooms. She doesn't have that stuff. She's had a great deal of our attention, but I don't think she has a lot of physical things."

Phil calmed down and said, "Ever since she was just a little tyke, we've never really been separated. Every time we went away, we took her with us because it was more fun with her than without her. She doesn't have the gadgets, but the togetherness we've had through the years seems to be more important than that."

The couple then discussed Jennifer's understanding of what would happen in the future. "It's funny," Phil said, "because Jennifer brought it up herself, right out of the blue, when we were taking a long family train trip together a few weeks ago. Jennifer asked me, 'If you passed away, where would you want to be buried?' I said, 'I would like to be cremated and buried out to sea.' Susan said, 'No, I want to be buried in the ground.' Jennifer then asked what would happen to her if we both died? I said, 'Well, we've already made arrangements for that; chances are that nothing will happen to your mom and dad. But you have to be prepared for everything. If anything happened to us, our insurance would take care of you, and you'd have money for college and that sort of thing.' She liked the fact that she could go live with Uncle Steve or my daughter Debbie, both of whom she is very close to."

Susan added: "Jennifer was very pleased by that. They all live close together; it's close to where we are planning to move in a few weeks."

Phil said: "For a 10-year-old kid, she's a good conversationalist. Unfortunately, at times I'm real busy and can't always listen to her."

Two weeks after this meeting, Susan was hospitalized, and Jennifer was thrilled that she was allowed to visit her mother in the hospital. After 10 days, Susan was discharged, but she had to be readmitted within 24 hours. Although Jennifer didn't know why, she was not surprised: "When Mom came back (home), she hadn't changed." Jennifer visited Susan one more time, and the interviewer asked her how the visit had been.

Jennifer said: "It was nice. She could tell I was there. She saw me, and she tried to talk—she could talk, but it was just like you were losing your voice."

"What did you say when you saw her?"

"I just hugged her."

"Did you have any idea then that things might get worse and that she might die?"

"Yes."

"How did you know?"

"I knew, I just knew. I didn't even cry when my father told me (she had died) because I just knew."

"Did you feel like you had a chance to say good-bye to your Mom?"

"Yes. She died the next day. She was in her sleep when she died."

"Do you wish you had been there when your mother died?"

"No, thank God. I didn't want to be!"

There was a three-day wake for Susan, followed by a mass. Jennifer said that the worst part was going to the funeral home, just seeing her mother lying there. It gave her the "the spooks." She had not wanted to go to the funeral home, but her friends Megan and Beth said they thought her mom would have wanted her to go, so she went. Jennifer then described how the three of them "got freaked because we went downstairs and went in this coffin showcase room and we're like, OH MY GOD!" Although Jennifer preferred a closed casket, she chose an open one because that was what the others wanted. Jennifer didn't like the way her mother looked because her mother's hair was not arranged properly, but Jennifer didn't want to rearrange it herself. She said the funeral was nice—she kept a cross that had been inside the coffin. She liked it, "but it feels funny." She was relieved that "at least they didn't lower her (in the ground) when I was there."

Bereavement and Reconstitution

After Susan's death, Phil tried to understand his own numbness. When he told Jennifer that Susan had died, he wanted to talk openly with her, but he sensed that she wanted to distance herself from intense emotions. He was tearful and sad as he described his life without Susan. He felt overwhelmed by his grief and by having to handle so many new responsibilities.

A week after Susan's death, he and Jennifer moved. Jennifer told the interviewer that she believed it was a good move because it was close to her other family. "It just felt good when I got everything settled. It felt settled when all the boxes were gone. The last boxes we unpacked were from my mom's room. I get all her jewelry. She has tons of jewelry; she has, like, 50 pounds of gold chains. This one has an emerald—it's my birth stone."

While talking about her mother's death, Jennifer said: "I know she was in a lot of pain, so it's better for her. The cancer had spread badly. It took over the whole liver, and I understand that the liver's an important part of your body. That made her weak."

Although she had moved, Jennifer maintained contact with her two best friends. She described a club they had formed, in which they did secret things such as burying treasure. "We have secret plans buried (in the park), and we have something really expensive buried there, some 14-karat-gold charms. Beth's mother gave them to us to bury because she didn't need them. The map shows where our hideout is and how to do stuff and where our treasure is buried." The club had been Jennifer's idea. "I just wanted to be like the Goonies, one of my favorite movies. And it's neat; I like it."

A father as a single parent-homemaker is fairly unusual, even in a bedroom community teeming with children, like the one in which Phil and Jennifer now lived. Phil developed a comfortable way of meeting Jennifer's needs for caretaking. "Jennifer's such a fashion plate," he chuckled. "She even wants me to iron her basketball shorts!" Then he added proudly: "I've had so many good comments about her from the mothers. They say Jennifer is just a dream, she does so well at other kids' houses."

Phil also was comfortable with Jennifer's growing independence: "She spends a lot of time out of the house. She always knows that I'm here."

Phil also was involved in Jennifer's after-school activities. "She's really into basketball. I wind up taking all the kids in my truck to her games. I was the official scorekeeper at her last game. She got a kick out of that."

Phil said the neighborhood was like Peyton Place: "There are so many single mothers around here. Three of Jennifer's best friends' mothers are all divorced." During occasional neighborhood coffees, Phil was the only father in a group of 18 mothers. At a Christmas-tree-lighting ceremony in the town square, all the mothers said, "Hi, Phil." He didn't know any of the fathers: "All the fathers are standing there probably thinking, 'Who is this guy?'"

Jennifer was also making many girlfriends at her new school. She didn't like any of the boys. She was a cheerleader and practiced three times a week for an hour; the games were on weekends. She liked her school: "Everybody likes me. I'm good at making friends. I'm a friendly person." She knew that the teachers also liked her: "They all yank my ponytail."

Jennifer was definite about how people had treated her since her mother died and how she wanted to be treated. "I hate people babying me, so I didn't tell anybody. I only told this one girl. I told her not to baby me, and she said 'Fine.' She didn't know she was doing it. She was about to say she was sorry, and I said: 'Can it. I don't like people pitying me. I just want to forget about it.'"

Even her teachers had learned not to say anything. She was sure they knew about her mother because, she said, "Mrs. Brown knows, because she said, 'Give this paper to your mon—I mean your dad.'"

When Jennifer received her first report card from the new school, her grades were lower than those she had received before. Phil reminded her that she made the varsity basketball team. Instead of being concerned about her drop in grades, he was supportive and told her that things were harder at first when you make big changes.

Although many children in Jennifer's age group worry that they may develop cancer when there is a family history of it, most refuse to think about it, let alone discuss their feelings. Jennifer, however, was unusually candid in discussing this as well as her thoughts about other family members dying. "It really spooks me to think it runs in my family. My grandfather had it, my mom had it. It's just spooky, because you don't really know, and you get frightened."

"Even if cancer is in your family, Jennifer, it doesn't mean that you are going to get it. The most important thing is to get checkups every year."

"That's why my mom got cancer. She wouldn't get a checkup. My grandmother says she'll be joining my mom (in heaven) soon. She doesn't think she'll live much longer. She is 72. She's lucky because I doubt it's gonna be another 50 years before she dies (the way it is going to be for me). I hope she doesn't die until I'm at least 20."

Unfortunately, Jennifer's grandmother was obvious to the difference between adult and child mourning and showed her intense grief over her daughter's death too openly. Both Phil and Jennifer complained to the interviewer about Grandma making them feel guilty and pressured. Jennifer said she had to tell her grandmother when she came to visit one month after her mother died that "I'm just a kid, and I need to be out with my friends" when her grandmother insisted that Jennifer stay home with her and talk about Susan.

"How has your father been since your mother died?"

"He's been O.K. I mean, he laughs and everything. He isn't down in the dumps or depressed." When asked to elaborate on her more intense grief experiences, usually talkative Jennifer became monosyllabic. When asked why she worried about something happening to her dad, she explained: "He's the only person I have."

Phil said that Jennifer was extremely concerned about him. When they went to the cemetery, he always got tears in his eyes, and Jennifer asked him if he was O.K. Phil explained to her that "I miss your mom and I get sad about it, as you are, and I get tears in my eyes, but you don't need to be concerned."

Phil worked hard to clarify the difference between his and Jennifer's needs in the mourning process. In discussing their talks together about Susan, Phil said that Jennifer liked to talk about the good times they had had together, not the hard times. Although he wished he could forget them, those thoughts and memories just came up. He didn't share them with Jennifer.

As Phil's mourning dissipated, his thoughts about Susan involved pleasant memories more often. He even found himself chuckling about some of the memories. He spent time looking at family photographs with Jennifer. She especially liked two pictures of herself with her mother. Phil put them in special frames for her, and she kept them on her dresser.

Phil found that it was easy to comfort Jennifer. Before doing her homework at night, she hugged and clung to him for a little while. Her mourning was sporadic: "Jennifer had a bad night last Sunday. She started asking me a lot of questions about how Mom died; who was there. She said that she should have been there, that she should have been a better daughter. She asked if she was a good daughter—and all those kinds of things. She sobbed a bit. I explained again that her mother was asleep and she just stopped breathing. She wanted to know the details. We both wound up crying a little."

Phil created rituals and ceremonies that helped Jennifer mourn. He also helped her limit traumatic, excessive grieving. Five months after Susan's death coincided with the Christmas holidays. "A few days ago, I found Jennifer lying in bed clutching Susan's purse. Stupidly, I kept it in the closet along with all her other things. When I saw her, I said, 'Come on, get up. It's not the right time for this. A new year is going to start in a couple of days, and you've got a lot of good things to look forward to.' I tried to break her out of that mood by saying, 'Jennifer, let's put it away.' She didn't overreact or underreact, she just said 'O.K.'"

Both of them went to the cemetery a few days later, taking some flowers and a couple of helium-filled balloons that said "Merry Christmas." Jennifer had seen that done before and thought it was a good idea. They returned a few days later to the cemetery to set the balloons free. Phil was comfortable with the pace of Jennifer's grieving. Jennifer occasionally accompanied him on his weekly visits to the cemetery but walked away a couple of minutes after she put flowers on her mother's grave. Phil elected not to have Jennifer participate in a bereavement group because he believed that she did better herself controlling her own mourning.

The reactions of 9- to 11-year-old children to a parent's dating follow a fairly predictable pattern. Initial apprehension is followed by gradual rapprochement, though laced with jealousy, recrimination, guilt, even pleasure, and, ultimately, acceptance. Jennifer had settled into a pleasant, predictable life when Phil made contact with Diana, who was a friend of Phil and Susan's who lived in Alabama. She planned to visit friends in New England so Phil invited her to spend a week with him and Jennifer. Jennifer knew Diana and liked her. Phil thought Jennifer would enjoy a woman's company, although he felt guilty about having associations with women because he was betraying Susan. Phil was surprised by Jennifer's reaction to Diana when she arrived. All of them had a nice time. Diana did Jennifer's hair and rubbed Jennifer's feet while they watched television. However, when Phil sat next to Diana, Jennifer "had her eyes and antenna out, and then when Diana was not around, Jennifer questioned me: 'Do you like Diana? Would you ever marry her?' I said, 'You are really pushing things.'"

Phil liked Diana more than he had expected. However, he felt that he still had a duty to Susan. Neither he nor Jennifer were ready for him to have a serious relationship.

The 9- to 11-year-old child's process of rapprochement to a parent's more serious involvement with a new potential mate is ambivalent. Jennifer, through her words and actions, was unusually open about her struggles concerning Diana. Diana had spent a few days with the two of them over the holidays, and Phil valued Diana's sensitivity to Jennifer's feelings. He quoted Diana as saying to Jennifer: "I would never try to come between you and your father. I could never take the place of your mother, nor would I want to, and I don't want you to think that I am."

Although Jennifer and Diana got along well, Phil sensed that Jennifer was a little jealous of Diana. As he explained: "Jennifer's not home all day, and if she is home, she's on the computer for hours. So, I'm watching TV, and she wants to snuggle. Sometimes Diana and I are sitting next to each other, and Jennifer will come in and sit between us, and that's fine. But then she'll say, 'You never have time for me' (he laughed) and I'll say, 'I never have time for you! Tell me about it! When do you have time for me?' I think she feels that someone is moving in on her dad! That's what it really is."

Phil and Diana were careful not to provoke Jennifer. "When we talk, we sit across from each other, and Diana sleeps with Jennifer in the other twin bed, so we're very careful to have Jennifer see that this is a platonic relationship. I'm not sure that is reassuring to Jennifer. When Diana left, I said, 'Well, you are probably happy that she's leaving,' and Jennifer said, 'No, I'm not. I really like her, and I'm not happy she's leaving.'"

Seven months after Susan's death, the reconstitution process was well underway. Phil had found an excellent job and planned to begin working soon. He had become more openly involved with Diana, and Jennifer had adjusted to the situation. She was rapidly adopting the concerns of the emerging adolescent. She had a greater need for autonomy, and Phil handled his apprehensions about this well. He was learning when and how to let go, and, as he said, "My daughter is a patient teacher." At school, Jennifer had settled in well. She received her report card and did beautifully, making the honor roll for the second time.

Unlike Phil's mourning, Jennifer's was increasingly episodic, usually brought on by a special occasion, a holiday, or a memory that triggered some tears. Phil continued to find solace in his weekly trips to the cemetery. Between those trips, he often thought about Susan, unless he was busy.

There were two more follow-up interviews: one 12 months after Susan died, the other 6 months later. Both Phil and Jennifer were doing well. Phil had a senior position in a major corporation that he enjoyed very much because it made him feel purposeful and connected. He was now clearly dating Diana, and Jennifer was much less possessive. Phil still missed Susan a great deal, especially during holidays and anniversaries. Jennifer made the honor roll three out of four times that year and played on a successful softball team. She went to a sports summer camp and enjoyed it immensely.

As part of the second, more formal follow-up visit, both Jennifer and Phil were interviewed by two psychologists, who noted how well Jennifer had adjusted to the loss of her mother, the move, and the new school. Each commented independently on how Jennifer and Phil were able to grieve and share memories of Susan. Their grieving process was one factor that had a favorable impact on Jennifer's adjustment.

Summary

Jennifer had recovered from this family tragedy despite the fact that she faced three risks. Her mother and not her father had died; her father was overwhelmed and somewhat distant before his wife's death; and the family moved to a new house, a new neighborhood, and a new school immediately after the death.

Phil learned to mediate and protect well. He decided to postpone starting a new job for seven months to care for Jennifer. He gained a significant understanding of his daughter, which few men achieve. His sensitivity and availability, his ability to be close to her, yet allow her to distance herself as she became engaged in outside activities was important. He taught her how to mourn by modeling through his own mourning but didn't overwhelm her with his powerful grief. He created opportunities for mourning by inviting her but not insisting that she accompany him to the cemetery, and he protected her when her own mourning got out of control. Phil enhanced her self-esteem by downplaying her initial drop in grades at the new school, by emphasizing her achievements, by supporting her interests, and by genuinely admiring her competence. And Diana? She joined these two good friends and respected Susan's place in Jennifer's heart. Because of Jennifer's innate strengths, her good relationship with her mother before the death, and her wonderful sense of herself— "Everybody likes me. I'm good at making friends; I'm a friendly person"—it is not surprising that Jennifer was doing well 18 months after her mother's death.

Mother and Three Children, Aged 7, 10, and 11 Years

"He's a Boy Friend, Not a Boyfriend!"

Grief and depression are easily confused. Kathy's story helps us understand this confusion. Depression, when full-blown, is stark, generally obvious, and usually cyclical. These cycles begin, last awhile, then dissipate. Kathy's depression was not like that. It was more insidious: the kind that sneaks in when a cascade of stressors get out of hand and when anger is bottled up. All her life, Kathy had tended to react to stress with mild depression and its frequent companion, lowered self-esteem.

Kathy's mother had a similar syndrome, and both shared a third characteristic: They unknowingly projected their self-devaluation onto their children. However, Kathy also had several unusual attributes: She was extraordinarily honest about her psychological self, was painfully honest with herself and with the interviewer, and worked hard to correct her unconscious tendency to underestimate her children because underestimating them was the last thing in the world she wanted to do.

Background

Kevin and Kathy met in college and married before Kevin graduated. Kathy was attracted to Kevin because he was competent, gregarious, athletic, and well liked. What attracted Kevin to Kathy was that she was supportive, sensible, generous, and extremely honest about herself. And she loved and admired him extravagantly. When they married, Kathy dropped out of college to help Kevin finance his education and early career. This decision defined the roles they would play in their partnership: Kevin would eventually become a corporate executive, and Kathy would devote herself to his career and to raising their children until they entered college.

The couple had three children: Courtney first, then Blair 18 months later, then Cynthia three years after that. Although Kathy occasionally resented postponing her own career, she usually was pleased about their decision to have children while they were young, to develop Kevin's career, and to enjoy the fruits of their labor after the children left home. The early years were not easy, especially after Kevin obtained an executive track job with a large multinational corporation that required the family to move every year or two. Kathy couldn't work because employers required more than one year's tenure.

By the time the interviewer met the family, Courtney was an 11-year-old sixth grader, Blair was a 10-year-old fifth grader, and both children had attended six different schools. Seven-year-old Cynthia, although only in the second grade, had already attended two different schools.

Family life was going well. Kevin attended various executive training programs, clearly excelled at work, and seemed destined to become an executive in his firm. In addition to being intelligent, gregarious, and well liked, he was an effective public speaker, another significant attribute in his job.

Kevin was devoted to his children, in part to compensate for his own parents' distance and emotional coolness. He and Kathy evolved complementary roles with the children. Kathy planned and organized; Kevin responded, understood, resonated, and encouraged. Courtney, the eldest, was like her mother—a thoughtful, intellectual, emotionally reserved little person—whereas her brother and sister were like their father: emotional, garrulous, even impulsive doers. Because Kevin had been successful in sports, he took a special interest in Blair's athletic development. He was a "Little League" father who often practiced with his son, boasted about his son's unusual talents, and fantasized about Blair having a professional baseball career. Kevin was also extremely fond of his daughters. He delighted in Courtney's academic prowess and the fact that she had many friends. When Cynthia came along, she quickly became "Daddy's little girl," going with him on household errands whenever allowed. Emotionally, Kevin and Cynthia seemed to be kindred spirits.

Kevin and Kathy were popular among their friends and often went out dancing. Kevin was clearly successful, and Kathy had mastered the art of making new friends quickly so that she had a support network wherever they lived, both for herself and for the children. Adding to the families' popularity was the fact that the children were bright, attractive, and active in sports and other activities.

Shortly before Kevin's cancer was diagnosed, Kathy's father had a stroke, and her mother was preoccupied with his care and rehabilitation. Her mother also took over the family business and ran it successfully. True to form, her mother accepted her success but didn't derive the kind of self-satisfaction from it that improves self-esteem.

Illness

When Kevin began having headaches accompanied by a slight drooping of his mouth, he was concerned but believed the cause was stress. He had recently entered a training program for employees destined to be corporate executives and assumed that he would master his physical problem the way he had mastered every other challenge in his life.

After a couple of months, his headaches became so acute that he went to the hospital emergency room. The diagnosis of a brain tumor stunned the couple. The physician said it was cancer but that it might be operable. Kathy and Kevin mobilized quickly to find the best treatment available and threw themselves into trying to master the new challenge. After surgery, the neurosurgeon told them he had been unable to remove the tumor completely, and Kevin transferred to a hospital that had an effective chemotherapy protocol, which controlled his tumor for 18 months.

Kathy's sadness, self-criticism, and fears about the future dominated her mood, although her actions were intelligent and thoughtful. All the children noticed their mother's changed mood, but typical of their age group, Courtney and Blair were less reactive to their mother's mood than their younger sister was. The one who voiced the family's emotional undertones was Cynthia, who became the family's truth teller.

Kevin decided to transfer back to the New York area, where they had previously spent two happy years and had many close friends. This move provided Kathy with some support and security, and she was able to calm her increasing fears by reminding herself that Kevin worked for a large, paternalistic corporation she could count on. The company, her "ace in the hole," would provide adequate money, medical benefits, and ongoing support if Kevin were unable to work.

Terminal Illness

When Kevin developed weakness in his right side, a CAT scan showed that the tumor was growing. After his second operation, the surgeon told Kathy that the cause of Kevin's symptoms was a large cyst, which was removed. The surgeon expected Kevin to recover after this episode, and he seemed better for about two months. A few weeks before Christmas, however, his speech began to slur markedly. Although he had returned to work, he was unable to accomplish anything. Additional surgery resulted in the paralysis of his right side. He became dysphasic and was unable to communicate effectively.

Kathy rearranged the family's life, ordered a hospital bed for Kevin and the other equipment he needed, and accompanied him each time he went to the hospital for experimental chemotherapy. However, his condition continued to deteriorate: He was less alert than he had been, was barely able to get around with a cane, and began to lose track of days and time. Finally, he was unable to get out of bed despite daily treatments by a physical therapist. At this point, Kathy requested another CAT scan to determine whether Kevin might benefit from additional chemotherapy. She received the results of the scan on the telephone during a meeting with the interviewer and was told that the tumor had spread so extensively that chemotherapy was unlikely to be effective. Because that day was their wedding anniversary, Kathy tearfully decided to tell Kevin the bad news on another day.

Kathy said she experienced waves of fear and rage. At night, she was afraid she would be unable to manage. In the morning, the pressure of taking care of Kevin and the children energized her and "Got me going." Kathy often ruminated about the time they had wasted paying their dues to the company: "Kevin worked so hard for so many years, and he will never attain his goal of being a senior executive."

Although the children were as distressed as their mother was, Courtney and Blair managed to perform reasonably well in school, whereas Cynthia did not. Their reactions to their father's deteriorating condition varied.

Courtney's Reactions

Eleven-year-old Courtney threw herself into her schoolwork and received excellent grades in the honors program. She was organized and enjoyed studying. She also enjoyed sports and attended an athletic summer camp. She did not like to talk about her feelings related to her father's condition; instead she learned about cancer and carefully watched the various caregivers who came to the house. She asked the physical therapist to teach her how to move her father, and she became expert at it. When Kevin returned home from a hospitalization, she instructed the ambulance workers about the best way to transfer him from the stretcher to the bed.

At school, Courtney's mid-term paper was about euthanasia, and her next paper was about the rights of the handicapped. Intellectual defenses were effective for her. She also maintained a circle of close friends that included one boy: "a boy friend, not a boyfriend!" She insisted that her friendship with him was based on a mutual interest in sports.

Courtney valued the fact that her mother kept her informed about her father's illness, but the closest she came to discussing her feelings about it was to express concern about the future: "I think about who will take me to the father-daughter dance and who will walk down the aisle with me when I get married." Although Kathy did not worry about Courtney, she had a difficult time figuring out how to elicit Courtney's feelings.

Blair's Reactions

Kathy was sad about the loss of Kevin's and 10-year-old Blair's dreams concerning their relationship. "Kevin was such an athlete! Blair missed Kevin during the baseball season. He is not having a very good year, and he wants to be a major-league player." She believed that Blair's innate intelligence was getting him through school with Bs. Unlike Courtney, Blair spent little time studying. His teachers believed that he could do better academically, and complained about his lack of organization. When Kathy informed Blair's teachers about Kevin's illness and urged them to take his stressful situation into account, their response was helpful and supportive. Although Kathy was unable to attend all of Blair's games, she asked her friends to go and cheer him on because he needed the support.

Unlike Courtney, Blair was more openly sad and tearful when he talked about his father's deteriorating condition. "Dad would have been an assistant coach for Little League the year he got sick. He came to every game I played in. Even in the off-season, he would practice with me in the basement. Now Dad is always sleeping, really tired. He used to be able to get up after chemotherapy, but now he can barely get off the couch." Blair overheard someone say his father had six months to live, but he thought his father might have more time because he had already lived for two years after the diagnosis.

Blair felt more vulnerable in sports without his father's guidance and support. He also felt isolated and empty because his father was no longer available to him. Yet he maintained his grades, his friends, and his after-school activities. Although he occasionally exhibited disruptive behavior at school, he was more disorganized and stubborn at home. Blair left his father alone when his father was tired. He just said hello and good-bye. Whereas cognitive mastery was helpful to Courtney, sports were helpful to Blair because they allowed him to identify with his father and to express his most powerful feelings safely through displacement.

Blair was concerned about his own anger: "I might go wacko when my father dies, might hurt someone." Then he retreated from this direct expression of his anger at his father's deterioration. Instead, he talked about his favorite house, the one they owned when they had first lived in their current area. He really loved that house. When they first moved back, he had hoped the family would at least live near the former house, but this did not work out. When he visited the house, he was shocked: "The people who own the house now cut down all the trees around it—everything. Just cut them down!" They had left his favorite tree, but it had died. "That house is in a valley and doesn't get a lot of rain. You have to water trees there. Then they painted the house pink on one side and brown on the other. How could you do that to a house?" Tears welled in his eyes as he tried to contain his rage. It seemed obvious that he was using his rage about the house to displace his rage about his father's deterioration.

Cynthia's Reactions

Seven-year-old Cynthia's reactions to her father's terminal illness contrasted markedly with those of her siblings. She was vocal about her unhappiness concerning what had happened to the family. She believed that because her father was no longer willing to let her sit on his lap or to play with her, he was rejecting her. Although Kathy tried to explain that Kevin was ill and couldn't give her the attention she was used to, Cynthia was unable to comprehend the relationship between his withdrawal and his illness and impending death: "Daddy doesn't love me anymore." Although she understood that he was sick, she believed that he would live for a long time. Her long litany of dissatisfactions included, "Dad is different now. He can't talk, he can't hear as well, he can't walk, he can't even get into a wheelchair. Dad used to fix things for Mom; he went to dances with her. Now Mom just has to stay home and work. Mom doesn't wear dresses and makeup anymore. She has a bad temper, too, because Dad is close to dying."

Cynthia also believed that her mother did not love her. She felt left out and said that no one listened to her. She also believed that her brother and sister received more attention than she did. "Mom changed a lot. Before Dad got sick, she was nice, talked to me a lot, bought me presents, and didn't yell at me." Cynthia was extremely angry at Kevin's physicians because she believed they had made a terrible mistake, which had caused her father's current problems. "He had a headache when he played tennis with Mom, then he got worse—not talking, not walking—and he lost his hair. The doctors did that. They just didn't know what they were doing." However, when asked what advice she would give to other children, she said they should talk with their mothers so they could understand what was happening to their fathers. Her ability to express emotion easily, her fixed ideas about what was happening and why nothing could be done, her preoccupation with her mother's affect, and the negative impact of all these factors on her schoolwork illustrated reactions that were typical of early school-age children.

Because Cynthia's grades had dropped, Kathy believed that she was not reading at grade level and wondered whether she had a significant learning problem. Kathy also struggled to understand and relate to Cynthia's emotionality.

Preparation for Death and Family Rituals

Kevin's deteriorating condition suddenly took a turn for the worse. His breathing became labored, and he was admitted to a local hospital. Kathy remained with him while the children stayed with two of Kathy's friends. Cynthia was tearful and frightened and confided to her mother's friend that she wanted to die so she could be with her father when he died. She could not understand why he was having trouble breathing if he had a brain tumor. Although the friend explained Kevin's situation well, Cynthia remained skeptical.

One night, while Kathy was napping at home after a late-night vigil at the hospital, she received the call that Kevin had died and returned to the hospital to be alone with him one last time. When she came home again, the children were in school, so she went to the school to tell them that their father had died.

Courtney's reaction surprised Kathy. She cried for a few minutes after hearing the news, then asked to stay at school for the remainder of the day. As Courtney later explained: "I knew it was going to happen; it was not a surprise. Mom was good about letting me know how things were progressing. I stayed in school that day because I had two tests. I just needed time to be with my friends. It was a hard day." She felt that she had been able to talk with her father before he became too sick and that he knew she loved him. "The hardest thing was having to get rid of all of Dad's things. Mom took care of most of it. The other hard part is that Dad can't share when good things happen. Like I got straight As on my report card in spite of the fact that Dad was so sick. He would have been real proud of that."

When Blair was informed about the death, he immediately decided to leave school and go home with his mother. He cried for a couple of hours. Kathy's cadre of close friends was at the house and talked with Blair until he seemed to feel a little better. Blair later said, "I couldn't believe it really happened. I went to the funeral so I could really say good-bye." He was stoical at the funeral and remained so. He wanted life to return to normal as quickly as possible, but he struggled with his sadness, when he looked at his father's empty chair at the table, for example. However, his school performance improved dramatically. By the end of the school year, he had made the honor role. At home, however, he remained angry, feeling that he had gotten a raw deal.

Cynthia also cried when her mother came to school to tell her that her father had died. Later, she said: "I couldn't believe it happened. I think Dad is in heaven, but it's not as special just having a mother without a father. Everything is different. Blair tries to be like Dad, but he's not." Unlike the polite but dismissive silence that characterized her brother's and sister's responses, Cynthia asked the interviewer probing questions: "Why did Daddy die?" "Why did God want to take him?" "Why did Daddy get sick?" She felt better when she thought, "Dad will always be in my heart." However, she also expressed anger toward him: "Why did he have to die anyway? It's not fair. I only got to be with him for six years, not nearly as long as Blair and Courtney."

Cynthia worried about her mother's ability to manage the family: "Will she be able to take care of me?" Much to Kathy's surprise, Cynthia's grades also improved markedly immediately after Kevin's death; she was on the honor role for the first time. At home, she often cried when she said her prayers, and she wanted to write a letter to her father.

Kathy found that as much as she wanted to be organized, she could not. "I felt weird going out of the house at first—a feeling of freedom and relief that I didn't have Kevin to take care of. But after the first couple of weeks, the reality really hits you. This is it! It's easier in some ways, but he is also not there for us." She visited the cemetery and was surprised by how difficult that was. The numb feeling that had shielded her from her intense grief was beginning to lift.

Bereavement and Reconstitution

Two weeks after Kevin died, a series of blows hit Kathy. Without warning, Kevin's company terminated the family's medical benefits and informed Kathy that she would not be entitled to his death benefits and life insurance because of "paperwork errors." Understandably, Kathy panicked. A month later, her father died following heart surgery, and her mother, deeply depressed, withdrew and spoke to no one, not even her old friends. The death of her father shortly after her husband's death, her mother's obviously deep depression, and the uncertainty concerning the family's financial survival left Kathy feeling angry, helpless, and defeated. She also talked less with her friends, who had been helpful in the past.

The children, sensing their mother's despair, were frightened. To Courtney's annoyance, Cynthia reported Courtney's fears directly during a family session: "Two people died—Dad and Grandpa—and Courtney said, 'What if Mom dies?'"

Courtney interrupted her, saying, "I never said that!" but Cynthia plunged on: "Dad was the big hero. He was the big protector."

Family Reconstitution Stalled

Kathy was hurt because Kevin's company disregarded her. Every time she called, they stalled and nothing was being resolved. Kevin's strong belief in and highly positive feelings about the company still influenced her judgment. However, the family session mobilized her. It had clarified how the financial uncertainty was undermining not only her feelings of security but those of her children, and that she would not tolerate! She was now furious at the company, and this feeling jolted her out of her immobility. She hired an attorney and began working closely with him, preparing all the paperwork he requested.

Another face of depression is an exaggerated fear of failure. Kathy was afraid that she might fail as a single parent and, even more frightening, that her children might fail. She was angry at Blair because he acted childish at times: "He won't even put his clothes in the laundry; he would rather wear them dirty." Because she was afraid that he was as irresponsible at school as he was at home and that his grades might drop, she asked the principal to have Blair's teachers call her about any problems they were having with him. The principal seemed surprised at her request, and informed her he hadn't heard about any problems.

Kathy was not concerned about Courtney, who was involved with cheerleading practice, studying, and spending time with her friends. When Kathy shared her grief with Courtney one night, Courtney comforted her. Afterward, however, Kathy observed that Courtney became more remote from her emotionally and she decided not to share her grief with Courtney again.

Family Reconstitution Restarted

Kathy's persistent work with Kevin's company finally paid off. The check for his life insurance benefits arrived four months after Kevin died. Kathy was elated and felt she could now get on with her life. She initiated long needed repairs on the house and worked out conservative but inventive plans to invest the insurance money. Although she needed to find a job to replace Kevin's benefits, she decided to wait until the children were more settled.

Courtney was heavily engaged in completing a science project about how chemotherapy affects the body. Kathy was concerned about Courtney's continued preoccupation with medical matters, in part because Courtney rarely talked about her father. To encourage Courtney's mourning, Kathy gave her a photograph that Kevin had taken of her when she was 3 years old, which he had given to Kathy as a Mother's Day present. Kathy hoped this would create an opportunity to talk about Kevin. Courtney thanked Kathy and hung the picture over her desk. That was it. The parents of Courtney's friends told Kathy that their daughters would never talk with them about something so emotional either! They reassured her that 11-year-old girls can be extremely private.

When Kathy asked Blair's teachers about his school problems, "They looked at me as if I had two heads. I felt he was like a walking time bomb, but apparently he is only having trouble at home." As a result, she began handling situations involving Blair differently at home: "I try not to pounce quite as quickly or as hard if he is doing things that are unacceptable. He still gets frustrated easily, but if I don't react so strongly, he seems to respond better. I think I had gotten into a vicious cycle with him. Now that I've gotten out of it, he's better."

Kathy noticed that Blair was behaving more and more like his father. The sports he was involved in, even the school subjects he was interested in, were similar to Kevin's. When Kathy received Blair's report card, she was surprised because he was on the honor role. He achieved higher marks than he had ever received before. Like Courtney, he rarely talked about his father.

Cynthia, rather than failing in school as Kathy had feared, also made the honor roll. Like her sister, she too became a cheerleader. Unlike her siblings, however, she liked to talk about her father. Kathy said, "Death is so final; it's such a hard thing for Cynthia to grasp." Cynthia still had headaches and nightmares, although these symptoms had improved. Kathy believed that Cynthia's improvement was related to the fact that she spent more time with Cynthia and was more patient with her. When Kathy mentioned returning to work, at least part time, Cynthia objected strenuously because she wanted Kathy home when she returned from school.

Although the idea of transporting three children to and from activities, managing the home, and working was daunting, Kathy recalculated the family finances and realized that the family could not remain in their current community unless she worked. She thought moving to another neighborhood would be too disruptive for the children. Also, her own friends were close by. Although she felt increasingly remote from her friends because her life had become so different from theirs, she also knew she could count on them for help. Eight months after Kevin's death, she described flashbacks she was having about some of the sad moments during his illness. She was mourning for the ill Kevin and remembering the traumatic aspects of his illness. When she participated in special activities with the children, she occasionally was overcome with sadness because she and Kevin had planned to participate together with the children.

At the one-year anniversary of Kevin's death, Kathy believed she was managing well. She was working full time and made good use of her friends' help and support. All three children remained on the honor roll, each one had a circle of friends, and all of them participated in after-school activities. Courtney heard that a boy was interested in her, but he was too shy to talk to her.

Eighteen months after Kevin's death, only Cynthia was having difficulty. Although she was doing better than she had ever done before in school, her headaches and stomachaches continued, and she and her mother continued to have arguments. The family physician recommended that Kathy take Cynthia for some psychological counseling because he was concerned about her physical complaints. Kathy planned to do so as soon as possible.

Summary

After grappling with the cascade of stresses confronting her, Kathy won the battle. The resolution of her battles with Kevin's company was a symbolic watershed. By the end of the first year, her depression was under control and her self-esteem had improved. She had a full-time job, had mobilized the help of friends, and all family members except Cynthia were doing quite well.

Although Cynthia had many strengths, she continued to have headaches and stomachaches 18 months after her father's death. Kathy better understood her older children's need for independence. Because both Cynthia and her mother had many strengths, a brief period of supportive therapy, suggested by the family physician, was likely to result in a more positive outcome.

Outcomes

By the final assessment, 8 to 14 months after the parent's death, 29 of the 37 children had achieved their previous levels of functioning in all of the major areas: psychological state, relationships at home, academics, athletics and after-school activities, and developmentally appropriate peer relationships. Five had a delayed reconstitution, one a compromised and two a symptomatic reconstitution.

Timely Reconstitution

Twenty-nine of the 37 children who had a timely reconstitution experienced declines in a number of areas of functioning during the patient's terminal illness. They expressed muted anger and sadness, and many had difficulty with schoolwork, usually a transient drop in grades. Some also demonstrated anticipatory grief. What was most characteristic of these children was that these symptoms and problems improved within a few months of the family's reconstitution. In fact, parents were often puzzled by their rapid improvement in school and rapid re-engagement with peers and activities. Their mourning was episodic and usually expressed as anger and a sense of injustice but also as sadness, disappointment, and longing for the patient's return. The surviving parent often had to initiate opportunities for mourning at holidays, anniversaries, and other marker events. Also characteristic of these children was that, although they avoided feelings, they certainly did not avoid facts. Cognitive mastery was their principal method of coping with the tragedy. For emotional support, they primarily turned to parents and other adults, not to peers. They related to peers through activities and adult-led peer discussion groups.

Delayed Reconstitution

By the final interview, five children had not regained their pre-illness level of functioning in at least one of the five emotional-behavioral domains. The factors associated with this slower recovery were similar to factors associated with slower recovery among early elementary school children: (1) complicated bereavement, (2) unusual stressors, and (3) polarized family situations.

Complicated Bereavement

Lack of information about the illness, treatment, and impending death functioned much as "suppression of bereavement" did with younger children. Because the 9- to 11-year-olds were able to experience anticipatory grief, they expressed anger, mistrust, and lowered self-esteem if they did not receive the information that would permit them to prepare for the parent's death. These reactions complicated the bereavement process after the death. Because one surviving parent encouraged the child's extreme avoidance of both facts and feelings before the death, the child's mourning and recovery were delayed.

Unusual Stressors

Poverty, multiple losses, and immigration, with its many associated stresses such as difficulty communicating with schools, hospitals, and formal support services, also delayed the recovery process. Several of these stresses often interacted with each other in a way that increased family conflict and deprived the child of vital sources of support.

Polarized Family Situations

Older school-aged children in polarized families were more aware of conflicts between parents, loyalties, and a parent's preference for one child over another child than were the early school-aged children. If these preferences reached the level of cross-generational coalitions, children of this age struggled with ambivalent feelings, resentment, guilt, and low self-esteem. It was especially difficult when the parent who died had been their advocate. The conflicted feelings, family realignments, and preferences that resulted were a source of considerable stress.

Compromised Reconstitution

The outcome of one child was compromised. This child was the eldest in a large immigrant family that was severely impoverished by the death of the father. The family lost their home shortly after his death and had to move into a relative's small apartment. Because of the family's immigrant status, they were entitled to few financial benefits. Because the mother's education was limited, she could only work in a low-paying factory job. The child was clinically depressed at the last evaluation.

Symptomatic Reconstitution

Two children developed symptoms after the parent's death that were qualitatively different from those they had had before the death. Although both had had adjustment problems before the parent's terminal illness, their symptoms after the death justified a psychiatric diagnosis. Their symptoms included severe, persistent school phobia; daytime soiling and enuresis; suicidal ideation; and temper tantrums that included head banging. In one family, the patient and child had a history of severe conflict, which the mother had been unable to mediate. In the other family, the parent who died seemed to be the only family member who could manage this emotionally troubled child.

DISCUSSION

The coping capacities of children in late elementary school reflected impressive advances in containing the emotions caused by the family tragedy. New protective defenses against anxiety were evident. Praise and approval, by the surviving parent and by other significant adults, served as an important protector by improving the children's self-esteem. Self-esteem was also enhanced by competence in schoolwork, sports, and after-school activities. Perhaps the most profound characteristic of this age group was identification with their parents, other significant adults in their lives, and peers. These identifications took on special importance in the children's relationship with the patient both before and after the death, particularly if the patient and child were the same gender.

For this age group, the content of mourning was different from that of younger children, and reflected the subtle but important change that had taken place in the relationship of child to parent. Whereas the 6- to 8-year-old children mourned for the parent as protector, caretaker, and supplier of self-esteem, these children also mourned the parent as friend, buddy, mentor, and person to chat with. Although there were some gender differences, the father as friend-mentor-coach was missed as actively by girls as by boys. It was primarily the girls who missed their mother as a person to chat with. The dreams of the children often reflected this aspect of their mourning.

These children had a thoughtful, logical, factual disposition. They welcomed the distractions of school, activities, and friends, and used them effectively. They coped by trying to master the information about the family tragedy confronting them and by reaching out for knowledge, skills, and understanding. Their beginning capacity for anticipatory mourning left them more in control. Because they needed information, they became angry and mistrustful if they were not given timely facts, which their cognitive skills could use to gain some control and prepare them for the actual death. When inadequately prepared, their bereavement was complicated.

Except for anger, the children rarely revealed strong feelings. Boys, more often than girls, displayed anger, usually to cover their fear, anxiety, and grief. However, even anger was more muted in this age group. Because the children tended to avoid all intense emotions, engaging them in the bereavement process was more challenging than it was with younger children. Some surviving parents misunderstood their child's emotional restraint as a lack of grief.

11

Children 12–14 Years of Age

Themes

This chapter describes the impact of terminal cancer on the lives of 38 children—22 girls and 16 boys—ages 12 to 14. They came from 35 families, and their surviving parents were 21 mothers and 14 fathers. (In this and the next chapter, when the word adolescent is used, it refers to 12- to 14-year-old early adolescents.) Before early adolescence, each new developmental advance made it easier for parents to help their children with the stresses of a patient's illness and death. As their ability to understand what was happening progressed, the children controlled their emotions and behavior better, communicated more effectively, and were easier to understand and support. Although they expanded their world, the family remained at its center. The entrance into puberty and adolescence produced such a level of disquiet in these youngsters that it was harder to separate the reactions evoked by the patient's condition from reactions related to developmental changes. While many non bereaved adolescents do exhibit minimal stress and disorganization during this developmental period, the event of parental terminal illness and death posed a significant challenge (Balk & Corr, 1996; Brooks-Gunn, 1992; Fleming & Adolph, 1986; Offer, 1987).

DEVELOPMENTAL THEMES OF EARLY ADOLESCENCE

The cognitive change in early adolescence is the initial development of formal operational abilities, the psychological change is the withdrawal of emotional investment in the parent, while the social change is the new importance of peer relationships. It is the interaction of these three domains, with the biological changes of puberty that create the complexity of this age. Cognitively, the early adolescents in this study were beginning to understand the full implications of the tragedy that was unfolding. But they appeared unable to manage their emotions about this loss. And while there was a much greater involvement with friends, they were unable to rely on them for emotional support about such a threatening event.

The adolescents' need to withdraw emotional investment in their parents conflicted with the greater needs of their families for help, emotional closeness, and support as the patient became terminally ill. The early adolescents' assertion of their need for privacy, their avoidance of disturbing facts and feelings, and their egocentrism became exaggerated in their effort to cope with the conflict between the obvious needs of the family and their own developmental task of individuation and separation. Even more than the 9- to 11-year-olds, their peers provided an ecological world that accepted the young adolescent's aversion to sharing feelings or information about the painful events surrounding the illness and death of the parent. Such discussions, when present, were generally limited to close friends.

Emergence of Formal Operational Thinking: Changing Needs for Information

A striking change in early adolescence was the diminished interest in, with some the active avoidance of, information about a parent's disease and its treatment from parents or professionals. With few exceptions, the young adolescents in the sample indicated that they had been adequately informed, that they understood both the diagnosis and the prognosis, and that they were not interested in discussing the matter further. Many times before the death, they said they didn't want more information. This was in marked contrast to the behavior of the 9- to 11-year-old children who listened behind doors and eavesdropped on telephone conversations to obtain as much information as they could because it made them feel less anxious and more in control. Not so among these adolescents, who found that such information provoked anxiety rather than relief.

Several convergent explanations for this new behavior among early adolescents are possible. First, their capacity for formal operational thinking enabled them to understand abstractions. Adolescents quickly grasped the abstract concepts of cancer, its treatment, its prognosis, and its alternative outcomes without needing all the specific details. Second, because they were struggling to control their new emotional volatility, detailed information broke through their defenses of denial and avoidance. Third, young adolescents were, in fact, informed more frequently than were younger children about their parent's illness because the parents viewed them as more capable of dealing with this information and therefore were less likely to withhold it from them (Siegel et al., 1996).

It was important for parents to realize that adolescents could still harbor disturbing misunderstandings because of their lack of experience and avoidance of the facts. Despite their protests to the contrary, the adolescents needed clarification more often than they realized or wanted. Establishing an optimal pattern of communication with them was a significant challenge for parents.

Challenge of Withdrawal of Emotional Investment in the Parent

Most difficult for early adolescents and their parents was the change in the emotional relationship between parent and child, which was certainly complicated by a parent's serious illness. Both before and after the parent's death, the adolescents struggled with wanting—or more accurately, needing—to distance themselves emotionally from their parents, while simultaneously needing to remain engaged with them. The conflict between this developmental task and the obvious situational needs inherent in the family tragedy resulted in a range of exaggerated behaviors and reactions aimed at protecting the adolescent.

It was the adolescents' extreme avoidance of feelings and disturbing facts and their exaggerated needs for privacy that were most disconcerting to parents. Parents typically complained that they had no idea what their young adolescent was thinking or feeling and were afraid they were missing something. Many parents wished there were some way to "look inside" their child's head. Because some boys and girls maintained a diary, parents guiltily found themselves "taking a peek" at it in a desperate attempt to gain some understanding of the child's adaptation.

Parents found it helpful to realize that the adolescent's privacy was part of the process of developing a separate identity. The stress and the implicit, if not explicit, pressure to engage more closely with the family only served to exaggerate their retreat from the family. Most of the adolescents said they felt more comfortable talking with peers and other adults rather than with their parents.

The paradox was that while adolescents were withdrawing emotional investment from their parents, they were completely intolerant of the parent's withdrawing from them consequent to the demands of the illness. The parent's preoccupation with the dying spouse threatened and enraged the young adolescent. They perceived this as abandonment.

Another characteristic very troubling to parents was the profound egocentrism of these adolescents. This apparent callousness and lack of feeling surprised and offended the parents because they had not perceived the children as lacking empathy when they were younger or in other situations. One explanation for egocentrism in early adolescence is the self-involvement that comes about as a result of the physiological changes of puberty. But its exaggeration in this situation may also be attributed to their fear of the strong feelings they would experience if they empathized with the parents.

> After 13-year-old Beth was told about her father's diagnosis in the afternoon, she attended a party with friends that evening. "What was I supposed to do?" she asked when her mother inquired, "Stay home and cry?" At another point, Beth became angry when her father was sick and unable to drive her to a school function: "If he could walk around, why couldn't he take me?"

> The mother of 14-year-old Carla was surprised by her daughter's apparent indifference to her father's terminal illness because she knew that Carla adored her father, and she resented the fact that Carla pursued her normal activities, seemingly without feeling.

When told that her mother would die, Angela, age 12, said, "Well, what can you do about it!" Such comments were not unusual. What was surprising was that many of these "callous and unfeeling" adolescents were among the 31 who had reconstituted well in all areas when assessed a year after the parent's death.

Many parents also said that their adolescent left the room when they cried. It helped parents when they realized that these comments and behaviors were attempts to control and contain overwhelming emotions. An almost ubiquitous assertion among the adolescents was, "I cry in my room alone, not with other people." Boys were more likely than girls to say this. Many girls said they saved their expressions of sadness for discussions with peers.

Finally, the adolescents struggled to find ways to manage their fears and overwhelming emotions. Distracting themselves with schoolwork and solitary activities was much more difficult than it was for the older school-age child. Thus, they used the defenses of denial, minimization, rationalization, and displacement. They used diaries, wrote poetry and fiction, and withdrew into themselves and into activities with peers.

Change in the Relationship to Peers: Social Changes and the Expanding World

Although the adolescents related to peers through a broad range of activities, much as they had in late elementary school, there were indications of a subtle change. The adolescents were usually able to talk more easily with friends about their parent's condition than with their parents, but this ability was less consistent than it was for older adolescents. Some youngsters were reluctant to discuss the details of the parent's condition with friends because they did not want to be perceived as different and therefore risk rejection. Sometimes friends did shy away from such threatening information. In the first narrative in the next chapter, Megan, an early adolescent, clearly had more fear of confiding in peers than her older siblings did, and she needed their encouragement to be able to talk with her friends about her mother's illness. However, Megan's mother noticed that Megan talked more openly within the family about the mother's terminal illness after she had talked with her friends.

Another difference was the degree to which boys and girls welcomed and participated in structured opportunities to share their thoughts and feelings with peers as well as adults. Many participated in individual sessions with a school counselor or in group sessions or rap groups. They perceived these opportunities as acceptable by their peers and as appropriate. Group sessions did not necessarily have to focus on loss to be helpful. Unlike the younger children, who needed to focus more on bereavement-related issues involving death or divorce, adolescents also benefited from more general discussions about their feelings and experiences. Because adolescents were more conscious than their younger peers of differences in social status and class, they could be upset when the family finances declined and they were unable to have as many material possessions as their friends. Discussions with peers gave them a sense of acceptance and normalcy and combated feelings of isolation and alienation.

Macrosystem (Bronfenbrenner, 1979) cultural clashes and estrangement from the immigrant parent, but also subtle nonacceptance of and by dominant-culture peers, impacted on their development. Although most marked in children of immigrants, this was also observed in non-immigrant minority children. This influence was more pervasive and profound than with younger peers, in part probably because of their formal operational cognitive abilities but also their growing emotional dependence on peers.

PATTERNS OF RESPONSES IN EARLY ADOLESCENCE

Terminal Illness

In the analysis of the adolescent's experience during the terminal illness, several factors described below emerged as particularly relevant. Some, like the exaggerated egocentrism and denial and avoidance of feelings, were also mentioned in the section on development because they were so pervasive throughout all three stages of the illness.

Adamant Optimism

Whereas the 9- to 11-year-olds avidly sought facts and avoided intense feelings during the parent's terminal illness, early adolescents maintained their adamant optimism by avoiding both facts and feelings. Most had been informed of the parent's illness by the time the interviewer met them. However, when she asked them exactly what they understood, at least some of the information proved to be incorrect. They had enough facts to know that the parent had a life-threatening illness, but many rejected or challenged information that countered their denial of the possibility that the parent would die. An apparent contradiction is that after the death, none of them complained about feeling unprepared or being misinformed.

> Thirteen-year-old Dorothy said she was surprised when she heard about her father's diagnosis. She hoped that the chemotherapy would shrink the tumor and that a cure for cancer would be found within the next couple of years. She asserted that she was not concerned or worried. When she talked about the fact that one of her father's lungs was filled with cancer and wasn't functioning, she asked: "If his other lung has only two small tumors, why can't the doctors take those tumors out so that lung will work? Can they remove just part of that lung? Can they do a lung transplant?" When asked what had changed for her since her father's diagnosis, Dorothy replied: "Sometimes I feel sad, but usually I just try not to think about it. I'm upset, but I don't cry. I go to a friend's house, and they cheer me up. Then I forget about it."

Adolescents used denial to maintain their adamant optimism, even in the face of contrary evidence. Very few mentioned the patient's more serious physical symptoms, nor did they express guilt about the patient's illness, as did their younger peers. Several decided to stop visiting their parent in the hospital because the parent forgot an important time they had spent together or could not remember their name. They stated that these lapses were too painful to bear.

Many young adolescents denied being worried about the parent's illness or the surviving parent's ability to take full responsibility for the family. Some boys worried about how much responsibility they would have to assume when their father died. One 13-year-old, who could have been a spokesperson for all, said he believed it was important to look on the bright side.

Denial and Avoidance of Feelings

Closely related to their adamant optimism was their denial and avoidance of feelings. Another explanation for why adolescents didn't talk about their parent's illness was because they were afraid they might lose control and cry. They didn't want to see their parents cry either. Many said they preferred to cry alone in their room at night. The reason they gave was that they felt that other people wouldn't understand what they were feeling.

Although the adolescents stated they knew they could talk with their well parent about their concerns, many chose not to. "It's better not to think about it," said one 14-year-old girl. "I keep my worries to myself." Indeed, their tendency to keep their sad feelings to themselves while maintaining a jovial, business as usual, or angry mood on the outside often bewildered and enraged parents. As one mother said: "(My 14-year-old) says she is 'Just fine,' and I can't understand that!" Parents worried that the adolescent's emotional unresponsiveness would result in future mental problems. Parents also resented their child's lack of responsiveness to their own apprehension.

Where there were pre-existing family conflicts and communication problems, the anxiety about the parent's dying was often displaced onto the existing conflict, causing angry, provocative interactions that sometimes spiraled out of control. When these interactions became established patterns of communication within the family, they interfered with family members' needs for support and diminished their self-esteem. In fact, avoidance of feelings was so characteristic of this age group that those who did not communicate in this way appeared to be in danger of experiencing a breakdown in their adaptive denial.

Muted Anticipatory Grief

Although the 12- to 14-year-olds maintained an optimistic attitude about the parent's possible recovery, they also were realistic enough to experience muted anticipatory grief. They sometimes cried when they told the interviewer how they had heard about the diagnosis and also when they expressed feelings of sadness about the possibility of the parent's death. However, their expressions of grief were usually subtle and sometimes contradictory. A 13-year-old girl asked her parochial school class to say a prayer for her father but asserted that she was sure he would recover. A 12-year-old boy talked about the importance of "looking on the bright side," then asked, "Why did this have to happen to my father?" After her father died, a 14-year-old said, "We really lost my father three months before he died when he couldn't talk any more."

Adolescents thought about the patient's role in the family and wondered how their life would be without their father's or mother's help. What would happen when they lost the parent who understood and defended them, who could handle Mom or Dad, what would happen when they lost the parent who was so much fun or was the strong one? They wanted to know why the illness happened to such a good person and questioned God's sense of justice and fairness. If they were religious, they prayed for the parent.

Reactions, Behaviors and Symptoms

Adolescents experienced an even broader range of reactions to the parent's terminal illness than did children in late elementary school. Typical symptoms of their distress included a drop in school grades; sleep problems, anger; sadness; and withdrawal from discussions about the parent's condition. Typical behaviors included oppositional, argumentative, and demanding behaviors. Less common symptoms in this age group included somatic complaints that had no identifiable cause; extreme anger, depression, guilt or separation anxiety; and serious misbehavior. Quite uncommon were refusals to attend school and avoidance of peers. When present such symptoms seemed to occur in the context of more severe stress reactions. However, it was frequently reported that at moments of intense anxiety, as when getting news of a change in prognosis, even adolescents slept with the parent. When adolescents slept with their parents for longer time spans, it generally indicated more serious problems.

As described in the development section above, most of the adolescents were angry or depressed about the withdrawal of both parents from the family consequent to the parent's preoccupation with the patient's worsening symptoms and changing treatment. This is only an apparent contradiction—adolescents needed to withdraw emotionally from the parents, but they resented the parents' apparent or real withdrawal from them.

The demands of the individual patient's illness and treatment regimen were important determinants of the degree of stress that impacted on the adolescents. The fact that girls experienced more emotional distress than boys seemed related to the fact that they were more likely to be asked to do household chores, while most boys were allowed to participate in activities outside the home. Adolescent girls were also more attuned to family dynamics, felt the impact of the withdrawal of parental attention more keenly, and struggled harder to alter yet maintain their relationship to both parents. This gender difference, of girls working to change their relationships with the parents while boys withdrew from the family, was even more marked in older adolescents.

Relationships with Peers

Most difficult during the terminal illness period was that early adolescents were often required to help with tasks at home in ways that interfered with their peer relationships. Although some adolescents (girls more often than boys) willingly took on additional household tasks, many did not. And all of them became intolerant when they felt that these tasks interfered with their need to escape through contact with peers.

Ann, age 13, was angry because extra chores kept her away from her friends. However, when it became clear that her mother's condition was terminal, Ann took more initiative and did much of the housework. After her mother died, she complained that she had to go for two or three weeks without seeing her friends, whereas her younger brother went out every night. She had maintained her grades during the crisis, but she felt that her father didn't appreciate her extra effort. When he began dating, he, too, went out every night.

After his father died, 13-year-old Andrew complained mildly about being given a few additional chores. His grades and overall functioning had rebounded. He said that sometimes he left his household chores undone, hoping his mother would forget, but she never did.

Death and Family Rituals

As the parent's death approached, more adolescents were able to talk about the fact that the parent was dying and were able to cry and express their sadness. Like younger children, they became highly anxious, but their anxiety was based on a more accurate understanding of what was about to happen and its consequence in their lives. The main preoccupation of many was how to manage their emotions.

Enabling Final Communication

Because the adolescents needed as much time as possible to prepare for the actual death, parents were urged to inform them when the death was imminent and when it was time to have a final conversation with the patient and to say goodbye. This was more or less possible, depending on how predictable the course of the illness was.

The day before her father died, 14-year-old Eve visited her father in the hospital after a two-week hiatus, because seeing him suffer had upset her. During the visit, he told Eve that he loved her. The next morning, Eve's mother called her from the hospital to say that her father was dying and was asking for her. Her father died while Eve was in the room. Later, she told the interviewer: "Now he has no pain. I know he is with me. In death, they are with you in spirit."

Francine's mother discovered that her daughter resisted visiting her father, who was being cared for at his mother's home near the hospital, because she felt helpless and useless. The mother suggested that Francine prepare tea and cookies for her father when she went to visit him, which helped her feel more useful and reduced the painful sense of helplessness. Francine was delighted when he told people that she always made him feel better: "She has the magic touch." However, sometimes adolescents refused further visits, based on their own emotional responses. For example, when Francine's father forgot an important trip they had taken together, she decided that his mental state was too painful for her and she couldn't visit him again.

In a few families, those with significant pre-existing conflicts, these conflicts and related emotions intensified and resulted in adolescents' expressions of extreme anger or withdrawal as the death approached. It was more characteristic that adolescents' anger, provocative behavior, and resistance to taking on new chores declined when the parent's death was clearly imminent. They seemed to try harder to comply with requests and to control their behavior. Expressions of hostility and intense conflict before death may have contributed to severe guilt feelings after the parent's death and therefore efforts to mediate these conflicts could be helpful.

> Although 12-year-old Gale viewed her father as her major supporter, she was hostile and combative throughout her father's terminal illness toward both parents and her younger sister, whom she viewed as the family favorite. As his condition deteriorated and she learned that his death was imminent, she refused to visit him in the hospital, and her rage increased. Because both parents responded angrily, they exacerbated the negative spiral of family behavior. After her father died, Gale felt guilty.

Telling About the Death

Parents found that it was less difficult to tell their adolescent children that the parent had died because they were generally better informed and prepared than were younger children. The adolescents' responses varied: Most of them cried, a few screamed. One 12-year-old boy cried most of one day, whereas a 13-year-old girl cried very little because her family and the religious denomination of the family valued a stoical approach to stressful events. The family had handled her grandmother's death the previous year in the same stoical manner. A 14-year-old boy cried, but then insisted on going to school to take an examination scheduled for that day. A 12-year-old cried, then returned to school to finish out the day with her friends.

Participation in Funeral and Burial Rituals

All of the adolescents in this sample attended the parent's funeral, sat Shiva, or participated in the wake, and usually returned to school a day after these observances. Many did not want to go to the cemetery because they felt that doing so would be too upsetting. Many had definite ideas about how they wanted to engage in the rituals. Although children in this age group were pleased to have their friends and teachers attend, some felt oppressed by the crowds of people and resented the time their surviving parent spent with visitors.

The adolescents were preoccupied with not crying at these events. "Crying won't help," said 12-year-old Hillary, who gave a eulogy at her father's funeral and was upset by her mother's crying. She refused to go to the cemetery, saying, "Why should I go to the cemetery? I talk to my father all the time anyway!" She also refused to look at a paper her 15-year-old brother wrote about the latest cancer treatments soon after their father's death. Andrew, age 12, said it was especially difficult not to cry at the funeral mass because he kept looking at his father's coffin. The wake was easier for him. He bravely chose to go to the cemetery.

More children this age wanted to participate in the funeral ceremonies than did younger children. Some delivered eulogies, some of which were written by the surviving parent; some wrote poems that were read by others; and some shared their thoughts with a speaker who conveyed them to the audience.

Like younger children, some early adolescents wanted to place objects in the parent's coffin, but their choices reflected more the parent's personality and interests, things that would have given them pleasure. One boy placed his father's library card; his father's favorite book, *Dune,* and a baseball into the coffin. Other youngsters placed family pictures there. Twelve-year-old Bob's father was buried with two small bottles of his favorite liquor, a pin from his local union, and a small teddy bear. One 13-year-old placed a picture of her father dancing with her during her *bat mitzvah* in his coffin.

Immediate Aftermath

After the funeral, the adolescents usually cried alone in their room at night because they did not want to upset their surviving parent. If the parent began to cry, they left the room.

In the immediate aftermath of the death, most children in this age group said they felt relieved because their parent was no longer suffering and in pain—that the parent was now resting in peace. As 12-year-old Irma said: "I wasn't worried that (my mother) would die because I knew she would be in heaven." And Ida said: "I was upset, but I rather him be at rest . . . he feels no pain. I know he's with me; it's just that I don't see him."

Many adolescents said they talked with the dead parent, some wondered where the parent was and what he or she was doing. Ida's more elaborate descriptions of her beliefs were less common, "I don't know if it's my imagination, but I talk to my dad, like, 'Oh, we're O.K. Don't worry about us.' He's worried about us—that we can't go on without him."

Thirteen-year-old Carl said he believed that his father was in heaven having a lot of fun, but he wished his father could come back. Denise, age 14, had numerous arguments with her ill mother about housecleaning. As her mother's condition deteriorated, Denise complained less. After her mother died, she initiated her own housecleaning regimen. She believed her mother was in heaven—cleaning. Fourteen-year-old Alex said he felt his father's presence both spiritually and personally. He felt his father looking down on him from heaven and felt his presence in dreams. These experiences comforted Alex.

In the immediate period after the death, however, most adolescents did not want to discuss their thoughts and feelings about the dead parent. They were generally able to defend themselves from their emotions more effectively after the death than younger children, and they devoted their energies to schoolwork, their friends, and additional chores. Their surviving parents observed that their child's life "went right on." They were surprised and sometimes resentful of the child's ability to conceal or avoid experiencing their grief.

Bereavement and Reconstitution

During the first year of bereavement and reconstitution of the family, the adolescents confronted the challenging tasks of grieving and of developing a new

relationship with the dead parent in their memory, while negotiating a new relationship with the surviving parent as a single parent. The adolescent's mourning, like that of the younger children, was generally episodic, often triggered by
specific events such as birthdays and anniversaries. They needed to adjust to the
newly reconstituted family while advancing in school, developing more intense
relationships with peers, and coping with their own intense and unpredictable
emotions. Most of them seemed to regard thinking or talking about the
deceased parent as interfering with their major preoccupation with school and
peers. Unlike younger children, who seemed to enjoy being interviewed and
having the opportunity to talk about their parent with someone who was interested and knowledgeable, a number of the young adolescents were resistant,
difficult to engage, and likely to decline to participate in at least one interview.

Adolescents selected adults other than parents to talk to. This exclusion was
difficult for parents who wanted more direct indications of how their child's
recovery process was progressing. They wanted to help the child grieve but
could not find a way to enter the child's experience. One mother said she was
worried that her son would "Blow some day because he keeps all his feelings
inside . . . He is in his own private world, with no one coming into his space
(with regard to missing his father)."

Displacement of Emotions on to Other Situations

Parents noticed that the adolescents became more angry or tearful about
other difficulties, such as pressures at school or having too much homework.
One 13-year-old said, "I can't cry about my father, but I think I use sad movies
as an excuse to cry for him." Many continued to say they preferred to cry alone,
if at all. Because it was so difficult for them to articulate their internal psychological processes, some aspects of their bereavement had to be inferred from
their behavior or indirect statements. A fuller range of reactions was elicited
when they were asked whether they had any advice for others whose parent
had died. They often responded with platitudes, such as "Getting on with your
life" and "Toughing it out." As one 13-year-old boy explained: "Kids shouldn't
take it so seriously. It is serious, but you have to get over it soon, or it will be
there forever and you won't be able to do stuff like face people without crying
. . . You have to take one step at a time." Another 13-year-old suggested, "Help
out at home as much as you can, cry if you have to." However, he said that
he preferred to cry alone in his room. And one girl the same age said, "Crying
doesn't help; it won't bring him back," a second said, "Just keep trying to do
your best," and a third said, "Be strong."

A Few Discussed Their Grief More Openly

The few early adolescents who were more expressive about their experiences seemed to come from families that fostered open expressions of emotion.
For instance, 13-year-old Edger, a member of a Greek family, was recovering
well after his father's death. He described his reactions as follows: "When it
happens to you, you don't have time to worry. It's about one month later that it
really kicks in. Then it is the pain and grieving. There are the memories,

reminders, pictures. It's little things that make me remember. I feel it is good to know you hold on to the person; it is normal to try to push these things away. Tell kids it is normal to feel this pain."

On the other hand, a 14-year-old from a troubled Hispanic family had an extremely difficult time recovering from her father's death. "I have so many feelings, I don't even know anymore. I'm moody. One moment I'm very happy and then I'm very sad. I know its hard for my mom. She talks about how it's going to be . . . I hate when she talks like that. My dad used to go dancing—he was always joking around. But that's all in the past, and I don't want to hold on to the past. Mom wants me to pray with her, but I don't want to. I want to pray by myself. I can't remember Dad the way he was before he got sick—he teased with insults, joking around. Mother can't understand that I can't remember."

> When told of his father's death, 13-year-old Dan, whose family had emigrated from Europe, burst into tears and sobbed. His 7-year-old sister comforted him. Subsequently, he was able to cry freely at special reminders. When he returned to school after the funeral, Dan asked his teacher if he could speak to the class about his father's life and illness.

Interestingly, the fact that these three youngsters and one other discussed in Chapter 13 are children of recent immigrants suggests one reason why so many adolescents avoided expressing emotions regarding their parent's death: American culture values rugged individualism and a stoical response to tragedy. Young adolescents reflected in stereotypic fashion the mores of the culture.

Importance of Reminders

Marker events, like birthdays and holidays, were as important to the adolescents as they were for younger children. Several acknowledged being reminded of the parent at unexpected moments and being overcome with emotion. Because they struggled so hard to control their reactions, these experiences were especially difficult for them. The surviving parent's mourning was also extremely threatening to many of the adolescents because the parent appeared to be more distraught than they had ever previously witnessed.

Identification With the Deceased

The adolescents exhibited early evidence of identifying with the dead parent. Wearing the parent's clothes was not uncommon. One 13-year-old chose a watch, several pictures, and her father's hat, which she had worn when her father had taken photographs of her. Another 13-year-old valued a locket her friends gave her that had a picture of her father on one side and a cross on the other, explaining that her father and religion were her two main interests.

A 14-year-old decided to attend an art school because art had been his mother's avocation, and he believed that art would be a way of maintaining his connection with her. Thirteen-year-old Edger began working in his father's diner. A 12-year-old took pride in being a good fisherman like his father. He chided his older brothers and his friends because they didn't know how to fish. He bragged that he was an expert fisherman because his father had taught him.

Identifying with the dead parent was disturbing for some youngsters. Those who came from families with a high incidence of cancer worried that they, too, would develop the disease. And adolescents could feel quite bereft when activities important to the deceased parent did not continue. For example, the deceased mother of one 13-year-old had loved the music he had written for his band. (Her husband played a tape of one of his songs to her as she was dying.) The boy became extremely upset when his band broke up eight months after her death.

Dreams and a Sense of the Parent's Presence

Although adolescents rarely talked about their internal experiences of grief, surprisingly, they frequently discussed talking with the dead parent, dreaming about the parent, and feeling the parent's presence.

Frank, age 13, was rarely able to discuss his feelings about his father and was clearly depressed. However, he did share a dream in which he was playing soccer and his father was standing on the sidelines. When Frank went to give his father a hug, his father disappeared "like a ghost." He woke up feeling upset and awakened his mother, who reassured him. Frank then said that he longed for his father to be with him at games and that it felt "eerie" without him.

Ida, age 13, said she dreamed that her father returned, but the dream frightened her. "If I think I want him to come back, he might hear me and feel bad (because) he can't come back." She was worried that her father was lonely and felt bad being by himself. Although she was doing relatively well, she had to deal with her mother's extreme withdrawal during her father's illness. Although Ida was close to her mother, her father had been the dominant, stabilizing force in the family.

Another 13-year-old girl whose father had been physically abusive to her had nightmares that her father returned. She heard noises at night "like pots and pans rolling" and thought it was her father. She sometimes thought she saw his face in the glow of the lamp at home and sought safety by sleeping with her mother. Although she cried at the funeral, she showed no open mourning, sadness, or distress. She was helped by the interviewer who assured her that negative dreams and thoughts about her father were normal reactions to the negative aspects in their relationship and that these frightening feelings would diminish with time. Her mother's inability to resolve her own ambivalence about her husband made it more difficult for her to support her daughter's grieving, especially her negative feelings.

Bob said he missed playing golf with his father and going to bars with him. At Christmas, Bob looked up at the sky and knew that his father was up there watching him. He thought his father was "the drunken star" that was moving haphazardly all over the sky.

Fourteen-year-old Greg said he felt his father's presence both spiritually and personally. He felt that his father was watching him from heaven and he felt his father's presence in his dreams. These experiences comforted him. Greg also said that his father had set an important example, and he felt empowered when he tried to live up to that example. Carl, age 12, recalled that his father had held his hand while he waited for the ambulance the final time. He thought his father had known he was there, and that made him feel good.

Thirteen-year-old Ida reported, "Last week I thought I felt him standing beside me, hugging me and saying 'I miss you.' My sister is mad at me because my dad liked me better than her and because he never comes to her." Francine dreamed that her father was making out a will and was leaving her several things. She had respected and looked up to him because he had helped her with math, cooking, and sports, and she worried about growing up without his guidance and help.

Meaning of the Death

Francine voiced the relationship that a number of adolescents had with their deceased parent and the specific meaning this loss had for them. Francine's father was her mentor and friend who had helped her in ways she felt would promote her independence in the future. Other adolescents mourned the loss of their parent as a teacher who would have helped them succeed, and they were afraid they would lose their "edge" in life because the surviving parent would be unable to fill that role. "Mom can't go to as many of my games as Dad did," said one 13-year-old boy. A 12-year-old girl worried that because her mother was not as good at math as her father had been, her mother could not really help her. Both boys and girls wondered whether their mother could earn enough money and manage it properly: "Will she be able to keep our house?" and "Will there be enough money for college and my future?" One thoughtful 13-year-old said he would no longer have some of the material goods his peers had and bravely accepted that fact, but "it's hard because they have a lot of things." For boys who wondered if they would have to "fill Dad's shoes" and seemed confused about what this would involve, discussing the matter with their mother, who clarified what their role in the family would be, proved to be reassuring.

Most adolescents commented about the unfairness of losing a parent who was such a valued advocate and friend at this point in their life. Some were angry at God. One 13-year-old pondered, "How could this happen to my dad? He was such a good person." The boy described how his father, who had coached his baseball team, aggressively argued with the umpire on his son's behalf, although his father was sick. Proudly, the boy added, "The ump could have blown on him and he would have fallen down; he was that skinny."

Both boys and girls missed the parent as a gender and social role model. The adolescents who lost their mother usually lost the organizing and nurturing figure that kept the family running, provided opportunities to be with their friends, and helped them with their homework. They deeply missed this relationship, in which the mother had begun to be a friend and confidant. In families in which the mother died, the girls usually took over some housekeeping functions—

albeit reluctantly and sometimes angrily. Girls commonly resented the lack of emotional support from their father, support which their mother had provided.

Commensurate with their developing ability for formal operational thinking, these adolescents voiced their thoughts and concerns in more abstract terms than did younger children. Some said they missed certain aspects of the lost parent's personality—e.g., the parent's sense of humor, entertaining activities, accomplishments, and recognition in the community.

Emotional and Behavioral Symptoms

During the period of bereavement, the adolescents commonly exhibited a broader range of transient emotional and behavioral symptoms than did younger children. These symptoms ranged from mild depression, anxiety, fearfulness, sadness, acting out, testing of limits, anger, emotional withdrawal, weight gain, stubbornness and rebellion, and transient somatic symptoms. Less common, but present in some, were serious suicidal ideation, clinical depression, enduring fearfulness, phobias, refusal to attend school, withdrawal from peers, use of drugs and alcohol, destructive acting out (e.g., stealing), aggressive behavior leading to personal injury or dismissal from school, school failure, serious accidents, severe regressive behaviors (e.g., lack of personal hygiene in girls), and enduring somatic symptoms. In some cases, such behaviors represented an exacerbation of already existing problems; in others, they appeared to be a reaction to secondary stressors that developed at the time of, or shortly after, the death. At times these symptoms were not evident before the parent died. The latter group of symptoms were most likely to persist in youngsters whose outcome was judged to be a symptomatic reconstitution.

Although many of the adolescents wanted to sleep with the surviving parent during times of extreme stress, this became a chronic pattern only among a few. When the surviving parent was the mother of a son, the situation was especially problematic. With the interviewer's guidance, one mother who initially had difficulty setting limits on her son was able to insist on his sleeping in his own bed. She also obtained therapy for him. Another mother actively encouraged her son to sleep in her room as a manifestation of her pathological clinging in the relationship. This adolescent developed new, severe, psychiatric symptoms for which he was hospitalized.

New Relationship With the Surviving Parent

Renegotiating the relationship with the surviving parent presented a major challenge to adolescents. The significant minority of early adolescents who were unable to negotiate a satisfying relationship with their surviving parent became discouraged and despairing, acted out impulsively, or developed even more severe symptoms.

The internal turmoil and instability that is so much a part of the adolescent developmental process created tasks for the surviving parent of setting limits; providing direction, nurturance, and support; and coping with the adolescent's increased need for independence, while coping their own grief, anger, fear, and, in some cases, lack of financial and social support. Some parents turned to their adolescent for sympathy, only to find that the youngster was so focused on the need to be independent that he or she withdrew even more.

Setting Limits

Adolescents this age normally required help in setting limits on potentially destructive regressive behaviors, acting out aggressively, or with drugs or sex. Firmness was even more important to the adolescent's well being as a consequence of their grief. When surviving parent and child were of different gender, some of the most challenging situations arose. Mothers sometimes sought guidance about how to set limits on a son's sexual explicitness at home; fathers wondered how they should appropriately respond to a daughter's sexually provocative dress, especially when it was not so different from that of peers. These were areas that the same-sex parent handled in the past and that arose out of the developing physical as well as psychological changes in the child. It was clear in this age group that for adolescents who had previous problems with impulse control, failure to set limits could result in escalation to more inappropriate and potentially destructive behaviors, and that firm limit setting could be an important correction.

> One 13-year-old boy, whose mother had always found it difficult to discipline him, began to steal from his mother and sister, to go into their rooms and even break locks on doors. He also wanted to sleep with his mother in an ongoing way. The father would have controlled this behavior, but he had died. The 15-year-old sister longed for her father to return to help them with this problem. The mother began to look more deeply into her reluctance to set limits, her fears that her son, like her brother, would fall apart after a traumatic experience if she did not gratify his requests. She also sought ongoing therapy for her son.

Having to find new ways to set limits frequently reminded the surviving parent of the parent who died. As one father said, "I tried to think of how my wife would have handled this, but then I realized she is not here. I can use some of her approaches, but now I must develop my own." When parents were not aware of the effects of their own grief reactions, they sometimes became overcontrolling and clung to an adolescent who was demanding independence and who often feared that he or she would be unable to attain it without the parent who had died. Parents also failed to set appropriate limits due to their unrealistic guilt and defensiveness about the grief the adolescent was experiencing. The adolescent often added to this guilt by lashing out at them, in effect blaming the surviving parent for the death of the patient. The challenge of setting limits for adolescents was the need to do it in ways that also supported their independent growth and maintained their self-esteem.

Importance of School and Peers

Because school and peers were these adolescents' major preoccupations, the academic performance of most of them improved quickly after the parent's death. Although most of the youngsters had communicated with their peers during their parent's terminal illness, they were able to talk more easily with peers about the parent's death than were younger children. Still, great variation existed in this regard. Some adolescents wanted to be close to peers, but they did not want to discuss their grief for fear of rejection. Boys were more likely to feel this way. For example, Herb said he did not discuss his mother's death in his rap group because he did not think it was appropriate. However, just by being able to talk with, feel connected to, and involved with peers, helped him. Girls were far more likely than boys to confide regularly in their peers about almost anything, including their feelings about their parent's death.

Parent's Dating and Remarriage

After initial resistance, most adolescents accepted the fact that their surviving parent was dating, especially if they had recovered their ability to function well at school and with peers. Some even expressed relief at not having to worry about the parent's loneliness. Their initial feelings about the parent's dating and remarriage varied a great deal. Some boys wanted their mother to get married quickly to a man who would have interests similar to their own, thereby providing a mentor replacement. However, most adolescents were unhappy if the parent began dating "too soon," from their point of view. This seemed to confront them with the loss of the parent in a way that could be very distressing. They also resented the time away from home that dating required. However, many were pleased if they saw that dating made the surviving parent feel better, that it improved the quality of their relationship with the parent, that the dating relationship seemed appropriate, and that some advantage of the relationship would accrue to them. For instance, Stuart resented the fact that his mother began dating an accountant within the first year after his father died—until he discovered that the accountant could help him with his computer.

RECOMMENDATIONS FOR PROFESSIONALS AND CAREGIVERS

Terminal Illness

1. *Provide the adolescent with information in a formal way and in ample detail.* Even if they resist hearing too much detail, adults can't assume that their child's understanding is as complete as it may appear.

2. *Facilitate discussions about the adolescent's feelings and concerns.* Although initiating such discussions with children in this age group is extremely difficult, parents need to ensure that these discussions occur no matter how brief or infrequent. When parents express emotion, they can explain that these feelings are time limited.

3. *Encourage the adolescent's anticipatory grief.* The fact that adolescents' anticipatory grief is usually muted does not mean that these children are not experiencing anguish and sadness about the parent's probable death.

4. *Make an effort to understand the adolescent's emotional volatility and develop-*

mentally related reactions. Remember that children this age may experience parental withdrawal as a rejection just as the adolescent is withdrawing from parents.

5. *Allow and facilitate adolescents maintaining support networks.* Parents may have to help them devise ways to communicate with peers and other adults. Parents also can encourage the adolescent to use the counseling services that may be available for this age group.

6. *Limit the number of caregiving and household tasks assigned to the adolescent.* Keep in mind that if the tasks interfere with their schoolwork and contacts with peers or require independent responsibility for difficult aspects of the patient's physical care, they are likely to become angry and antagonistic.

7. *Accept the adolescent's ambivalence about hospital visits.* Although some contact with the hospitalized parent can be clarifying and reassuring, because of their ambivalence and fear, adolescents often resist such visits and want less contact with the patient than the other parent or older siblings believe is appropriate.

Death and Family Rituals

1. *Inform the adolescent when the parent's death is imminent.* Because these adolescents often avoid visiting the hospital when the parent's condition deteriorates and death nears, it is important for the well parent to be clear about when final visits are required.

2. *Reduce high levels of family conflicts when they markedly intensify as the patient's condition deteriorates.* Such conflict may indicate a reactivation of earlier episodes, but its expression at this time can seriously compromise needed constructive communication. Crisis intervention and/or family counseling may be helpful to reduce conflict levels.

3. *Prepare the adolescent for funeral and burial rites.* Adolescents need to know what their role might be, to the extent they are able to be involved. The choices concerning how they participate are broader than those of younger children: they can deliver a eulogy, offer their thoughts for others to articulate, be a pallbearer, or greet guests. Because the presence of friends, teachers, and coaches at the funeral is important to them, the surviving parent can help them notify these people.

4. *Support the adolescent's desire to return to school.* They may fear the rejection of peers who find it difficult to talk about a parent's death. Parents should not view the adolescent's rapid return to normal activities as an indication of callous indifference. Instead, they should view it as a vital continuation of development and as a way of avoiding intense grief until the adolescent is prepared to confront his or her painful feelings more directly.

5. *Allow the adolescent to select mementos and clothing that belonged to the dead parent.* Because children this age are often similar in size to the lost parent, they may enjoy wearing the parent's clothing. Thus, parents need to permit them to select appropriate mementos of the dead parent that can serve as linking objects and bring solace as well as aid the grieving process.

6. *Encourage the adolescent to express grief.* Young adolescents often need to be reassured that intense expressions of grief are episodic and relatively brief.

Bereavement and Reconstitution

1. *Recognize expressions of grief in the adolescent.* Unlike adult grief, it will be episodic and of shorter duration. Adolescents will follow their own timetable.

2. *Normalize the grief process for the adolescent.* It is important for adolescents to recognize that the experience of talking with the parent who has died, dreams of their return as well as negative dreams, a sense of their presence, feelings of pain and feelings of no pain are all components of a naturally occurring healing process that we call mourning. While it is difficult and painful, over time it becomes less so.

3. *Provide opportunities for grieving.* The parent needs to provide opportunities for grieving during normally occurring anniversaries and other family gatherings. Emphasize positive memories, especially around achievements, like "Your Dad/Mother would have been as proud of you as I am".

4. *Begin the process of altering the relationship of the parent or parent substitute with the adolescent to include some of those functions previously performed by the parent who died.* For mothers, this generally includes learning new ways to set limits, support discipline, growth, and independence. For fathers, this often includes learning to provide nurturance, understanding, and support around family relationships and social situations.

5. *Set limits to prevent destructive behavior, and support continued growth and independence.* The stress of the grief process can result in acting out that could become destructive.

6. *Be aware of the level of family conflicts, pre-existing family preferences and cross-generational coalitions.* Modifying these interactions can reduce stress, improve communication, and improve the adolescent's functioning. Family therapy may be helpful to moderate these struggles and strengthen the family's ability to cope.

7. *Support the adolescent's participation in age-appropriate activities.* Encourage continuing mastery of school, athletic, and social skills.

8. *Identify positive outcomes for the family and the adolescent from this family tragedy.* Emphasize positive growth that comes from having gone through a mourning process, as well as acknowledging the profound loss. The deepened understanding of oneself, others, and the world; the appreciation of friends and family; and the receipt of an important legacy of attributes, hopes, and dreams from the parent who died are some examples of positive outcomes.

9. *Draw on the support provided by the adolescent's peer group and on the services provided by counselors and agencies to facilitate the adolescent's grief process.*

10. *Referral to professional counseling or therapy is advised when uncommon, enduring and/or severe symptoms occur.* In our programs, these included serious suicidal ideation, clinical levels of depression, enduring fearfulness, phobias, refusal to attend school, withdrawal from peers, use of drugs and alcohol, destructive acting out (e.g., stealing), aggressive behavior leading to personal injury or dismissal from school, prolonged school failure, serious accidents, severe regressive behaviors (e.g., lack of personal hygiene in girls), and enduring somatic symptoms.

11. *Parents should seek counseling if they are experiencing prolonged or severe problems in mediating family conflicts or in managing their own grief.*

12

※

Children 12–14 Years of Age

Narratives

As we saw in the previous chapter, the confluence of the adolescent's developmental shift with a parent's terminal illness and death presented an awesome challenge to both the adolescent and the surviving parent. As we will see in the descriptions of two families in this chapter, both surviving parents reached out and offered nurturing closeness. This allowed their adolescents' mourning *and* ongoing developmentally syntonic separation to continue. Before reviewing how a surviving mother and her adolescent son dealt with all these factors, we will look at how a surviving father exerted an extraordinary amount of effort to guide his two adolescent children through their mother's death despite the additional problems of poverty and acculturation.

FATHER OF 12-YEAR-OLD GIRL AND 15-YEAR-OLD BOY

"Now There Is No One Here to Talk to Me about Girl Things."

I chose this family because Roberto Ruiz, the surviving father, was unusually articulate in describing the experiences of his family. He taught us a great deal about the dilemmas of the immigrant family when faced with the added problem of a terminal illness. This father helped his extended family in Mexico in many ways, help for which his culture would have honored and respected him and his wife and children would have gained reflected respect. These same actions are less valued in the United States. This confronted Roberto with the American choice of providing more for his nuclear family or the Mexican choice of providing for the extended family. The costly illness of his wife resulted in his experiencing gut-wrenching ambivalence as he made his choices: He was proud of his children's acculturation but was angry and hurt when they rejected his values. Although he felt like Sisyphus at times, he was actually more like Hercules.

Rosa, his wife, also had attributes that were highly valued in the Mexican culture. She dearly loved and admired her husband and children. She knew how to defuse arguments that erupted in this vocal, emotive family. She valued the children's education and delighted in their intelligence and academic success; and she had a special way with her daughter. Although boys are highly valued in Mexican culture, she helped 12-year-old Michelle feel special—to feel good about being a girl.

Both Michelle and her 15-year-old brother, John, coped amazingly well with their mother's illness and death, with the subtle prejudice against Mexican-Americans, with having less money than their middle-class classmates, and with the added problem of Michelle's illnesses.

Background

Rosa and Roberto were born in neighboring villages in Mexico. Both came from large, emotionally close extended families. Roberto's mother, the village school teacher, pushed hard to leave the working class. Among her many children, Roberto was her favorite son because he was the bright one, the one who finished one year of college. This had required a considerable sacrifice on her part. Roberto respected his mother and believed he had a life-long obligation to be the family's backup support. In addition to financial support, he provided support in many other ways. "Mi casa es su casa" ("My house is your house") was one of his strong ethical beliefs. These attributes, which are highly valued and respected in Mexican culture, contributed to Roberto's standing in his extended family and to his mother's pride in him.

Rosa's family was a more traditional peasant-class family. The men worked the fields, and the women cared for the children, the home, and their men. Rosa and Roberto met and fell in love when Rosa was 13 and Roberto was 15. They married after he finished one year of college.

Roberto had a powerful ambition: He wanted to be an architect. However, because remunerative work and opportunities for further education were impossible for the young couple in Mexico, the only solution was to emigrate. Close relatives of Roberto and Rosa were already living in New York City, and they had told him that good, well-paying jobs and free education were available in the United States. He and Rosa left Mexico on their second wedding anniversary and moved close to the relatives.

Roberto found a job as superintendent of an apartment building. A second job as a plumber's assistant covered their living expenses. Roberto believed he needed to learn English and save money before he could resume his education. Rosa added a bit their income by doing housework. But their money was also spent helping with various family emergencies in Mexico. In addition, Roberto regularly sent money to his parents, who had health problems. Five years after their arrival in New York, John, their first child, was born. Three years later his sister Michelle was born. Roberto's dream of college and a career as an architect gradually faded and was replaced with a strong desire to provide a good education for his children.

By the time the couple had lived in New York for 16 years, they had settled in. Roberto was respected and valued in both his places of employment, and the children were doing well academically in parochial school. Although the family's income was limited, Roberto's union provided health insurance, and the school gave partial scholarships because of the children's excellent grades. By these means Roberto was able to provide for his family. He took great pride in paying all of his bills and *always* on time. He had learned this from his mother. By this time, Roberto's English was relatively good, but Rosa's was more limited. Their friends and neighbors, those Rosa was close to, were all Spanish speaking.

Diagnosis

Rosa was in her mid-30s when she began losing weight, had trouble swallowing, had double vision, and had pain in one of her legs. The doctors who examined her insisted there was nothing physically wrong with her. Although their Spanish was worse than her English, her distress did not seem to warrant using an interpreter. Three months after her symptoms appeared, the pain in her leg became so severe the she was unable to walk on it, so she returned to the clinic. This time the doctors ordered a CAT scan, which revealed a pathologic fracture. After a series of tests and a lung biopsy, they diagnosed her as having lymphosarcoma.

Roberto felt angry and guilty. He was convinced that because of language and cultural differences, he had been unable to advocate on Rosa's behalf with the doctors, which resulted in the delay: "By the time they found the cause of her illness, it was too late," he said. Rosa was treated with chem otherapy and radiation. Unfortunately, this only resulted in short-lived remissions.

Michelle was 10 when her mother's cancer was diagnosed. When interviewed, Michelle said her mother had lymphoma, "a type of cancer." She did not know much more than that and really did not want to know more. She did not like it that her mother was receiving chemotherapy because it made her mother so sick. Furthermore, her mother's illness meant more housework for her. Michelle had always done extremely well in school. Roberto proudly said that "Michelle is almost the top in her class; she always has a 95 percent average." Michelle was friendly and outgoing, had many friends, and all the kids and teachers liked her. Roberto explained that she was more like he had been when he was a young man, not serious like her brother. Roberto thought John inherited his disposition from Roberto's mother. When the interviewer asked Michelle how she got along with her brother, she said that since her mother became ill, she and John fought a lot. They fought even more when their mother was in the hospital. Michelle said sadly that their fighting made her mother cry, and her aunt told her that their fighting made her mother sicker.

During this first interview, Michelle said feeling responsible for her mother's illness made her depressed—sometimes she even thought about suicide. A psychiatric evaluation determined that she was not seriously suicidal, but individual therapy to supplement the parent guidance intervention was recommended. Roberto agreed, and despite the added expense, obtained individual therapy for her.

Terminal Illness

Two years after the diagnosis, the doctors told Roberto that Rosa's cancer involved her liver and brain, and there was no longer any hope for a cure. Roberto did not share this information with Rosa, explaining that in Mexico "a man must carry this burden alone." During the final six months of the illness, Rosa's treatment was primarily palliative. Her mobility gradually declined as a result of pathologic fractures in her arm, leg, and hip. As a consequence of her brain metastases, she developed seizures, which were especially frightening to the children. When she was examined for severe abdominal pain, more tests showed that she now also had gallstones.

Roberto wondered whether they should try a different treatment. He had heard about a poison from a snake in a capsule that someone from Mexico had developed to treat cancer. "It's poison against poison," he explained.

Extended Family Arrives

Rosa's mother and two adult male cousins arrived from Mexico shortly after the doctors told Roberto that Rosa could not be cured. They stayed four months. Because the apartment was small, Michelle, Rosa, and Roberto shared one bedroom, his mother-in-law slept in Michelle's small bedroom, and the two male cousins and John slept in the living room. As Roberto explained, the cousins did not work, they were just underfoot. They did not contribute to the household expenses. In Roberto's opinion, his mother-in-law was no help either: "She cries when Rosa cries, and then Michelle starts crying!" For Roberto, the final blow was that his mother-in-law criticized him for not raising his children properly, claiming that they were discourteous to her and their uncles. However, he could not ask them to leave because that would be unforgivable. He was hurt that neither John nor Michelle understood that basic Mexican ethic of hospitality, and they wanted these relatives to leave.

Increasing Financial Pressures

Another pressing problem was that Roberto's mother became ill with diabetes. She wrote from Mexico that she wanted to die because it cost too much to keep her alive. It was clear to Roberto that he needed to send her more money. In addition, the hospital was pressing him about unpaid bills, which the insurance company would eventually pay. He felt it was useless to explain his extended family obligations—they would never understand. They seemed to act as if he were "a dead beat." It was difficult for him to discuss this with hospital personnel. He felt intimidated by them: "I'm talking with someone, but we don't seem to understand each other. We were raised in a different world. We were not prepared for these things. The cultural difference is the most important thing (that affects) us now. We just take things as they come. We cannot express ourselves (or fight) the way you do here." Roberto took a third job, working several hours each night, more on weekends.

An Adolescent Response—Anger and Disappointment

Michelle's response to her mother's illness had all the self-centered characteristics of the young adolescent. She complained to her father that her mother was not really available to her anymore, that no one helped her with her homework. She confided to the interviewer that she was afraid her mother would never get better and was going to die. She said she felt sad, nervous, like crying. Her mother used to help her with these kinds of feelings, but now there was no one to talk to about such girl things. She told the interviewer that she would like to go out more—to go shopping, to the movies, to buy ice cream—things she used to do with her mother. She said she wanted to do some of those things with her father, but she could not because he was so busy. Roberto said that Michelle told him: "Poppy, you don't love me, you don't praise me or like anything I do. You only like my brother."Roberto admitted to the interviewer that he felt closer to his son than to his daughter. When Michelle asked him who would take care of her if Mommy died, he tried to reassure her that he would take care of her, and reminded her that she had female relatives living close by who were about her mother's age and with whom she could talk.

Michelle's Ambiguous Medical Problems

Roberto was worried and confused about Michelle. She stayed home from school, not only because her mother needed her help, but also because she often did not feel well herself. He took her to a pediatrician on an average of once a month, but the pediatrician said Michelle's problem was nervousness. Then Michelle's stomach pain got worse and she had cold sweats. When her father took her to the clinic again, she was diagnosed with hepatitis. Everyone in the family, including Rosa, received hepatitis shots.

Despite her medical problems, Michelle continued to do well in school, both scholastically and socially, but her frequent absences upset Roberto: "If worse comes to worst, I will take her out of school for good. It is not so important that women go to school." Michelle was first in her class for the first time just before she was diagnosed with hepatitis. When she returned to school, she went right back on the honor roll again. Roberto said: "She is so bright, she can pick up fast. Her average is still above 92 on all the subjects, and after the three-week absence, she got 95 on a math test!"

Michelle again developed severe stomach pains. She was hospitalized and diagnosed as having gallstones; the original hepatitis diagnosis had been a mistake. One morning when he was visiting the hospital Roberto discovered the doctors were planning to operate on Michelle for her gall stones even though he had actively opposed this approach. He was able to stop them but became even more suspicious of doctors after that.

A Middle Adolescent Response: Pragmatic and Empathic

Fifteen-year-old John's entry into a private high school on full scholarship coincided with his mother's terminal illness. John was an excellent athlete and became an important member of the track team. The coach's hope of finally beating the rival school rested on John's contribution to the team. But John was unable to participate in the first track meet because his mother's illness suddenly became worse and he was needed at home. Missing the meet was a big blow to John. His mother's illness weighed heavily on him, and, typical of middle adolescents, he was able to be both pragmatic about the situation and empathic to her suffering. He felt helpless at times: "My mother looks so down and tired. I get scared when she has seizures. I guess the best thing I can do is just help around the house and keep on loving her. You have to make the best of it. I get depressed, and I try to calm myself down. I pray a lot and ask God to give me strength to carry on. It feels like the whole world is going to come down on you because someone you love is going to be gone."

John took care of his mother while his father worked his night job, which was why he could not participate in sports after school anymore. Sometimes he worried that he could not help his mother as much as he should because of his schoolwork.

Death and Family Rituals

First Vigil

In late summer, Rosa's condition deteriorated. She suffered excruciating pain in her abdomen, and the doctors found more gallstones and a new pathologic fracture in her arm. She needed to be admitted to the hospital again. As her pain became unmanageable, Roberto was terrified about what was happening to her. The doctors said her death was imminent. Roberto set up a round-the-clock vigil and negotiated with the hospital so that both Michelle and John could be part of the vigil during the day. When Rosa rallied briefly, the doctors recommended transferring her to a hospice, but she adamantly refused. She wanted to die at home. The insurance company agreed to provide home hospice care.

Two More Vigils

Both children stayed home from school for a second bedside vigil. Rosa's death seemed imminent again. After a week, however, Roberto insisted that they return to school. As Roberto sadly described his plans for the funeral, he told the interviewer he hoped her agony would not go on too long.

Again, Rosa's condition became worse. Rosa's mother and one of her cousins returned to New York, and with Roberto, John, and Michelle, began a third 24-hour vigil. This one continued for 14 days. Although Roberto had heard several times in the past that Rosa was going to die, this time the situation felt different to him. When the priest came Sunday morning, Rosa opened her eyes and said to Roberto and her mother: "Take good care of my children. Treat them well. Make sure they get a good education." She then slipped into a coma and died a few hours later.

Roberto said that his family and the church members were wonderfully supportive. All the family attended the wake and went to the cemetery, where Rosa's ashes were placed in a niche.

Bereavement and Reconstitution

Adult Mourning: Numbness, Relief, and Yearning

After an initial period of numbness, Roberto felt extremely sad and cried more. He missed Rosa and had regrets about all the things they had not done together. In church, he prayed for Rosa to give him strength to keep on going. He described how bleak and empty he felt without her and recalled all her good qualities: He missed her ability to keep track of what everyone in the family was doing, her insistence that family members should let go of conflicts, and her wonderful way of stopping fights and arguments. She was someone he could talk to and depend on.

Roberto described a dream in which he was dancing with Rosa. Although she was young and healthy, he told her not to jump because the doctor had said she was ill. Rosa told him not to worry; she had been cured a week ago. She said she was not dead and no longer had any pain. She was having a good time, and Roberto should just take care of the children. When he woke up, he felt relieved and comforted because Rosa was finally at rest, and although they were separated now, he would see her again some day.

Roberto said that he was relieved because he no longer had financial problems. He was putting the children's Social Security survivors' benefits and Rosa's life insurance money in the bank to pay for their college education.

An Early Adolescent's Mourning: Bouncing Back with Muted Emotions

Michelle continued to do well in school. Her grades were back up again However, her father worried because she had a boyfriend, and he was afraid she would be taken advantage of by boys. He said Michelle looked exactly like her mother—she had her mother's face and was about the same age Rosa had been when they met. Roberto was pleased that his sister was teaching Michelle to cook; he felt cooking was important in case Michelle had a poor husband. Although Michelle did not talk to him about her mother, he knew that she longed for Rosa and missed her. Michelle often reassured him by saying, "Don't worry, Poppy, Mommy's resting."

Four months after her mother died, Michelle was interviewed alone. She obviously was not too happy about the extra chores she had to do around the house, but she said she liked learning how to cook. Although her grades had dropped during her mother's illness, they were now improving. She missed her mother and said it helped to talk to her friends and her guidance counselor. However, she did not like to talk to her father about her feelings because she did not want to worry him. She was concerned about who would take care of her if anything happened to him.

A Middle Adolescent's Mourning: Intense Grief

At mid-semester, shortly after Rosa died, the school threatened to dismiss John if he did not catch up quickly. Three long vigils for his mother had kept him out of school, and he was nearly failing all his subjects. His teachers believed he was no longer motivated, needed to contribute more to the school, socialize more, and be active in sports. Roberto was distressed about this and thought that the school was denying the impact of Rosa's death on John and how badly it was affecting his concentration. Because few minority students were enrolled in the school, Roberto believed the faculty simply did not understand the family responsibilities John was expected to assume during his mother's terminal illness. According to his father, John was moody, sullen, uncommunicative.

Reallocation of Roles and Responsibilities

Without Rosa, the family was not yet settled. Roberto returned to work the week after Rosa died and said that it was difficult to care for the children and do all the cooking and cleaning while holding two jobs. He had quit the third night job shortly before Rosa died. He wanted the children to help and felt they were not doing enough.

During a family meeting, Roberto expressed concern because his children did not talk to him. The children agreed. Michelle said she did not talk to him about her feelings because she did not want to be a burden to him, so she talked to her aunt instead. Her brother said that when he tried to talk to his father, "All I get is a lecture; he doesn't understand."

All three family members agreed that life at home felt disorganized; they all missed Rosa's way of maintaining the family's equilibrium by keeping family life organized. Michelle complained: "I'm expected to fill mother's shoes. That is too much for me! I want to be with my friends." She began to cry when she said she wished her mother were there to take care of everything. "If she was here, I'd be having a great time. Instead, I have more chores to do than any of my friends. No one understands!"

Challenge of Setting Limits as a Single Parent

Seven months after the funeral, Roberto began enjoying his jobs and his friends. He contemplated the possibility of dating but was concerned that John would be upset: "My kids are my first priority." Roberto wanted his children to appreciate how much he was doing for them, but they gave him a hard time instead. He was concerned because he believed that the children were not mourning their mother with the intensity that he did. He missed his wife's gentle touch with them and spent many hours thinking about how she would have handled them to insure that Michelle would remain a good girl and John would be happy and have friends.

Roberto was concerned about how to handle his daughter's emerging adolescence and budding independence, which frightened him because 'something bad might happen to her'. Although Michelle was doing well in school, she seemed to be far more interested in her appearance, her many friends, and boyfriends. "I told her Mother wouldn't want her to dress the way she is dressing!" He certainly didn't want her to date: "She is only 13!"

Michelle explained to the interviewer how she had tried to talk to him about what was happening with regard to boyfriends, but her explanations seemed to confuse him. As Michelle told the interviewer, by the time her father remonstrated with her about the boyfriend, the boy was out of the picture! The relationship had ended because the boy became interested in one of Michelle's girlfriends. Michelle had ended her friendship with the girl, but renewed it when the girl broke up with the boy a few weeks later. Both girls now were best of friends and had different boyfriends. Michelle was convinced that her father was unable to understand how dating was done in the United States.

Michelle explained: "He won't let me see my boyfriend after school every day because he says that will interfere with my homework and my responsibilities at home." It was hard for Roberto to communicate sufficiently with the mothers of her friends and learn that daytime socializing was accepted by most parents as long as the child's grades were O.K.

During another family session, Roberto's struggle concerning his daughter's budding independence surfaced in a number of subtle ways. For example, Roberto complained: "The apartment is really a mess! Rosa used to do all the housework." The messy apartment made him feel out of control.

Defensively, Michelle said: "Poppy, housework is new to me. And anyway, I like to be with my friends—this is the best time of my life. Sometimes I have more to do than my friends, and they don't always understand."

"I get mad when nobody helps or picks things up. When I really get mad, I walk out sometimes."

"I feel guilty when he does that," Michelle responded. "But sometimes I just tell him to chill out or calm down."

"Why should I calm down? I'm just asking you to do the dishes!"

This interchange indicated how quickly discussions deteriorated into mutual recriminations. Roberto was unable to assume his wife's role of de-escalating conflicts. Who was responsible for housework remained a touchy and unresolved issue. On the other hand, Roberto permitted both children to confront and contradict him. He ran a very democratic household, and allowing the children to confront him helped limit conflicts, and supported and empowered the adolescents.

Additional Challenge of Cultural Difference

Approximately one year after Rosa's death, Roberto's mother contemplated moving to New York to stay with him. Although Roberto acknowledged that such a move would complicate his life, the added responsibility would make him feel proud. Because his mother valued her independence, the fact that she considered living with him was a sign of her love and her trust in him.

Michelle, who was almost 14 years old, was open and talkative with the interviewer. She said she was very popular at school and was not seeing a counselor because both she and the counselor had agreed that it was no longer necessary. She still felt responsible for her mother's illness and felt isolated at home because no one was available to talk to her about "women's things." However, her aunt and a cousin, who lived a few blocks away, were important figures in her life and were available to her.

Michelle summarized her situation by saying that in addition to problems caused by her mother's death and her father's depression, many of the problems she had with her father were caused by the demands of her life in New York versus her father's desire to raise her in traditional Mexican fashion.

At the end of his sophomore year, John transferred to another school. He was angry about the demands the first school had made on him and their lack of support during his mother's illness; therefore, he decided to leave them. He was doing quite well at the new school. Roberto said that although John occasionally had nightmares and slept with him for a night or two, John was doing well in other respects.

New Changes and Life Transitions After the Death

Three years after Rosa's death, Roberto requested a couple of additional sessions to discuss recent events: "Well, actually to talk about how angry John is about my new girlfriend." The fact that John would be leaving for college soon made him anxious because he would feel empty without his son, but he felt better about his leaving because the new girlfriend would fill that gap.

Roberto said that Michelle was in high school and was doing extremely well academically. She had many friends. However, she still had physical problems and was again scheduled to have tests for gallstones.

Summary

Understanding Michelle's adjustment to the death of her mother is complicated by the role of acculturation and limited financial resources. Michelle was a bubbly, joyous person who had formed a close relationship with her mother. What was complicated was that Michelle was now trying to renegotiate a different type of relationship with her father. They mutually provoked each other. Her anger and frustration led to depression rather than acting out. What helped was that Roberto had attributes that are so important for children this age: he was quite obviously a very caring and loving parent, he tried hard to set limits, and he was very proud of her intellectual accomplishments.

There were two stressful aspects of the death for Michelle. First, her mother's long illness at home. It was a small home, where all details leading to the final agonal moments were in evidence. The family, including Rosa's mother, participated fully in this final dance. This is a very Mexican way to die—quite opposite from the Anglo way described in the next story. However, this extended family responded with attention, love, and assistance. Sometimes the extended family was not as helpful as John, Roberto, and Michelle would have liked, but it clearly mediated the most stressful aspects of the dying process. In addition, both children were helped to prepare themselves for the future without their mother. Michele mourned her mother, both before and after her death. This anticipatory mourning, encouraged by Rosa being home, prepared her for the loss. She had peers and close relatives she could talk to about her mother or with whom she could escape from the pain of her grief. John said he believed he had helped to keep his mother alive longer by his attentiveness to her, and this alleviated any guilt he might have felt. Both children were also supported by the extended family, who helped as much as they were able.

Not only did Roberto work hard to keep his family together and progressing in their development, but he also never hesitated to use whatever help was available. He fully involved himself in the intervention, and he readily paid for Michelle's therapy, which appeared to be of significant benefit to her.

Michelle had a positive self-image. When asked, she summarized for the psychologist when last interviewed that she was popular, liked by peers and teachers, and a good student.

MOTHER AND 12-YEAR-OLD SON

"Is this Really a Dramatic Change, Mother?"

Background

We are accustomed to hearing about a strong family history of cancer in women, but the Green family reminds us that men also are subject to familial disease. The relatives of 12-year-old Josh carry this burden, which prompted an older male cousin of Josh's father, Allan, to say: "This family should not propagate!" Two men in Allen's immediate family and two in his father's family had died of cancer. Allan, a financier, and Rita, a middle management administrator in a government agency, married in their early thirties. Both came from families of high achievers, and both pursued their respective professions with success. Five years after they were married, the couple was overjoyed when Rita became pregnant and had Josh. After taking several months off from work after Josh was born, Rita decided to postpone her career ambitions and to raise her son. She began working part time.

Illness

Allan was diagnosed with lymphoma when Josh was a year old. His vague fatigue, cough, and sore lymph nodes led his physicians to perform a biopsy immediately because of the strong history of cancer in his family. Allan quipped that "some families have a family doctor; mine has a family oncologist." Allan's diagnosis seemed to be a favorable one because of the excellent prognosis associated with the newer treatments available for the disease. At first he responded well, but two years later he began experiencing new symptoms, as it turned out they were symptoms of a second cancer. This more ominous prognosis was a severe emotional crisis for the couple.

More treatments followed, and Allan did fairly well for the next seven years, despite occasional bouts of infection, fatigue, and weakness, which usually improved after additional treatments. As Josh grew older, his parents gave him specific, age-appropriate information about the illness. Thus, he understood why his father received regular medical checkups but otherwise seemed relatively unaffected by his illness.

Faced with two cancers, Allan developed an ability to live fully in the here-and-now while maintaining a commitment to the future, embodied by Josh. Although he worked full time in a time-consuming, demanding job, Allan complemented Rita's parenting by helping Josh with his homework and by reading to him. Father and son subsequently began inventing stories together; then they began writing books, which Allan typed on his computer. Because of his father's help, Josh believed he had an edge over his classmates, especially in math. Allan also encouraged and participated in Josh's interest in sports. Their relationship was a warm, loving one that supported Josh's emerging independence.

Terminal Illness

Allan had been ill for 10 years when he had a life-threatening brain hemorrhage. Although he rallied to some extent after a few weeks, the family had to face the reality that Allan was now terminally ill. Allan clearly understood and accepted his fate. He struggled with the need to give up his work and with the progressive reduction in family life caused by his increasing debility. He spent so much time in the hospital that the staff seemed like an extended family. When hospitalized, he maintained contact with Josh, especially about his homework, and telephone contacts and visits to the hospital on weekends became the routine.

In contrast to Allan, Rita was extremely anxious and was having a difficult time coping with the uncertainty of Allan's illness. Her detailed, methodical mind was a crucial element in her success as an administrator, and she continued to work part time. Her employer regarded her work as so valuable, he gave her maximum flexibility regarding her schedule. She plagued herself and the interviewer with endless questions and preoccupations in an obsessive search for definite answers to questions such as "What is the best way to handle Josh? Will this experience irrevocably injure him? Will growing up without a father make him a homosexual?" and on and on. Her anxiety was palpable.

Limiting Discussion Around Illness and Death

Rita wanted to be with Allan in the hospital and with Josh at home. When she came home, she wanted to share every minute detail of Allan's disease and the laboratory findings with Josh. Finding this situation intolerable, Josh handled it by insisting, "I need to concentrate on my homework, and hearing about Dad's medical problems makes me lose my concentration." Rita suspected that he worried at night and had difficulty falling asleep. She also said that he devised mental games to keep from thinking and worrying about his father.

Josh finally set a limit on his mother: He would not allow her to discuss his father's current medical status unless there was a dramatic change and, even then, she could talk about that no more than twice a week. Whenever she was about to begin talking about Allan's condition, Josh reminded her about their agreement by asking, "Is this really a *dramatic* change, Mother?" Because he was able to criticize her in a humorous way, his criticisms were acceptable to her.

Negotiating a New Relationship with the Surviving Parent as
Death is Anticipated

Because of Allan's many months in the hospital, Josh began to mourn his loss before his father's death. He also began to work out a new relationship with his mother as a single parent without his father's influence. When Allan was no longer able to help Josh with his homework, Josh wanted more help from his mother, but her style was different and, somehow, it did not work out as well. Josh wrote the following poem for school during this time. It illustrates so clearly the adolescent's need for optimism and certainty.

> Things are bad, Things are good
> My Dad is always sick.
> What would be best?
> If someone would tell me
> My Dad's going to be O.K.

Josh was doing well in private school, both academically and in sports. Although he had friends, his mother thought he was not gregarious enough because he had one special friend and a couple of acquaintances. She also was concerned because he was not discussing his feelings about Allan's illness with her. During a session with the interviewer, however, he gave a clear, accurate, and sophisticated description of the illness and expressed concern that his father would die. He hoped for another miracle like the one that had occurred after the hemorrhage, when his father had nearly died, and he reminisced about playing basketball with his father just before Allan had been rehospitalized. Josh vaguely wondered whether the game had caused his father's relapse. Rita reassured him successfully by providing facts, which she always did well.

Josh had mild asthma, and Rita worried it was getting worse. Her anxiety about Allan's gradual deterioration and how she would survive when he died made it progressively more difficult to know when her concerns about Josh were realistic and when they reflected her own anxiety. During a family session, Josh reassured her that he was sure she could handle things if his father were to die. He did not want her to get sick, certainly not sick in the way his father was. When Rita said that Josh seemed to be jealous of other boys whose fathers attended their ball games, she began to cry. With his typical droll humor, Josh said, "I cry too, but only when the computer disk with my homework on it freezes up." Clearly, he had learned how to handle his mother's emotionalism. Although she did not show it at this point, Rita also had a good sense of humor and enjoyed Josh's way of cajoling her. They were clearly beginning to negotiate a relationship with each other that did not include Allan's involvement.

Death and Family Rituals

Muted Anticipatory Responses

After Allan had been hospitalized for several months, he was progressively becoming weaker. Rita told the interviewer that Josh was making more demands on her. He wanted her to help him more with his homework but was angry when she didn't provide the specific answers. She realized that she was in a period of anticipatory mourning and was concerned that Josh was not because he never mentioned that he was worried that Allan was dying and that he was afraid of how life would be without his father. However, she knew that Josh was having more trouble sleeping at night and then getting up in the morning on time. She thought he was having difficulty concentrating on his homework. He also was becoming a perfectionist regarding what he expected of himself: His recent report card was excellent, containing comments such as "He is happy," "He is a good writer," "He is unusually gifted." He also won a tennis tournament.

Privately, Rita began making funeral plans and wondered whether Josh should participate in the funeral. Some family members had urged her to send him to stay with close friends, but, agreeing with the interviewer's counseling, she decided against doing that. Her concern then shifted to money; she was uncertain about how she should negotiate with Allan's firm to insure access to the funds she believed were part of his partnership.

Active and Limited Participation in Funeral and Burial Rituals

Allan suddenly suffered another severe hemorrhage and died. Josh had visited him earlier that day and was surprised by all the tubes Allan had in him. Rita was alone with Allan when he died. Later, she picked up Josh at school, and they had a quiet half hour at home before friends and neighbors arrived. When Allan was buried two days later, many people attended the funeral. A family friend spoke during the service, and Josh was grateful to him because he said all the things Josh wanted to say. Rita had arranged for Josh and his cousins to return home from the cemetery before the casket was lowered, but then she changed her mind. Josh threw a handful of dirt on the casket after it was lowered. Rita sat Shiva for five days, and although she and Josh felt a great sense of support from friends and relatives who sat with them, the sheer number of people overwhelmed them at times. Josh returned to school after the first day, as did most adolescents his age.

Anxiety About His Own and the Family's Survival

Josh was uncharacteristically "clingy" for two days after Allan died. He did not want Rita to go out at night or to leave him alone in the house. He wanted to know why the doctors could not save his father—why they could not do something extraordinary as they had done after his first hemorrhage. But he began to go out with his friends and gradually became more autonomous.

Rita decided to go back to work full time. Because the family finances were unclear, the extra money would be helpful. Josh's after-school activities fit well with her new schedule, and she enrolled him in other activities twice a week so she would be home when he got there.

Rita was surprised when Josh expressed concern about how much money they had. She said he tried to figure out their monthly expenses and wanted to be more involved with her investments. She thought he wanted to take over his father's role as the family's money manager. This immediate emulation of the patient was quite typical of early adolescents in our studies. Josh also worried about who would teach him advanced math so that he would maintain the edge he had over his classmates. Then he remembered that he had an older cousin who "knows even more math than Dad did."

Bouncing Back and Initial Efforts to Avoid Grief

Rita had letters from Allan and audiotapes of books Allan and Josh had written together, but Josh did not want to look at or listen to them. She was worried because he did not seem to be mourning enough and was only partially reassured when the interviewer explained that adults mourn continuously, whereas children mourn gradually and sporadically.

Josh confided to the interviewer that he wanted to cry but could not. He missed his father most intensely at night before he fell asleep because he remembered things they used to do together. As a result, he liked to stay up until he was so sleepy he would not have to think about his father too much.

Bereavement and Reconstitution

Apparent Differences Between Adult and Adolescent Mourning

According to Rita, Josh showed evidence of developing new interests: He was combing his hair carefully, showing a new interest in clothes, negotiating with her for more spending money, and showing increased interest in being accepted by peers. Rita also noticed that he was seeking, appropriately and successfully, men's attention and affection, and the fathers of his sports buddies were responding and reaching out to him. It took Josh approximately two months before he felt comfortable talking with Rita about Allan, although she had to initiate these discussions.

During a family session, Josh's eyes teared a bit when he and his mother reminisced about Allan, but he quickly blamed his tears on his allergies. In school and sports, he continued to do extremely well, and he was getting caught up in the social world. He had two double dates brewing, and his mother was relieved. She observed that his greater feeling of acceptance followed his peers attending the funeral and the Shiva.

Rita had difficulty talking about her own mourning, focusing instead on the many tasks that needed to be done. Only occasionally did she describe her pain. She focused more on how to deal with Josh's possible inherited vulnerability to cancer, not only from Allan's side of the family but from hers. Several women had been successfully treated for cancers in her family as well. She felt that Josh was doing so well at this point that it was not the time to bring up a bone marrow harvesting procedure, which Allan's oncologist had recommended because he predicted that Josh had a 10 percent chance of developing leukemia during his lifetime. Rita believed that the oncologist's estimate was probably optimistic—there was simply too much cancer on both sides of the family.

Anger and the Search for a Replacement Mentor

About four months after Allan's funeral, Josh's math teacher said Josh had become argumentative in class, but his other teachers said that, although challenging, Josh was not a behavior problem. According to Josh, his greatest concern was losing the two latest baseball games because his pitching arm was below par. Rita talked to two men whose sons were on the same team as Josh. They then talked to Josh, man-to-man, pointing out that although his pitching was not as good as it usually was, his batting was better. Rita hesitated to tell Josh that missing his father might have something to do with his recent slump because, during previous discussions, he had denied missing his father. With typical 12-year-old finesse and insensitivity, Josh talked to his mother about marrying Jim. Jim had been a family acquaintance for many years. Because Jim had been a semi-professional baseball player, Josh thought Jim could give him good tips and perhaps help him solve his pitching problem. What better choice of a stepfather? Rita told Josh that Jim was a nice person, but she was not interested in marriage at this time.

Rita also worried about how Josh would in fact react if she began dating and how he would react if she did not. Recently, Josh had come home agitated and told Rita that Jim had a girlfriend. He worried that Jim might marry the woman before Rita had a chance.

Challenge of Setting Limits as a Single Parent

Rita worried about how to set appropriate limits on Josh's social life. He planned to invite a group of friends to a graduation party at their house. Because she was afraid that some of the boys would become rowdy, she insisted on being at home during the party, which made Josh grumpy. When the parents of the girls Josh had invited called Rita to ask whether the party would be adequately supervised, she was pleased and reassured regarding her own good sense.

When Josh went to summer camp for two months, Rita was annoyed because he did not help her get his clothes ready. When the interviewer pointed out that his behavior might represent a mild regression, a reaction to separation so soon after his father's death, Rita understood. Four weeks later, she drove to the camp for Family Day, and the camp director told her that Josh was doing well. Rita said she should have known that he was doing well because she had received only two postcards from him. She was angry because people kept asking whether she missed Josh. "I don't miss him, I miss Allan!" She was mourning her husband deeply at this point.

Talking About the Parent Who Died, But with Sparse Emotion:
the Parent Misunderstands

During an interview about seven months after the funeral, Rita said that Josh had entered eighth grade and was doing well. He had enjoyed camp and shortly after returning home, he asked to see his father's letters and listen to the tapes he and Allan had made together. Although Rita was reassured by the fact that Josh talked so freely about Allan, the fact that he did not talk about being sad or about missing his father concerned her. Although she knew he was sad and missed Allan, she wondered whether his mourning was inadequate and, if so, whether he would have severe problems as an older adolescent. "He might even join some religious sect!"

Josh had many friends, and the extended family was a good support system. The research psychologist described him as a pleasant young adolescent who related warmly and thoughtfully to her. In her opinion, Josh was adjusting well to his father's death. Like Josh, Rita was functioning well but was not dating. During the interview, she cried; her feelings about Allan were still raw.

Continued Dis-synchrony Between the Adolescent's and the Adult's Grief

At the time of the final interview, approximately 14 months after the funeral, Josh was functioning well both academically and in sports and was popular with the students at his new junior high school. Although he expressed some fears about developing cancer, he seemed to have an easier time talking with strangers about the matter than with his mother. He had no difficulty talking with the research psychologist about his father's illness and death or about missing his father, but the content of these discussions was thoughtful rather than emotional.

Rita was having problems with her daily social adjustment: She was lonely, she missed Allan, and found it difficult to be single in social situations. She had not dated yet and was not sure whether the reason was that she had not met any appropriate men or whether she simply was not ready.

She felt that because Josh was entering adolescence, she was in for a stormy time, more so because she was a single parent. Although he was doing well, he was not visibly grieving, and she worried about the future.

Rita had been working full time for a year when she was offered a promotion. Her employer had encouraged her to take his own job. Although the promotion would lead to a significant career, she decided not to take the job because she would lose the flexible work schedule she currently had, and she believed that Josh was not ready for that. He still did not like to be left alone at home, and she needed to prepare herself for what she was afraid would be a stormy adolescence, like the one she and her brothers had.

Summary

Because a parent's long illness is stressful, it is not unusual for children to show signs of distress under those circumstances. Why did Josh do so well? He did well for a number of reasons. He had important attributes—he was intelligent and did well in school and in sports, and he was well liked by peers and teachers. But perhaps more importantly, his father handled his double cancer and progressive disease maturely, and he left an important legacy of grace and courage in the face of adversity. He was a role model for acknowledging the tragedies in life without becoming overwhelmed by them, valuing and investing in those relationships that are important, using humor, and achieving personal growth through life's trials.

Josh thought he had an "edge," especially in mathematics, but also in baseball, *because* his father had helped him. When his father died, Josh looked for and found replacements. Should the adolescent look for a mentor replacement or should he internalize his father's attributes? Should he believe *in his own* ability to develop his own edge? No, not yet. Josh's need for a mentor replacement was quite typical of 12- to 14-year-old adolescents. It was in the well-functioning 15- to 17-year-old adolescents where the emphasis began to shift, and the replacement mentor was less urgently needed.

Was Rita correct? Should we be concerned about Josh's future because he seemed unable to mourn his father as she thought he should? No. We learned that the quiet way Josh mourned was not uncommon, especially in boys and especially during early adolescence. Young adolescents still have significantly different patterns of mourning than do adults.

Setting appropriate limits, appreciating and fostering the child's skills and abilities, and walking that fine line between nurturing and allowing and encouraging appropriate moves towards independence were parenting factors that were associated with a better outcome in this age group. Despite her anxiety, Rita contributed to her son's good adjustment. Like Allan, she appreciated and fostered Josh's abilities.

What of Josh's developmental task—to reduce his emotional investment in his parents? Rita was emotionally intense and found the history of family illnesses threatening to her sense of control. However, Rita was able to respond to Josh's needs. It was perhaps fortuitous that she could channel her energies into her work. This seemed to allow Josh his necessary distance.

The real specter in Josh's life was his inherited risk for cancer. Both mother and son have to live with this reality, as did several of the men in his father's family. Not until the next developmental stage will Josh begin to comprehend fully its meaning for him.

OUTCOMES

By the final assessment, 8 to 14 months after the parent's death, 21 of the 39 adolescents had achieved their previous levels of functioning in all of the major areas: psychological state, relationships at home, academics, athletics and after-school activities, and developmentally appropriate peer relationships. Eleven had a delayed reconstitution, four a compromised reconstitution, and three a symptomatic reconstitution.

Characteristics of Early Adolescents with a Timely Reconstitution

The 21 adolescents who had the most timely reconstitution experienced transient declines in functioning in a number of areas, most often before, sometimes after the parent's death, but regained their equilibrium in all major domains at the time of their last evaluation. Their level of productivity in school and in after-school activities returned to previous levels. They dealt appropriately with parents and other significant adults, and related well to peers. Their mood and the range of their emotional expression was normal. Syntonic with the developmental tasks of this age group, they were less emotionally involved with their parents and withheld their thoughts and feelings about the death in ways that were worrisome to many parents. They demanded that the tragedy be confined to a limited place in their lives. They tended to accept "reasonable" added chores required by the reality of the changed situation. At times they enjoyed being able to help out. On occasion they even expressed emotions other than anger and criticism to the parent. However, if they believed their chores were excessive and removed them too much from peers, they complained. Their grief occurred episodically, but the parent often needed to initiate opportunities for mourning at times, such as anniversaries and other marker events. It was difficult to engage young adolescents in therapy relationships, although some were responsive to the intervention. Parents of well-functioning adolescents readily accessed whatever therapies were available for their children, most often using school guidance counselors, school bereavement and rap groups, and other community groups.

Characteristics of Early Adolescents with a Delayed Reconstitution

Eleven adolescents, those with a delayed reconstitution, were also adapting relatively well to the parent's death. However, they were still struggling to regain their equilibrium in at least one major domain. Some had not returned to their previous levels of academic proficiency, some were depressed or expressed intense, persistent anger at parents, siblings, and peers; others exhibited regressive behaviors such as withdrawal, separation anxiety, or impulsiveness.

The factors that characterized the adolescents and families in which the adolescent had a slower reconstitution included: (1) pre-existing adjustment problems in the adolescent and/or, (2) persistent adolescent-parent-family conflicts.

Pre-existing Adjustment Problems

About half of these adolescents with a delayed reconstitution had pre-existing learning or social problems that were exacerbated by the parent's illness and death. The problems included bouts of depression, severe learning problems, and significant problems with impulse control.

Persistent Adolescent-Parent-Family Conflicts

The other half had severe and unresolved parent-child conflicts. It is note-worthy that in all but one of these families there were siblings, mostly younger, who had a timely reconstitution. In some family situations the conflicts were exacerbated by the child's entrance into adolescence. Their parents seemed less tolerant of their emotional withdrawal, of their anger and criticism, and of their coexistent needs for dependence and independence. In short, these parents seemed less tolerant of the adolescent's separation process. In other families, there was a more complicated pattern: Some adolescents had elicited a stronger relationship with one than with the other parent based on abilities, interests, gender, temperament, and/or early behavior problems. Not uncommonly, a sib-ling developed a stronger relationship with the other parent. When this prefer-ence locked into a cross-generational coalition, and the adolescent's coalition parent died, spiraling conflicts with the surviving parent often resulted. Some of the adolescents were scapegoated by the surviving parent. More often, the sur-viving parent was the recipient of displaced anger that really belonged to the deceased patient. These patterns also led to spiraling conflicts. In these more conflicted families, the parent's death seemed to upset a fragile equilibrium that had been established. This suggests that whether an adolescent had a timely or delayed reconstitution was, with some, a matter of "fit" or "lack of fit" between the surviving parent and the adolescent.

There were also characteristics of the surviving parent that contributed to the delayed reconstitution. When the deceased patient was one on whom the surviving parent had been highly dependent, the parent often became quite depressed and withdrawn, and, not uncommonly with fathers, very quickly started dating. This constellation of events often aroused strong and persistent resentment in adolescents. Another pattern was evident in which the surviving parent was unable to structure and direct the household. In such situations there was a good deal of household chaos. In short, where the surviving parent was less able to provide the support, structure, and direction that were needed, it took longer for the parent to gain control, to restructure without the day-to-day intervention of the deceased parent; it also took longer for the adolescent to reconstitute. An important distinction between parents of adolescents who had a delayed reconstitution and those with a compromised or symptomatic recon-stitution was that the surviving parent in the delayed group tried and eventu-ally succeeded in changing the patterns. The parent also readily used available resources within and outside the family that might help the adolescent.

Characteristics of Compromised Reconstitution

Four adolescents girls had a more compromised reconstitution and did not experience the improvement in mood and functioning after the parent's death that was observed in the timely and delayed reconstitution. During the final assessment, they exhibited continuing serious symptoms of depression, of school failure, major weight gain, and/or alcohol abuse. All four came from families that became much more chaotic and disorganized following the death of the primary caregiving parent. The surviving parents had been almost totally uninvolved in the day-to-day parenting prior to the parent's death. They did not assume a warm, caring, effective parenting role before or after the death. All four girls expressed profound longing for the warmth and engagement they had with the parent who died and that was no longer available.

There were additional stressors in these families, ranging from substance abuse in older siblings to a history of domestic violence. In addition, all of these families had three or more children, and all were struggling with financial problems. The surviving parents assigned primary care taking and housekeeping responsibilities to these girls. The young adolescents were angry with the surviving parent for what they perceived as excessive demands. The parents withdrew even further or retaliated angrily. A destructive interactive spiral ensued.

Characteristics of Symptomatic Reconstitution

After the patient's death, three adolescent boys developed psychiatric symptoms that were severe and qualitatively different from symptoms they had exhibited before the death. These included one or more of the following: severe phobias, major clinical depression, acute homosexual panic, stealing, and physical assaults on peers that resulted in repeated school dismissal. In two families, what distinguished these situations from those with a better outcome was the presence of mental illness in the surviving parent, which seriously affected parenting ability. While serious mental illness occurred in the families of adolescents with better outcomes, either the illness did not significantly affect parenting skills or there were moderating factors present, such as closely involved extended family members who supplemented the parenting and reduced the family isolation so common in single-parent families, in which the parent is seriously mentally ill. A second constellation of factors included the presence of severe behavior problems in the adolescent from an early age. One temperamentally difficult child was also adopted. Only the father seemed able to exert some measure of control as the boy grew older. When the father died, the adolescent's behavior seriously deteriorated. The family had also adopted a girl who had a timely reconstitution. This mid-adolescent girl was able to negotiate a new satisfactory relationship with her mother.

DISCUSSION

Puberty and adolescence disrupted the relatively smooth adjustment seen in the 9- to 11-year-old group. Clashes between the emotional developmental tasks of this age group and the tasks of meeting the family needs during the terminal illness and death were ubiquitous. What was surprising was that 31 of the 38 adolescents and their families collaborated enough to result in a timely (21) or delayed (10) reconstitution. The developmental tasks included the start of emotional withdrawal from the family, beginning to negotiate a different, more adult relationship with the parent, and learning to become more emotionally involved with peers. These are daunting challenges for adolescents that often exacerbate pre-existing vulnerabilities. Equally daunting were the family tasks that began to fall more directly on these adolescents who were confronting parental death: meeting a new set of responsibilities and maintaining an appropriate level of involvement with the family during the illness, death, and reconstitution stages.

These adolescents retained the intolerance of strong emotions seen in the younger group, but now added intolerance for information, especially for bad news. While the younger group used intellectualization as a defense, seeking explanations and information, the emerging formal operational stage of development of the early adolescents forced a clearer awareness of the implications of information. The adolescent was not able to deal with both emotional withdrawal and the guilty reunification that they feared was required by their parent's illness. The usual difficult behavior of early adolescence was exaggerated, compounding the problem unless the parent was quite skillful at de-escalating conflictual interactions.

The terminal stage of the illness, with its attendant uncertainty yet with increasingly clear signs of the impending death, was, for this group, as it had been for the younger children, the most difficult period. More unique was the extent of their self centered, egocentric perspective, or, as many parents decried, 'their callous, unfeeling selfishness'. The parents had to set appropriate limits on the behavior of the adolescent; this was critical but was generally more complex and difficult with adolescents than with younger children. Adolescents were bigger, and at times quite adult in their thinking and deportment. Their behavior was not only confusing, but also more provocative, especially in their challenges of authority and in their "eye rolling," barely hidden contempt of the parent. Toward the end, most adolescents changed this behavior and showed a greater empathy for the patient and parent, and they became more helpful.

The early adolescents thought of the dead parent as being 'out there', perhaps watching, an interested listener to their monologues, certainly interested in their achievements. Like their younger peers, they mourned the parent as a mentor and supporter, but now also as gender and social role model, limit setter and de-escalator of conflicts. This age group was the oldest that often placed objects in the coffin. These objects were more practical, and focused on special interests of the parent—the parent's favorite book, a little liquor, a picture of good times—objects to take on a long, one-way trip.

Like their younger peers, these adolescents sought control of their grief through outside activities. The ecological system of the early adolescent is more complex than that of their younger peers. Religion, bereavement counseling with peer groups, finding replacements for supports previously supplied by the deceased parent, cultural and subcultural values, all were more important and more personally relevant to this age group. Still, the family, especially the relationship with the surviving parent, remained crucial, as was particularly apparent in youngsters whose outcome was more compromised.

13

Children 15–17 Years of Age

Themes

This chapter describes the impact of terminal cancer on the lives of 35 mid-adolescents–20 boys and 15 girls—aged 15 to 17. They come from 31 families, and their surviving parents were 16 fathers and 15 mothers. (In this and the next chapter, when the word adolescent is used, it means 15- to 17-year-old mid-adolescents.) This chapter surveys the important developmental themes observed in this age group, the responses of the adolescents and their families to the parent's terminal illness, preparation for the death and family rituals, and the period of family reconstitution. Chapter 14 describes the experiences of two families and ends with a summary of the characteristics of the children and families that constitute the four possible outcomes when last interviewed, 8 to 14 months after the parent died.

DEVELOPMENTAL THEMES OF MIDDLE ADOLESCENCE

In the analysis of the data, five areas of development emerged as important in understanding the way middle adolescents coped with the death of a parent. These included the maturing of cognitive abilities, the change in mourning, gender differences in parental relationship deepening and changing peer relationships, and a significant increase in the capacity for empathy. Each of these is described below.

Advancing Cognitive Abilities: "He Gets It!"

The solid abilities of middle adolescents to use abstract ideas and to interconnect the various aspects of the illness and death more comprehensively than their younger peers were striking. These abilities were observed in their clear capacity to anticipate the death and simultaneously to project its impact on them not only in the present but in the future as well. In the mid-adolescent, the early adolescent's adamant optimism was replaced with more flexible and pragmatic thinking about the disease, the symptoms, and the probability of death, all of which led naturally to a more profound anticipatory mourning.

Fifteen-year-old Scott's mother said that she thought Scott "got it," whereas his 12-year-old sister remained optimistic, despite her father's advancing symptoms of colon cancer. Scott hugged his father more often than he had done before and asked his mother, "How long does Daddy have to live?" He hoped there was time for one more fishing trip. Scott talked about the injustice of his father having cancer and expressed his feeling that life was not fair. At the same time, he received excellent grades in school. Scott wrote a report on colon cancer for school, interviewed his father's physician, and learned about a new drug. His early adolescent sister did not want to read his report.

Mourning in a More Adult Manner

The adolescents' advanced cognitive abilities also resulted in their experiencing a more complex mourning process. They automatically thought about and integrated their past relationship to the parent who had died, what the parent had expected of them, and how they might live up to those expectations in the future. However, their advanced cognitive abilities also led to more painful grief because they were able to comprehend the enduring consequences of the loss more fully than could younger children.

The mourning of adolescents differed from the mourning of early adolescents in two major ways. First, they experienced anticipatory mourning more consistently during the parent's terminal illness because they understood that the death was imminent. Second, the adolescents experienced more persistent and prolonged periods of mourning after the death than did younger children, whose grief was more episodic. In quality and timing, their mourning approached the mourning of adults, and their strong grief responses after the parent's death affected their concentration and functioning.

Gender Differences

For adolescent girls, a parent's death interfered profoundly with their developmental task of changing their relationship with the surviving parent rather than only withdrawing emotional investment from the relationship. Some current theories about adolescent development suggest that males and females have different relationships with their parents. Girls emphasize a change in the relationships with their parents, especially the relationship with their mother. Boys, on the other hand, are usually engaged in more fully separating from both parents (Blos, 1962; Gilligan, 1982; Kaplan, Gleason, & Klein, 1991; Miller, 1991).

Empathy, Allocentrism, and Altruism

The capacity for a more allocentric perspective—that is, the ability to see a situation from another person's perspective—replaced the characteristic egocentrism of the early adolescent. The adolescents were more aware of and more empathic with their parents' feelings and concerns. They were more comfortable with a broader range of emotions and were able to express and analyze their thoughts and feelings better. They could talk about sadness and fears of vulnerability; this was evidenced in many comments expressing concern and caring for both the patient and the surviving parent. They also perceived and were more apprehensive about the parents' vulnerabilities. At times, they tried to help with the family tasks left undone because of the patient's illness and death. This extended to caring for and supporting younger siblings, sometimes in a touching and effective way.

> Diane, age 15, and her younger brother were home with an older cousin when a nurse called from the hospital, told them their father had died and said that their mother was on her way home. Diane's brother became extremely upset, and Diane was pleased that she was able to comfort him.

> Seventeen-year-old Brian was considerate of his mother after his father died. He asked her if she wanted him to stay home so that she would not be alone in the house. He offered to cancel an activity to do this.

> Fifteen-year-old John took care of his mother while his father worked at a night job. An excellent athlete, John gave up all his after-school sports activities to help. Sometimes he worried that he couldn't help his mother as much as he should because of his schoolwork. When his mother broke her hip, he was afraid she would lose a leg and tried to reassure her by saying, "It really doesn't matter if you are disabled or not because I will always love you."

What sometimes confused parents was how their adolescent fluctuated between allocentric and self-centered thinking. Their ability to be concerned about the needs of others was a gradually evolving perspective rather than a solidly established capacity.

Deepening Personal Relationships

Aided by increased social understanding, adolescents were more selective in the choice of people outside the family with whom they shared their grief. They formed more intimate and mutual relationships than their younger peers. Many sought a classmate whose parent also had cancer. Several had girlfriends or boyfriends who helped them cope with stressful periods both before and after the parent's death. The group friendships of early adolescence were giving way to more intimate, deeper, and more enduring relationships with individual peers. The deeper trust in their friends seemed related to greater trust in themselves and in their emerging capacity to function independently.

> When 15-year-old Heather's father told her that her mother had died, he hugged her and then let her go to her friend for comforting. The fact that the friend had lost her mother to cancer made her more understanding about Heather's feelings. Heather also knew two other people whose mothers had died and another person whose father had died.

Some adolescents had difficulty finding friends in whom they could confide. The unavailability of friends or the withdrawal of friends was a significant stressor for these adolescents. Often, problems were encountered if the adolescents transferred to a new school or moved to a different school district. They were reluctant to share tragic news about their family with peers they did not know and distrusted.

Social-ecological Development

Although the more personal and intimate factors in the life of the adolescents are emphasized in these chapters, other factors—planning for college and thinking about moving away from home, getting a drivers license, their changing dependence on a significant friend—all moved them into a different involvement with the world outside the home. Sports and school continued to be important, but their ecological world became wider, with greater and more direct and indirect influences on their development.

PATTERNS OF RESPONSES IN MIDDLE ADOLESCENCE

Terminal Illness

Four areas reflected the changes in the way adolescents experienced the parent's terminal illness: (1) their ability to comprehend the realities of the terminal illness, (2) their ability to experience anticipatory grief, (3) their constrained reactions, behaviors, and symptoms, and (4) their increasingly stabilized relationships with parents, siblings, and friends.

Comprehension of the Realities of the Parent's Terminal Illness

Adolescents were more realistic, practical, and flexible in their thinking about the parent's terminal illness than were their younger peers, and they usually received more facts about the parent's illness at an earlier point in its course. They also were more likely to understand the facts and to grasp the implications associated with them, and they did not need to maintain an unrealistic optimism in the face of the parent's advancing symptoms.

Seventeen-year-old Jesse said that his father did not want to talk with the younger children in the family about his illness, but he did want Jesse to know more. Because he had difficulty talking about his personal feelings, Jesse's father gave him a book about a cancer survivor. The fact that a number of his father's relatives had died recently from cancer contributed to a high level of apprehension in the family. At the mother's urging, his father gradually shared more facts, but few feelings, with Jesse. Jesse had a sophisticated understanding of the disease and its treatment. He worried that because his father had been hospitalized on an emergency basis several times recently, he might not be eligible for an experimental treatment that had been scheduled for him. Jesse explained that the emergency hospitalizations might mean that his father was too sick to receive that treatment. This explanation reflected Jesse's understanding of the realistic problems associated with being eligible for experimental treatment.

When it became clear that the chemotherapy her father was receiving for stomach cancer was ineffective, Diane was told that he would die. Diane was close to her father, and they had a mutually enjoyable, teasing relationship. When she learned of his poor prognosis, she scheduled an appointment with her school principal and had a long talk with him about the situation. She also talked directly with her friends about her father's imminent death.

Most parents were able to discuss the facts and feelings associated with the illness with their adolescents with less fear and apprehension than they experienced when talking with younger children. Avoiding such discussions interfered with the adolescents' ability to engage in anticipatory grief, which was important in preparing them for the intense, more adult mourning they would experience after the death.

Todd's father avoided giving his 15-year-old son information about his mother's prognosis, fearing that the information would overwhelm Todd and cause him to perform even more poorly at school. The father's avoidance may have been related to his own depression, which had been treated for a number of years. Although Todd refused to discuss his mother's illness with the interviewer, saying, "I understand perfectly fine," the interviewer noted that he had many distorted and unclear ideas. He said his mother had an infection in her stomach, although what was actually wrong with her was an intestinal tumor.

When his mother died, Todd was angry with his father for not telling him about the seriousness of his mother's illness sooner, especially shortly before her death. When last seen, Todd was angry and defiant and was struggling with family and peer relationships.

Anticipatory Grief

Although adolescents articulated a broader range of feelings than their younger peers did, they were more likely to explore these feelings after the death than during the terminal illness. Before the death, they tended to be thoughtful and realistic and expressed some anger and defiance and, less often, sadness. They thought about what life would be like without the parent. Helping out with household tasks and caring sometimes for the patient helped them contain their anxiety.

Seventeen-year-old Jimmie understood what was happening to his father. He said that they had often gone to baseball games together, and he imagined it would be difficult when baseball season came and his father wouldn't be there. His father had progressively withdrawn from Jimmie and his younger brother, and had recently become impatient when the boys made noise in the small apartment. Although this was annoying, Jimmie knew that his father's irritability was part of the disease.

Jimmie was aware that his mother was tense, but he felt that she was available to him. He resented his grandparents because he felt they were trying to "take over" and "baby" him. He said that when his father died, he made a point of not crying or showing excessive emotion in front of his brother, although he was worried because his brother was not expressing his feelings enough.

Fifteen-year-old Brendan, the oldest of four boys, prayed that his father would get better, but he wondered what would happen if his father died. "I'm not going to have a father. Mother will be alone and upset. If she gets remarried, I don't want another father; it will never be the same as it was before he had cancer." His advice to other adolescents in this situation was to "Look on the bright side, don't get down, and have faith. Try not to be a pessimist, try to help out your parents as best you can, and stay out of trouble."

Like Brendan, Diane wondered what life would be like when her father died. "It will be hard to believe it is final." Her advice was to "understand that it is a hard situation, but knowing someone who is going through the same thing can help." Because her household responsibilities had increased, she was resentful, but she also understood.

What was apparent in the recommendations of the adolescents was the personalized thoughtfulness rather than the more egocentric platitudes so typical of early adolescents.

Reactions, Behaviors, and Symptoms

During the parents' terminal illness, the adolescents' reactions, behaviors, and symptoms were more constrained than those of the early adolescents, unless they had pre-existing emotional problems or the illness situation involved unusual stresses. They were able to confront the reality of the parent's terminal condition cognitively and often emotionally. Although maintaining their grades, activities, and peer relationships were their highest priorities, they were more understanding than younger adolescents when the demands of the illness interfered with their activities. Although resentful, they accepted the need for their help. They also were not angry when their parents' attention shifted as a consequence of the ill parent's deteriorating condition. As one adolescent put it: "So much has changed. . . . Things will never be as they were." This statement characterized the adolescents' comprehension of what was happening. They did not personalize the situation; they did not feel responsible for the parent's illness. They were more inclined to express sadness and a sense of awe about the loss rather than look for a scapegoat.

Although the adolescents were more helpful than their younger peers, they struggled to balance their own wants and needs with those of the family:

When his father's disease became worse, Jesse drove him to work. He also enjoyed taking his younger brother and sister out to dinner when his mother was with her husband in the hospital. His mother told the interviewer that it was difficult for Jesse to accept his father's fatigue and inability to participate in activities the two had planned together. She also said that Jesse argued with her about his interest in going to Europe for the summer. She thought that was too far away, given his father's medical condition. However, during his father's most recent hospitalization, she observed Jesse taking his father in his arms and letting him spit out phlegm. She was surprised that her son could handle that.

School performance.   Maintaining their competence in school was important to the middle adolescents, because they and their parents believed that their grades would have a crucial impact on their future opportunities. The adolescents complained about the problems they were having with concentration and welcomed efforts to help them develop skills in this area. Although concentrating was a struggle, most of them experienced only transient problems with schoolwork before the death. In addition, they worried about "falling off" and "losing my edge" in sports, especially when the father had been heavily involved with them in these activities. For girls, asserting leadership in activities and maintaining relationships with friends also were areas in which they could continue to achieve and to feel effectual and normal. Some adolescents improved their school functioning and general behavior as a way of giving a gift to their dying parent.

Fears, Anger, and Guilt.   Fear about the future was a prominent theme in the adolescent's thinking. Sometimes the fear was practical: "Will I have enough money for college? Will I be able to get all the things my friends have? Will we be able to keep the house?" Eldest sons, especially, were worried about living up to the dying parent's dreams. Many of the adolescents were afraid that they would lose an entire stage of their development, that their futures would be compromised by what they would be missing: Some said, "I will lose my adolescence." They understood the concept of limited time and opportunity.

Although the adolescents' anger was generally muted during the parent's terminal illness, most of them were irritable. They usually focused their anger on their inability to be with friends and to maintain their mastery in sports and academics. Girls were often angry because their responsibilities at home greatly exceeded those of their brothers. When guilt was present, it focused on regret about their misbehavior, their anger at the patient, or their desire to separate and be independent at a time when the family needed them to be closer.

The father of 16-year-old Donald was concerned about some dangerous behaviors his son had engaged in on a dare from a classmate. He noticed that Donald had been angrier and had received lower grades since his mother was hospitalized for several months with recurrent cancer. Donald said he had been extremely upset about all the changes that had occurred since his mother's cancer had progressed because he was afraid she would die.

When his mother began having seizures, his father was afraid that something would happen to her if she were alone and insisted that Donald stay with her every afternoon after school. This upset Donald because it meant that he had to give up after-school sports and had little time to see his friends. He said his grades were going down because he couldn't concentrate. Furthermore, he felt guilty because he was angry with his mother because of all the changes her illness had made in their lives.

When the interviewer confronted his father about Donald's inability to manage all these demands, he made alternative arrangements for his wife's care three afternoons a week. As a result, Donald's school performance and feelings about himself improved: "I'm trying to put my life back together and help my mother and hope she gets better. I'm trying to deal with two things at once—help my mom and help myself. It's hard, but I'm toughing it out."

Adolescents tended to be intolerant if their ill parent engaged in clinging behavior. When the patient, usually the mother, became excessively controlling during the terminal phase of the illness, wanting the adolescent to remain close to home or becoming afraid or angry when the adolescent came home late, the patient's behavior provoked the adolescent's resentment, anger, and guilt. At the same time, the adolescent was sad about these changes in the relationship with the ill parent.

Externalizing Behaviors. Several boys reported having problems with alcohol after the parent's diagnosis but before the parent's terminal illness. When they entered counseling or were confronted by family members about the connection between their behavior and the parent's illness, some were able to see the connection and to change their behavior. One 15-year-old stopped skipping school and improved his attitude about completing his homework when he elected to switch from a public to a Catholic high school that was far more structured. A 17-year-old and the older sibling of another adolescent had serious problems with drugs and alcohol at an earlier point in their mothers' illness. They entered a drug treatment center and had recovered by the time the mother's illness became terminal.

Severe school problems, aggressive behaviors, severe regression, and suicidal preoccupations seldom occurred. Most of the adolescents who acted out had experienced problems before their parent's terminal illness, the relationship with the well parent was troubled, and/or there were multiple stresses in the family.

Relationships with Parents, Siblings, and Friends

Previous conflicts between the adolescent and parents, siblings, grandparents, and other extended family members often intensified during the terminal illness. Because the adolescents had the capacity to maintain control, they were likely to become self-critical and contain their anger rather than express it openly at this time. They understood what was happening and tried to help the family.

The conflict between 16-year-old Gayle and her father increased when he returned home after his cancer diagnosis. Although her parents had separated the previous year, her mother agreed to care for her husband when he became ill. Gayle viewed her father as difficult and demanding. She clearly had not resolved the anger she had felt after her parents' separation, but she did not express her feelings openly until after his death.

What was different in this age group was how the adolescents reached out for help from friends and adults—some even reached out to parents. They sought out individuals who had gone through similar experiences. Although some participated in counseling groups, they were more likely to engage in individual counseling relationships, formally or informally.

Death and Family Rituals

The adolescents' more adult reactions and responses were evident at each stage of the parent's illness. As they prepared for the death, they demonstrated advanced cognitive abilities. They were less self-preoccupied than their younger peers were. Helping them to describe their intense emotions in words helped them achieve a measure of relief. They automatically took an active role in the funeral and burial rituals. Although most of them returned to school quickly, they were unable to distract themselves with schoolwork and contacts with peers the way early adolescents were able to do, they could not escape their sorrow.

Impending Death

Most adolescents were told about the parent's probable death in a timely way. Being prepared for the death and undergoing anticipatory grief helped them cope with the period of sustained, intense mourning after the death. Those who were not informed in a timely way tended to experience more difficult mourning.

Discussing the impending death was so expected that failing to do so reflected strong denial on the patient's or surviving parent's part, the parents' complete self-absorption, or the parents' unrealistic thinking about the developmental needs of 15- to 17-year-olds. Parents who were struggling with such avoidance were often undergoing a pathological grief process related to their own earlier losses. In most situations, only after the patient died was the surviving parent able to understand fully the impact of the earlier loss on their own ability to communicate with their children.

Heather's father struggled with telling her about her mother's advancing cancer for a number of reasons. His wife couldn't accept her own impending death: She worked full time until five weeks before she died, and adamantly refused to go to a hospice. She also refused to obtain a handicap sign for her car and was reluctant to use the word cancer when talking with Heather until the interviewer challenged her denial.

In addition, Heather's father had lost his own mother when he was 18 years old and said, "A lot of questions were unanswered at that time." Although he had been with his mother when she died and was the family member who informed relatives about her death, he didn't know the cause of her death. This experience had been extremely difficult and painful for him; thus, he unconsciously treated Heather the way he had been treated.

Although Heather's father's failure to inform her in a timely way created conflict, his ability to recognize his problem and change his pattern of communicating with her after his wife died contributed to Heather's improved school performance and reduced her intense sibling rivalry. She and her father developed open communication and a more satisfactory parent-child relationship.

Saying Good-bye

Adolescents visited the patient in the hospital or hospice more consistently than early adolescents did. They were able to deal with the patient's symptoms and assumed responsibility for maintaining contact. However, parents still needed to let the adolescent know when it was time to say good bye. Most parents appropriately did not protect the adolescent from the reality that the death was imminent.

Sixteen-year-old Greg knew that his mother's cancer had spread to her brain and spine. He visited her four times a week when she was in the hospice. The night before she died, his brother paged him at work and said she would not make it through the night. "We were up most of the night. The next morning she was gone. My father woke me up. He was crying. It was a hard way to wake up, and I was in shock. I just sat there and thought for awhile about the good and bad times we had had. The good times were when I was small and we went to the park, bowling, or to the movies. The bad times were when she had to get me out of trouble." Greg's father, Greg, and Greg's two older brothers went to the hospice to view the body and say their good byes. Then they left to make funeral and burial arrangements.

Brendan was devastated when his father died. As the eldest child in the family, he also struggled with feelings of responsibility for his siblings. All the children had visited their father, who was conscious and aware of them, to say good bye. Brendan and one brother remained at the hospice until late at night. Brendan's mother and his father's sister then took over the vigil and were with his father when he died.

Scott, his mother, and his sister made an audiotape with his father the night before his father died. His mother asked the questions prepared by the two adolescents. She later said she believed that her husband had expressed all the feelings he wanted to express before he died.

Telling adolescents about their parent's death was easier because they understood the situation better than younger adolescents did and were able to control their emotions better. Most of them cried and a few screamed, but very few claimed to be surprised. Some adolescents participated in the patient's care during the final days. They struggled most with appropriate ways of expressing their emotions and were more comfortable helping plan the funeral and deciding how they would participate. It was helpful to talk with their surviving parent and other adults about what had happened and how they felt. Many had already made contact during the terminal illness with a friend's parent or another adult who had had cancer or whose parent had died of cancer, and they returned to this person for solace. In addition, most spoke with a close friend or a girlfriend or boyfriend.

Adolescents' ambivalence about new chores and their anger about all the changes in family life diminished considerably as their parent's deteriorating condition became clear. Although they expressed anger and irritation, they rarely engaged in intense sibling rivalry or in conflicts with parents because they recognized the patient's fragility.

> Brian had endured an abusive relationship with his father. His mother and two siblings had acknowledged that his father was a different person at work and at home, which confirmed the father's abusive behavior at home and alleviated any guilt Brian may have felt after the death. Brian felt he said his good-byes to his father and was at peace with him when he died. His father was given a hero's funeral by his colleagues, and Brian asked his mother if he was expected to cry during the funeral. However, he felt good about the public recognition of his father's positive attributes and was pleased when his mother gave him a special gift his father had left for him.

Funeral and Burial Rituals

All the adolescents attended their parents' funerals. Many played an active role, and most went to the cemetery for the burial. They felt a keen sense of responsibility to honor the parent's life and a keen sense of responsibility for the surviving parent, the family, and themselves. They tried to convey what the parent had meant to them and to express their sorrow. Unlike their younger peers, most of them remained at the wake or sat Shiva as long as it lasted. Whereas many early adolescents avoided the intense sadness of the burial, their older peers looked for ways to control or express their feelings by participating in that ritual. Many parents helped their adolescent compose a eulogy and they described details of the funeral. One mother asked her two sons whether the burial should be delayed so that it would not occur on the younger son's birthday. They mutually agreed to postpone the burial. Some adolescents wrote poems to be read or to be printed in the program. Most adolescent boys were pallbearers.

Most of the adolescents were automatically included as an important part of the proceedings. If they were not, the usual reason was that the surviving parents were too overwhelmed by or involved in their own feelings to consider the adolescents' need to express their grief actively in this way.

The funerals for many parents were large, elaborate affairs that included many tributes to the young parent's life. This was extremely important to adolescents, who valued the idealization of their parent. When the relationship between the adolescent and the dead parent had been a severely conflicted or abusive one, the adolescent felt that the homage paid to their parent helped them remember the public image of the "good" parent more powerfully than the personal image of the painful and destructive parent. The outpouring of support from the community also was reassuring because the adolescents appreciated the fact that people cared for the family and wanted to help.

Support During the Early Mourning Period

The adolescents' more adult mourning process began soon after the parent's death, and the intensity of their grief often overwhelmed them. As Scott said: "The first week wasn't that bad, but the second and the third week, I began to realize he was really gone for good." This timing seemed to reflect what many adolescents experienced—an initial brief period of numbness followed by intense mourning. Unlike early adolescents, these adolescents were generally not interested in placing objects in the coffin to accompany the parent on his or her journey. Although they received some of the parent's possessions, most of them did not feel an urgent need for these transitional objects. Instead, they were preoccupied with mourning the internalized parent.

They thought about what the parent had meant to them and how difficult it would be to replace some of the parent's functions now and in the future. Their mourning included integrating past, present, and future.

Greg said that his family got mad at his girlfriend during the funeral because she would not leave him alone. However, he said he had asked her, "When my mother dies, I don't want you to leave me. I ignored their anger." When he thought about drinking (a previous problem), she kept him on track. "I miss my mother bossing me around, telling me to get my act together. My father does that some now." Greg described how his father and his older brother got him to stop drinking so much. He thought that some of his drinking may have reflected his anger toward his mother because she had been ill for so many years: "a revenge." He was clearly looking for people who could help him "keep my act together."

At his father's funeral, Scott said that although his father was his buddy, he was his Dad first. He was glad he saw his father's body at the wake because he thought his father looked perfect. About 200 people came to the wake, and there was a lot of crying. Scott was pleased to see that his entire family was present; he had not seen many of the family members for a long time. He did not know what to say to people or exactly how to react. But his best friend was there because Scott had asked him to come. "That helped—a lot."

Fifteen-year-old Lisa felt good about her father's funeral service. Old family friends spoke. She felt the loss of her father most intensely when she had arguments with her brother because her father had come to her aid at such times. Her family was bi-racial and conflicts arose with her father's relatives about the funeral and the religious differences. She remembered that her father used to handle these conflicts well. She said she had become more cautious about choosing friends since his death. Although she participated in activities, she felt shy and private. She did have one special teacher who, as an assignment, asked the class to write down questions for which there were no answers. He made this assignment the week after Lisa's father died. He praised her response, which made her feel good. Her father had made her feel special, and she missed his advocacy and was having a difficult time finding another advocate.

Bereavement and Reconstitution

Adolescents had three major tasks during the period of bereavement and reconstitution: working through the pain of mourning, renegotiating a relationship with both the dead parent and the surviving parent, and establishing relationships outside the family in preparation for greater independence and leaving home. Accomplishing all three at the same time presented a formidable challenge to the adolescent and the surviving parent.

Mourning

The adolescent's mourning continued well into the bereavement and reconstitution stage. Although more brief than the surviving parent's mourning, the intensity, persistence, and the more adult, uncontrollable quality of the adolescent's grief made this the period during which the adolescent's productivity and emotional equilibrium were affected the most.

The adolescents demonstrated a broader range of affects and behaviors as part of their mourning than did their younger peers. Their affects included sustained and profound sadness, crying, anger, bitterness, depressed mood with sleep disturbances, and a sense of helplessness and of being overwhelmed.

Scott described how he watched through his tears as they wrapped his father's body after the death. Everyone on the block where they lived came to their house. Scott went to bed early that night and remembers waking up exhausted about 1 A.M. He looked into his father's room and kept looking in whenever he woke up for the next three weeks. In retrospect, he thought that the first week wasn't that bad, but his grief kept increasing over the next several weeks.

Six months after her father's death, 15-year-old Jennifer said she had crying jags at home and even at school. She also was having some difficulty falling asleep at night because she could not stop thinking about her father. She asked her school to say a special mass for him. She also wanted to go to the cemetery more often.

Because most adolescents were unable to distract themselves with school, sports, and other activities, they tended to experience a decline in all these areas after the parent's death.

Jimmie was worried about his pitching in baseball. Pitching had always come naturally to him. Since his father's death, however, he was having more trouble with it and was no longer on the team's starting roster. However, he maintained his functioning at school and in other areas. His mother believed that his distress might be related to his close involvement with his father concerning baseball and that Jimmie missed his father, especially now that he couldn't consult his father about his pitching.

Typically, surviving parents worried about their adolescent's intense, persistent grief. Whereas many surviving parents of early adolescents complained about their child's apparent callousness and lack of concern, the parents of middle adolescents rarely expressed such complaints. Many of these parents helped their adolescents by encouraging them to express troubling emotions in words as a way of attaining some relief. They also turned to trusted friends, other adults, and, occasionally, siblings for support. Some parents also suggested professional counseling for the adolescents at this time.

The adolescents also demonstrated other behaviors that were less clearly recognizable as grief. These included externalizing behaviors such as transient episodes of drinking, bouts of anger, arguments with parents, and testing limits by demanding more time away from home with friends, girlfriends, or boyfriends. These behaviors seemed to be a mixture of mourning, reactions to the turmoil involved in reconstituting the family, and the process of establishing independence and separation under adverse circumstances. Although the adolescents demonstrated a basic sense of responsibility and empathy, they disregarded their parent's needs on occasion and refused to do chores. Another confusing dynamic was that they sometimes displaced their anger at the dead parent on the surviving parent.

Visiting the Grave

Most of the adolescents visited the gravesite, sometimes with the surviving parent but often alone. They described wanting to be alone, to think about and talk with the dead parent, and grieve in their own way. This behavior differed from the behavior of early adolescents, who were usually reluctant to visit the cemetery for some time and then usually visited it with the surviving parent. For the adolescent, visiting the grave provided a sense of closeness to the dead parent and some solace for their grief.

Sixteen-year-old Brendan made an urgent call to his mother during her session with the interviewer a few weeks after his father's death. He was in tears and wanted her to take him to the cemetery because he wanted to 'see' his father. Brendan was so distressed that she complied with his request. Subsequent grief counseling on an individual basis helped Brendan understand his mourning process better and develop ways of feeling more in control.

Dreams

Adolescents' dreams were more complex than those of early adolescents. Whereas the dreams of younger adolescents reflected fulfillment of the wish that the parent was still alive, the dreams of middle adolescents concerned separation, ambivalence toward the dead parent, and feelings of guilt.

Heather dreamed a lot about her mother after she died. Her mother had become controlling of Heather as she was dying. She seemed to be desperately trying to hold on to her own life through holding on to Heather. She clung by asking repetitive, intrusive questions. Although her husband tried to intervene, her fear was so great that she couldn't hear him. After her mother died, Heather was relieved that her mother was no longer in pain and realized that her mother had hidden the extent of her distress from the family while she was dying. The last time Heather had gone shopping with her mother, just two weeks before her death, her mother had to sit down in every store they were in. In one dream, Heather was standing in a theater line with her friend and her mother, and her mother said the embalming fluid made her feel better. However, Heather was unable to get a ticket for her mother, who became angry with her about this. In another dream, Heather had a birthday party with all her friends. Although her mother was there, her friends didn't know who her mother was, so her mother got up and left. "I feel guilty because I had an attitude problem at the end," Heather said. "I don't know why, but I think she would understand." Heather said she had a lot of confidence in her father. He was much less intrusive than her mother had been and supported her growing independence.

Bill, age 17, integrated the experience of his father's illness and death into the personal statement on his college application in an inventive way. He ended the application by writing about his determination to grow from the experience and to move on the way his father would have wanted him to. A few days after his father died, Bill dreamed that he heard his father in bed moaning, then getting up and going into the kitchen to make pancakes (as he had done on weekends). Then Bill woke up and thought, "Somehow, I knew my father was dead and it was just so sad to have to accept that."

Meaning of the Loss

Although by the time of the final interview most adolescents remained too involved in a sense of the tragedy, injustice, and unfairness to derive a positive meaning from their parent's death, a few did.

As John said: "The disease has helped me understand what it's like to help someone go through this. I don't think it's a good idea to rebel at this time. It feels good to help somebody. What's the use of fighting or doing something bad? It just causes more problems. What you are trying to do throughout life is get rid of your problems or control your problems."

Bill described his grief as follows: "Inside, I feel so much pain that I can't come to terms with my dad's death. I think: he's gone; he won't see me graduate, go to college, get my first job, get married." Then he added: "Dad would be disappointed in me if I ruined the rest of my life by not living my own life."

Many adolescents left for college within a year or two after their parent died. This transition reawakened many of their feelings about the death. They were ambivalent, glad to be moving on to a new stage in their lives and to a place that did not have the negative reminders of the death, but feeling guilty about leaving their grieving parent and, sometimes, about leaving younger siblings. Primarily, however, they seemed apprehensive about their ability to succeed. They had more self-doubt than other graduating seniors who were not bereaved, and experienced renewed questions about the meaning of the parent's life and death in their future.

Reactivated mourning, although common, was not universal. For some adolescents, leaving home for college seemed to be an effective reprieve and a distraction.

> Jessica described a more adult mourning after her father died. She had sleeping difficulties, often cried, and her thoughts raced. She prayed for her father and attended a bereavement group. Her mother's preoccupation with the fear that Jessica would get married too young (as the mother had done after her own father died) also was difficult for Jessica. As Jessica prepared to leave for college, her functioning and sleeping problems improved, and she said she was feeling better and not thinking as much about her father's death. Although her mother was ambivalent about the fact that Jessica was going away to college, Jessica looked forward to it as an important step toward independence. She and her mother had often talked about their relationship, and her mother understood that her own experience made her less objective about Jessica. As a result, her mother sought counseling to understand the impact of her own father's death.

Factors that Complicated the Mourning Process

Extraneous factors complicated, or even derailed, the normal mourning process. Events that affected the adolescent's self-esteem were especially difficult during the process of early mourning.

> Diane was overwhelmed by the fact that her father had died only four months after the diagnosis. Their relationship had been a close one. They had played tennis regularly, and he was a lot of fun. Her mother, a chronic worrier, was especially apprehensive about Diane's adjustment to the death because a relative's two children were recently hospitalized for depression after their parents' divorce, and she was afraid that Diane would become depressed.
>
> Diane's mourning appeared to be proceeding normally. After her grades declined briefly, they improved. Although her feelings were relatively guarded, they did not appear to interfere with her functioning. Diane wondered what it would be like growing up without her father. She missed him, dreamed about him, and worried about celebrating holidays without him.
>
> Shortly after her father died, Diane's boyfriend and her best girlfriend began dating, and Diane felt terribly betrayed. She began to sleep regularly with her mother, attributing this to her need for the air conditioner in her mother's room because of her allergies. She worried about her grandfather's

health and cried when reminded of her father. She said she felt that she was less acceptable without her father. Although her mother was worried and supportive, she didn't urge her daughter to function more independently. When Diane was evaluated 14 months after the death, she was suffering from increasingly disruptive phobias. She was afraid of heights, of her mother becoming ill, of being alone in the house at night, of being alone with no one to take care of her. She also had lost a considerable amount of weight.

The confluence of 'small stressors' such as these on top of the 'large stressor' (the parent's death) was especially difficult.

Renegotiating the Relationship with the Parents

After their parent's death, the adolescents renegotiated their relationship, not only with the surviving parent, but, through the bereavement experience, with the dead parent as well.

The adolescents needed to renegotiate a relationship with the surviving parent as a single parent. This process was different for boys and for girls and with fathers and mothers.

The process of renegotiation seemed to be less complicated for boys than for girls. After the worst period of grief ended, boys negotiated their independence, autonomy, and pursuit of schoolwork, activities, and friendships. When the mother was the surviving parent, she was likely to have arguments with her son about his not being home enough or about her being too intrusive, curbing his independence too much, or setting new limits on his use of the family car. When the father was the surviving parent, sons often tested limits. They also displaced anger onto the surviving parent.

> After his mother died, 16-year-old John went shopping for school clothes with his father Roberto. Roberto looked forward to this event as a pleasant time to be together with his son. However, it did not turn out that way. John became frustrated and angry with his father because his father did not understand current fashions and could not help him select colors and styles that helped him fit with the group and made him look good the way his mother had done.

More difficult in father-son dyads was the fathers' limited understanding of the sons' dependency needs and the intensity of the sons' mourning. The competitive nature of their relationship also interfered with emotional sharing and often required negotiation, especially regarding father's dating.

Although issues of control, of limit setting, and curbing excessive independence were important factors with girls, other, more muted issues, emerged. Many parents had come to rely on their older daughters during the patient's terminal illness. As single parents who were struggling with their own grief, they tended to turn to these daughters for comfort and support. As a result, the parent-child boundaries and roles became blurred at times. This pattern was more typical when mother-daughter dyads were involved. In some situations, the surviving parent, usually the father, was unable or unwilling to establish an empathic and caring relationship with his adolescent daughter. These fathers either had been emotionally distant before the death or became so in reaction to the death, and buried themselves in their work or remarried quickly.

Changing the Relationship With the Dead Parent

Adolescents automatically thought about and continued to internalize their past relationship with the dead parent, what the parent had expected of them, and how they might live up to those expectations in the future. Because they were better able than early adolescents to comprehend the enduring consequences of the loss over time, their grief was more painful.

Adolescents also mourned a broader range of the parent's roles and characteristics than did early adolescents. Adolescents talked about the parent as their "buddy"—the one who set limits, "helped me keep my act together," knew how to mediate conflicts; who provided the "lightness" and humor in the family; the strong one, the calm one, "the one who makes me feel special." Unique to adolescents this age was their yearning for the parent as "believer" in their independence, in their capacity to succeed on their own.

Unlike early adolescents, who desperately wanted to wear the dead parent's clothing, the adolescents did not. Rather than emulate the dead parent, they appeared to be more concerned about becoming the person the parent wanted them to be, about living up to the parent's expectations—expectations that were overwhelming at times. Rather than look for a substitute for the dead parent, as early adolescents tended to do, mid-adolescents seemed to need time to mourn. Then they turned their attention to becoming the person they believed their parent valued.

Understanding the dead parent's legacy and expectations for the adolescent was an important task.

Seventeen-year-old Louis was extremely pleased when he and his younger brother played in a baseball game as pitcher and catcher because his father had told him that having his sons play baseball together was his dream.

William spoke of his father's legacy as follows: "Dad gave me his talent and love for sports, music, reading, writing; he gave me his sense of humor." He explained that although his father's death was the worst thing that had ever happened to him, he found that it helped him define his most important value—to live his own life rather than reach for goals just to please others.

Even when the adolescent's relationship with the dead parent had been a hostile one, it was still possible to construct a positive legacy. For example, although Brian's father had been extremely abusive, the fact that his mother acknowledged this and blamed his father was helpful.

For a few adolescents, a positive outcome such as Brian's was more difficult because the reality of the relationship with the surviving parent was so problematic they could not fulfill the dead parent's dream.

Susan, age 16, desperately wanted to graduate from high school as her mother had requested. Her mother had been Susan's strong advocate with her father, a distant, hostile man. After her mother died, Susan's father became increasingly distant and verbally abusive. Susan began dating a divorced man who was 10 years older than she was and eventually ran away with him.

After the parent's death, adolescents also became concerned about their genetic vulnerability to cancer. This was especially true when several family members had the same disease. Discussing the matter with an expert was extremely helpful in clarifying facts and in identifying possible preventive care. Failing to discuss this problem, which families often did, left adolescents alone with their questions and anxieties.

As she was preparing for college, 17-year-old Carolyn, the eldest child in the family, began to worry about her own vulnerability to cancer, which had killed her mother and grandmother. She began feeling profound sadness, had difficulty sleeping, and wished she could be with her mother.

For a number of children, the burden of high expectations was sometimes overwhelming in the context of the parent's death. Two boys with strong, successful fathers were overwhelmed by the sense of responsibility and the fear that they could not succeed in the way their father had wanted or expected them to.

Preparation for Independent Living

Separation is another developmental task that presents its own problems to adolescents who have lost a parent to cancer. Because they understood the surviving parent's loneliness and need for closeness, they often felt guilty about wanting to separate. They worried about how the surviving parent would manage when they were out on their own. They revealed their worry and guilt in their muted discussion about going to college and their lack of visible excitement, expectation, and enthusiasm. Boys, in particular, went through a period of exaggerated independence and conflicts with their surviving parent over the time they spent away from home. A few adolescents, such as Diane, went through a period of greater dependence and fear of separation. The conflict between these different needs resulted in a cauldron of emotions, including frustration, disappointment, anger, and sadness.

RECOMMENDATIONS FOR PROFESSIONALS AND CAREGIVERS

Terminal Illness

1. *Provide the adolescent with information about the patient's illness and prognosis as soon as possible.* It is especially helpful if the patient can speak directly to the adolescent about the illness.

2. *Anticipate some temporary reduction in the adolescent's ability to function well.* This situation may occur regarding school, athletics, or after-school activities.

3. *Recognize additional stressors, such as a change of school or conflict with peers.* Although adolescents can cope with many stresses, they can be overwhelmed by an accumulation of stresses, which prevent them from being able to deal with each stressor, one at a time.

4. *Keep in mind that adolescents are able think about the future in relation to the present* Initiate a discussion about how their future plans will be affected by the present situation and provide realistic reassurance.

5. *Be alert to adolescents' fears about their own vulnerability to cancer.* If several family members have had cancer, adolescents may wonder whether they are genetically vulnerable to the disease. (They usually express this concern after the parent's death.) Thus, surviving parents should discuss the matter with their adolescent if they feel knowledgeable about the subject. If they do not feel knowledgeable, they can ask the patient's oncologist or another trained professional to discuss hereditary and other sources of cancer. Adolescents find that these discussions reduce their anxiety enormously.

6. *Discuss specific ways that the adolescent can be helpful during the parent's terminal illness.* Adolescents are more likely to engage in forms of help that are consistent with their own interests and proclivities.

7. *Consider counseling for the adolescent who exhibits troubling behavior.* Such behavior may include serve or prolonged anger, sadness, or depression, potentially destructive acting-out such as substance abuse, physical aggression, or extreme changes in weight; or severe problems with peers. In addition, a preexisting learning disability, physical illness, or mental illness is likely to be exacerbated by severe psychological stress. Some of these problems may occur before, some after the death. Early therapeutic interventions can be extended into the even more stressful period of mourning after the death. Adolescents who have had previous counseling may welcome opportunities to reengage with a counselor concerning the stress of the parent's illness.

8. *Parents may benefit from professional evaluation if they are experiencing difficulty in discussing the parent's probable death with their adolescent.* Such inhibition may be related to more recent illnesses and stresses, early childhood losses of their own, pre-existing psychological problems, or intense fears of not being able to manage after the patient dies.

Death and Family Rituals

1. *Inform the adolescent about the parent's impending death soon enough and in enough detail to permit them to prepare to say good bye.*

2. *Identify an active role for the adolescent during the funeral and burial.* Active participation in the funeral and burial rituals was often helpful for adolescents. Roles they commonly assume include writing a poem for someone else to read at the funeral, writing and delivering a eulogy, playing music, or being a pallbearer.

3. *Recognize the importance of the adolescent's need to idealize the dead parent.* This need was as important to adolescents as it was to younger children. The surviving parent's confirmation of the dead parent's negative characteristics was also important, especially if the dead parent was abusive or if the relationship was severely conflictual, because it facilitated the adolescent's expressing both negative and positive feelings with reduced guilt.

4. *Communicate with the school.* Acknowledgment of the death and expressions of sorrow by friends, peers, and school personnel are enormously supportive to adolescents. The surviving parent should make certain that these people are informed appropriately after discussing the matter with the adolescent. Adolescents easily misinterpret lack of participation by peers as a rejection.

5. *Anticipate the adolescent's intense mourning and facilitate expression of these feelings.* Encouraging them to express their feelings; explaining the nature of the grief process can be helpful.

6. *Select appropriate mementos and clothing belonging to the dead parent.* Although the adolescent's need to have possessions that belonged to the dead parent is less urgent than that of early adolescents, they should have the option of selecting possessions that are meaningful to them. When one 16-year-old refused to take any of her dead mother's jewelry, her father told her that he would put it away for her until she had had more time to consider what she wanted to do.

7. *Use available peer group and individual professional counseling.* Adolescents benefited from participating in peer, informal, and formal counseling experiences.

Bereavement and Reconstitution

1. *Normalize the mourning process.* Because their grief is more adult, adolescents need specific education about the nature of their mourning process to cope more effectively with the work of mourning. Although most adolescents welcomed talking with the surviving parent, another trusted adult, or friends, they especially appreciated receiving bereavement counseling and educational services. Keep in mind that adolescents who don't recognize the symptoms of grief may become extremely frightened about what they are experiencing.

2. *Communicate with the adolescent's teachers and other school personnel.* Although most schools are now better informed about children's mourning, the surviving parent should ensure that school personnel have been notified about the death and are aware of the adolescent's need to mourn. School personnel may need to be reminded that a marked temporary change in performance can occur.

3. *Discuss the adolescent's plans for the future.* Adolescents may have misconceptions of how their future plans and opportunities will be affected by the parent's death.

4. *Anticipate conflict regarding family responsibilities and independence.* Parents are often provoked by their adolescent's anger and withdrawal, especially if the adolescent refuses to help with household chores or to be supportive of the surviving parent's grief. These behaviors reflect the adolescent's mourning process and ambivalence about separation. Such conflicts were alleviated by negotiation of clearer limits and clarification of future plans.

5. *Support the adolescent's need for independence and separation.* Although surviving parents often have difficulty encouraging their adolescent's continued movement away from the family at a time when they themselves feel the need for support, they need to recognize the necessity for such encouragement. Provide unqualified support for the adolescent's ability to function independently.

6. *Recognize the adolescent's potential for anger if the surviving parent begins dating early.* Discussing the desire to date with adolescents ahead of time helps to prepare them for that actuality and encourages them to express their thoughts and feelings about this change in the family's composition.

7. *Surviving parents should seek therapy if they have unresolved previous losses or are encountering unusual conflict with their adolescent.* Supporting the adolescent's independence under these adverse circumstances can be especially challenging.

8. *Identify positive aspects of the parent's legacy to the adolescent.* This can include a broad array of attributes of the dead parent that the adolescent admired, gifts left for them, and their dreams for the adolescent. Clarify positive outcomes such as a deepening understanding of self and others and strengthened capacity for coping

9. *Refer the adolescent with severe symptoms for evaluation.* Adolescents who have symptoms such as the following should be referred for professional evaluation: problems functioning in school; phobias; eating problems; severe withdrawal from peers, teachers, and family; symptoms of depression, including suicidal thinking; potentially destructive acting out such as abuse of alcohol or other substances; accidents; and severe aggression. In the context of a parent's death, such symptoms are potentially more threatening to the adolescent's well being.

14

❦

Children 15–17 Years of Age

Narratives

The two narratives in this chapter illustrate how adolescents experience more adult mourning. In the first, a 15-year-old boy and his 16-year-old sister confront the death of their mother. They have a 13-year-old sister as well. What can be observed are differences between the early and the mid-adolescents in the timing of their most intense mourning, differences in their symptoms, and their ability to recover after a few months of intense grief. In the second narrative, a 16-year-old girl loses her beloved father and tries to negotiate a new relationship with her mother, who was herself in the midst of her own troubled mourning.

Both stories illustrate major features of adolescents who face a parent's death: allocentric thinking fluctuating with self-centeredness, the presence of anticipatory grief, the evolution of adult mourning, elaboration of thinking made possible by cognitive advances, the crucial role of supportive peers, the role of the legacy, the renegotiation of the relationship with the surviving parent, and the struggle to separate in the midst of loss. The intention of these narratives is to complement the previous chapter, which described the range of responses of the 36 15- to 17-year-old adolescents, with a more detailed description of the complexity of the interactions within the family system, which also provides a clearer perspective of change over time. The characteristics that define the different outcomes when the adolescents were last seen 8 to 14 months after the parent's death are discussed at the end of this chapter.

FATHER, 16- AND 13-YEAR-OLD DAUGHTERS AND A 15-YEAR-OLD SON

"Your Mother Never Gave Up, and You Can't Either!"

Background

It seemed natural that Vincent and Elizabeth would marry. Both came from large, working-class Catholic families; both excelled at athletics in high school, where they met, and both worked to support their families. Both had large extended families in the neighborhood who dominated the local construction trade and the police and fire departments. Construction was a natural job for Vincent. He worked for one construction company during the week, and was able to do freelance work on weekends for his cousin's company. Elizabeth was the administrator-bookkeeper at another cousin's company.

Savings from their combined salaries made it possible for them to buy their own home before their first child, Lisa, was born. Bruce came a year later, then Megan three years after that. Elizabeth remained home with the children until Megan entered first grade. Then she began working as an administrative assistant. Both Vincent and Elizabeth advanced in their positions, in part because of their natural intelligence and high energy, in part because of their outgoing, social dispositions. Vincent's great sense of humor was an asset not only on the job and in contacts with customers but also at home with his children. The Romanos were viewed as strict but caring parents who knew what their children were doing and where they were. Family life was good and evolved around work, school, church, child-care, and constant contact with many members of the extended family who lived in the surrounding neighborhoods.

Vincent's and Elizabeth's approaches to parenting were complementary. Elizabeth tended to be strict, particularly with Lisa, with whom she had some conflict. If the truth be told, Lisa's disposition was very much like her mother's: assertive, responsible, independent, and determined to do the best she could, but she was also stubborn. Vincent deferred to Elizabeth "in order to keep the peace." He thought he could be more effective by reaching out to Lisa and developing his own relationship with her rather than arguing with his wife over the rules. It was a well-known family secret that he often bent the rules in the children's direction.

Illness

Two years before her death, Elizabeth found a small lump in her breast that the doctor initially believed was a cyst, but the biopsy proved otherwise. Elizabeth was stunned and terrified by the cancer diagnosis but was not completely surprised. Her mother had been diagnosed with breast cancer a year before, and her grandmother had died of the disease. Her physician said a good treatment was available, and she should be optimistic about her prognosis. Her initial approach to her illness was characteristic of her: "Give me the facts and begin the treatment so that we can get on with normal living."

Vincent and Elizabeth told the children about the diagnosis and the upcoming treatment in a matter-of-fact and optimistic way because both believed that all three children were old enough to know. Treatment would begin, and they would all be hopeful that it would be effective. Life would proceed as if nothing had changed. What was uncharacteristic was that both Elizabeth and Bruce, who was then 13 years old, felt strongly that the family should keep her diagnosis and treatment to themselves. Elizabeth did not want a lot of sympathetic telephone calls. Although Vincent did not agree, he felt that the decision was

"Elizabeth's call." Thus, the family maintained the secret for two years. This became a problem, however, as Elizabeth's symptoms progressed.

Terminal Illness

When Elizabeth began seeing the interviewer, she was receiving experimental treatment in a neighboring state, where she remained one out of four weeks each month. She had high hopes for its success, although her disease had metastasized to her lymph nodes and brain. She cooked food ahead for the week she was away and chatted regularly with the children on the telephone. Vincent called her every evening when all the children were home to hear about her current condition. The children increasingly asked: "Why isn't the medicine working? Why is Mom coming home later than she planned?" When interviewed, the children described their mother as increasingly moody, contentious, and tearful. Because they thought she was upset with them, they responded by feeling angry, hurt, and guilty. They were unaware that her brain metastases could cause such symptoms.

Lisa was 16 years old and was steeped in her academic work. She received As and Bs in her honors classes, yet she worried unnecessarily that she was not doing well enough. Neither her mother's nor her teachers' reassurance alleviated her strong need to achieve. She ran track, was a cheerleader, and had many friends who often appeared at the house on weekends. Lisa felt that her relationship with her mother had always been strained. The usual renegotiation of the mother-daughter relationship in adolescence had not really taken place because Elizabeth's anxiety about her disease and her efforts to keep things normal and deal with her treatment had made her more distant and less emotionally available. In response, Lisa had become more independent. Now they argued over her messiness and her curfew hour. Lisa thought her mother tended to "take out her moods" on her, and she was distressed about this. Her father described her as stubborn sometimes but socially skilled, capable, and responsible. Elizabeth was annoyed about Lisa's unwillingness to help with the housework. Vincent was annoyed about both Lisa's and Bruce's failure to offer to help their mother when she was so sick: "I don't think the kids realize that things are not status quo." However, the parents were desperately trying to act as if nothing was different. The interviewer asked them if they had told the children that things were not "status quo." Clearly, they had not.

Lisa had two best friends and desperately wanted to talk with them about what was happening to her mother. She also thought that her brother needed to talk with his friends. Lisa felt close to her father, but she worried about him. She also worried about her younger sister, who was close to her mother. "How will Megan and Dad manage if Mom dies?" Clearly, Lisa had anticipated her mother's death and was feeling sad and worried.

Bruce was an engaging, well-liked, bright 15-year-old who was far more interested in athletics than academics. He was a champion wrestler, but he also played soccer, football, and basketball. He maintained his grades, but did so, according to his mother, with a limited amount of studying. Vincent and Elizabeth usually attended his sports events. Bruce had Vincent's sense of humor, and they often engaged in entertaining banter. A neighbor commented to Elizabeth that "Bruce loves Vincent. I watch how he follows him around in the yard." Because Bruce tended to keep his feelings to himself, he sometimes thought he was going crazy over his mother's illness. He wanted to stay away from her because of her moodiness, but felt guilty about avoiding her. Elizabeth found a book about cancer and the family, gave it to him, and noticed that he read it frequently.

Megan, the 13-year-old, was everyone's "good child." She received good grades, had many friends, was neat and kept her room clean, and did not challenge limits. As Vincent put it, "Megan always got a lot more yes's than Lisa did." Megan also was close to her mother's sister, Donna, whom she saw several times a week. Megan said she felt bad about her mother's moods and was afraid that she might be responsible for them in some way. She felt guilty about her mother's illness and worried about what was going to happen next. She thought maybe she wasn't good enough or wasn't helping enough. Rather than expressing her anger about her mother's inevitable withdrawal, Megan seemed to be turning the anger inward.

After their first meeting with the interviewer, Elizabeth and Vincent gave the children permission to talk with their friends about her cancer. Vincent led the way by talking with his colleagues at work about her illness and reported to the family that no longer having to make up excuses for some of his absences from work was a big relief. Lisa and Bruce immediately begin talking about the illness with their best friends. Elizabeth reported that they both seemed relieved. Megan, however, was hesitant: "I just don't know how to start." Bruce tried to help her by explaining that it was not easy to tell your friends until you "got into it. Starting is the hardest part." Megan's friends were a little hurt because she had not told them sooner, since Lisa had already told her friends and the news had spread. Elizabeth told the interviewer that after Megan began discussing the disease with her friends, it was easier for her to talk about it in the family.

During the summer, the children helped more around the house in response to Elizabeth's severe exhaustion after her last treatment. To Vincent's relief, Elizabeth finally quit working and went on disability. Lisa continued to test her father's limit setting concerning her curfew. When Vincent grounded her for a couple of days, she seemed to respond. When Bruce tested his father by leaving things lying around the house, Vincent blew up and Bruce improved—for a while. Vincent explained his strategy as follows: "I try not to let things get out of control, but I also laugh with the kids. Sometimes I realize I am being grumpy. They make me realize I have to lighten up a little." Elizabeth also tried to temporize and maintain her perspective by saying that their children tested limits in small ways compared with other children she knew about. Both parents clearly enjoyed their adolescent children and listened to them.

The children's almost frenetic schedules continued throughout the summer. Even Megan was gone a lot, and Elizabeth missed her. She was taking track and was being a social butterfly. The extent of the children's activities seemed to reflect an effort to avoid the worrisome sight of their mother sleeping on the couch, her fatigue, her cough, and her discomfort. As summer continued, the children helped out even more when they came home. Opening up communication with the children seemed to have helped them to perceive their mother's frailty. However, Bruce did not want his friends to see her without her wig, which she often took off in the house because it was hot and hard to wear when she was cooking. With good humor, he and his mother worked out a system: He would ring the front doorbell three times when he brought friends home so she could put on her wig. Elizabeth understood his age-appropriate concerns about the importance of appearances.

Death and Family Rituals

The end of the summer was complicated further by the advancing breast cancer of Elizabeth's mother, who finally died after a few weeks of hospitalization. Although her death was expected, the timing was traumatic for the entire family. The family held a wake for her, and Vincent tried to help his father-in-law make arrangements for his wife's funeral and burial.

At this point, Elizabeth was obviously in a great deal of pain and her cough had become worse. When she was admitted to the hospital for treatment of what she believed was pneumonia, Vincent realized that she was dying. He stayed with her during the day and had the children visit her at different times. One nurse urged him to get some rest. He looked exhausted and admitted that he was not sleeping. One Saturday morning, he and all three children visited Elizabeth. When they went home, Vincent fell asleep, Megan stayed around the house, and Bruce and Lisa visited friends. At 2 o'clock in the afternoon, the hospital called, and Megan and Vincent went to the hospital. Fifteen minutes after they arrived, Elizabeth died. Bruce and Lisa, Elizabeth's father, and her two sisters arrived about 20 minutes later. Lisa went in to view the body with one aunt, and Bruce went in with his other aunt.

Vincent was in shock and only six months later was he able to reflect on how he had handled the children during those difficult early moments. "Was enough done or was enough said to them in the hospital? Did I do the right thing? I hope I didn't ignore them. You think: Did you have your arm around the shoulder at the right time? Lisa and Bruce were with their aunts. I just felt so bad. That must have been such a terrible thing for them to go through. I don't even remember what happened on the car ride home."

The children attended the two-day wake and felt supported by the huge crowd of people that included many of their friends. Megan was pleased that her mother's face was made up and that she looked so much better than she had looked in the hospital. Because Elizabeth had been careful not to talk about the pain and discomfort she experienced, the children had not expected her to die when she did.

When the children returned to school, their lives began to have some semblance of normalcy and order again. Vincent was occupied with burial, financial, and other death-related arrangements. His biggest support was Elizabeth's younger sister, Donna. He called her several times each day to share feelings and obtain information and advice on how to handle the children. He felt numb and yet was able to organize, an ability that rarely failed him.

Bereavement and Reconstitution

Communicating their feelings presented special challenges to this action-oriented family. They organized, they discussed facts and events, and the children continued to demonstrate their developmental achievements. But the family members struggled to find ways to talk about the overwhelming feelings evoked by the deaths of Elizabeth and her mother. They used activity to avoid and deny feelings—a strategy that was protective during the period immediately after the death but was less helpful during the period of mourning and reconstitution.

Lisa initially denied the impact of her mother's death, saying that nothing much had changed at home because her mother was gone a lot before she died. The traumatic impact of both mother and grandmother dying of the same disease, of an illness that she might be vulnerable to herself, can only be imagined. Lisa was not ready to acknowledge this, let alone discuss it. She acknowledged that she thought about her mother all the time. She was able to concentrate at school, however, and that remained a source of gratification. Although Lisa became even more responsible at home, she stayed busy and was away from home as much as possible.

Bruce was quiet and withdrawn at home, and his grades began to drop immediately. He stayed involved with sports, but seemed more distant. Vincent seemed to be communicating his fear of additional loss indirectly to the children, who experienced his fearfulness as clinging, which exacerbated their own vague worries.

Megan remained helpful at home, but she clearly demonstrated the ability of early adolescents (described in Chapters 12 and 13) to distract themselves with school and friends. Although her grades declined a bit, her teachers said this was because she was overly social, talking a lot with her friends. She also was becoming interested in athletics. She said she thought about her mother a lot, especially about the things they did together.

Just before Elizabeth died, Vincent was playing football with some friends when he reactivated an old knee injury. The doctor insisted on crutches and daily physical therapy, so he took sick leave. After he was home a couple of months, the children, only partly in humor, told him he needed to return to work "so he won't be on us all the time!" However, all of them appreciated the fact that he took over some of the housework, while limping around on crutches, which reduced the number of their chores.

Mourning

Once his initial numbness wore off, Vincent described the power of his feelings. Six weeks after the wake, Megan asked him to go to the cemetery with her. "When I saw her grave, I was a wreck. I must have walked at least half a mile. It was raining, so Megan waited for me in the car. I couldn't stand it. I just don't feel like I'm ready to go to the cemetery yet." He was completely unprepared for the overwhelming emotion he experienced. At another time, he was ironing when he heard a song on the radio and began to cry "Just out of the blue!" He was afraid of losing control in front of the children and was unaware that men also often have such surges of emotion.

Vincent handled single parenting by trying to involve the children in planning how family life would proceed. He called a family meeting and asked: "Do you want to have Christmas dinner here (for the whole family) as we always have? Christmas is going to be very different this year because Mom's not going to be here, but I think we should have Christmas dinner anyway." They agreed, and he talked with them about how they would decorate the house. He noticed that Megan "got a little blue and very quiet, but then she came around a couple of hours later. I think what hit her was that I said that Christmas is going to be very different because Mom's not going to be here. That hit her very hard." Once that was settled, he told them he had been negotiating about their mother's tombstone and had tentatively picked pink granite. They preferred black granite instead, so that is what he ordered. His conversations with the children were characteristically direct, even blunt.

Vincent tried to do things the way Elizabeth had done them. Christmas decorations were one such example. Elizabeth had always decorated the inside of the house while he put the lights on the outside. The children brought the boxes of decorations down from the attic; then all of them looked at the family picture albums to see where Elizabeth had put the decorations in previous years. Everyone pitched in, a bit sadly, but the end result was good.

After the children went to bed, he put the gifts under the tree, "and then I let go; it was too much. I just had it. The kids were upstairs, and I said this is it. I just let go." Although such bursts of emotion alarmed him, Vincent did recognize that he was much better the next day and was able to be in a festive mood. He woke the children in the morning and entertained family and friends all day: "The only thing that keeps me going is keeping busy."

Vincent noticed that no one wanted to take pictures on Christmas Day. "I think it was because we wanted to have the holiday, but it wasn't a great day. Not a holiday you want to cherish in your mind. I was determined to do it because I wanted things to go on. People came over, but we didn't play games. We just stayed in the living room and talked."

Setting Limits as a Single Parent

By Christmas, both girls were having some minor problems at school. Bruce's school problems, on the other hand, were quite severe. His grades worried Vincent because they might prevent Bruce from being accepted by the college of his choice. Vincent was stymied by Bruce because he felt that nothing he said seemed to be getting through. Bruce procrastinated on his assignments, had to be reminded about them, and sometimes had to be grounded.

Vincent also was annoyed with Bruce and Lisa for failing to keep their rooms clean. "I say to Bruce, 'You have to clean your room. You're doing nothing tonight, so why don't you just do it?' But he doesn't. I just close the door. I'm thinking about taking the doorknobs off his door because he hangs so many things on the knobs." Megan maintained her previous pattern of helping with housework and picking up her clothes.

Vincent kept thinking: "What would Elizabeth do about this?" But then he realized that because she was not there, he had to make the decisions alone.

Because he had always been more liberal than Elizabeth about setting limits, he decided to give them all an extra half hour on their curfew. However, he followed Elizabeth's pattern of checking with their friends' parents about "current standards." Lisa wanted to go away for 12 days with a friend and her family over Easter vacation. He spoke with the parents, then said O.K., even though he believed that Elizabeth might have said no. He reasoned that she was 17 now and would be going away to college. He made a package of Easter eggs and candy for her to take with her. When Bruce asked if he could go on a ski trip with friends, Vincent called the father of one of Bruce's friends whose parenting skills he admired and asked him if he approved of the trip. He did; therefore, Vincent let Bruce go.

Fear of Other Losses

Vincent was surprised by how much he worried about the children. For example, he gave Lisa a 1:30 A.M. curfew on weekends. At 1:30 one night, she called to tell him she would be five minutes late. It was an hour later when he found her friend's telephone number and called. He was told that she had just left the house. Vincent was frightened and angered by her lack of consideration and grounded her for two nights for creating a situation in which he had to stay up an extra hour and worry. Later, he relented and said she could go out until 11:30 P.M., but she decided to stay home anyway.

Six Months After the Funeral

Vincent wondered why the children did not talk much about their mother anymore. Lisa had gone to the cemetery with a cousin. On another occasion, Megan and Lisa visited their grandfather, who showed them some pictures he had found of their mother. They were excited and wanted to keep the pictures. They talked about the fact that the pictures were "exactly like Mommy. Remember how she use to get so excited?" At times such as these, conversation about Elizabeth flowed more freely.

Vincent finally overcame his reluctance to visit the cemetery and went there with his sister-in-law, father-in-law, and the three children. "It was nice. Bruce liked it. They walked around the cemetery. It wasn't somber; there was humor. We were joking about the fact that some people had the date of birth but not the date of death, indicating that they were ready and waiting! It was a nice day—a positive approach. It has to get easier every time. It's like you're approaching something unknown, then someone begins to talk and it's O.K."

Mourning Becomes Depression

Megan's and Lisa's grades went up in all their classes, whereas Bruce's grades kept going down; his situation was now extremely serious. Vincent spent hours on the telephone with his teachers and coaches. The English teacher said that Bruce behaved as if he simply did not care and did not hand in his assignments. Vincent's first reaction to Bruce's report card was to keep him from playing soccer. But after speaking with the coach, he decided that would be counterproductive. The coach said he had great ideas for Bruce this year; he was going to be captain of the team. So they decided a better approach was to require him to write down his assignments every week, with the teachers signing when they gave him the assignment and when he returned it. He also had "responsibility sheets" to be signed by the coaches concerning punctuality, effort, and so forth. If Bruce failed to submit work that was appropriate and on time, he would be kept out of soccer.

Vincent talked with Bruce about his discussions with the teachers. He reminded Bruce about his mother's legacy and challenged him to live up to her expectations. "You're just quitting on yourself. You're only letting yourself down. Your mother gave you strength and all this courage, and you're giving up. You have to make *her* happy, not just me. You have to continue to strive and not give up; continue to fight, not quit. She left a nice legacy for you, and you have to be as good as she was, if not better. You are quitting. You are so capable and you are just throwing it away." Vincent pointed out: "Your mother never gave up. Even when she knew she was dying, she never gave up, and you can't either. The teachers really care about you. They really put in a lot of time trying to get you to do well. They think you can do well. Show them you can do well."

Bruce told the interviewer that his father's plan made him feel relieved. He knew his grades had been going down for a couple of months, but he didn't know how to tell his father or how to reverse the situation. Because he was afraid his father would keep him off the wrestling team, he could not tell him. However, he knew he was having trouble even in wrestling, a sport he loved: "I wasn't really into it, my heart wasn't in it." When the interviewer asked him if he minded his father's plan, he said, "No choice really, but I would have done the same thing." He said he was thinking about the past a lot, about vacations with his mother. He longed for the happiness again. He was indeed mourning.

One Year Later

Twelve months after the death, Bruce's English teacher and his coach wrote the following note:

> For the second 10-week marking period of the year, Bruce received a 65 in my class, and that was a gift. Nothing I would say or do would move him. When challenged on why he refused to hand in work, he would sit stone faced and not answer. Perhaps a little shrug of the shoulders. When I offered every bit of my time for him, asked if I could help with the work, sit with him, give him extra time to complete the work, come and talk to me as a confidant, the response was always the same. Both his Dad and the gym teacher required him to have a daily responsibility sheet to be signed by all his teachers regarding attendance, work, attitude, and grades. At the end of each class, Bruce faithfully came to me and I would write the appropriate comments. During all of this time and the time previous, he was never surly or disrespectful, just uncommunicative.
>
> About two months ago, he started doing all of his work again. He was still getting his responsibility sheet signed, but there was a silent though dramatic change. It was as if he had found his will to live again. Since that time (and we

have not discussed the whys or wherefores) Bruce has become the student he can be. His work is very good. It shows study and care. In short, he is a terrific kid who has had a most unfortunate twist of fate in his life. Here's hoping for the best.

Fourteen Months After Elizabeth's Death

Vincent reported that all the children were doing well in school, sports, and social activities. All of them spent a large amount of time with their friends. Vincent had begun to date, and discussed the matter with his children. Because Bruce seemed a little concerned that "she" might move in before he finished high school, and Megan was upset about what she viewed as the replacement of her mother, Vincent decided to slow down his relationship with this woman in deference to their feelings.

Bruce showed no more evidence of depression. He felt that his relationship with his father was a good one. Occasionally, he feared that someone else would die. On the whole, however, Bruce maintained a positive and hopeful outlook. On the other hand, Lisa was more depressed, probably because of her upcoming separation from the family when she would go away to college. She was not sure that things would work out for her. She cried every day, privately, and had trouble sleeping many nights. However, she went frequently to the cemetery by herself, integrating this easily with other activities. Her father was pleased to hear her say, "I'll be home a little late after Mass, I'm going to stop by the cemetery to see Mommie." She maintained an active, positive social life and had a good relationship with her father. At times, she wished that she had died with her mother. She was surprised that her Easter trip with another family had been difficult for her. It had highlighted how different her own family was now and would be in the future. It was so different from what she had come to expect and hope for. Although she was concerned about whether she would "make it" away from home, these concerns did not seem to be interfering with her plans. She had been accepted by a college some distance from home and experienced renewed mourning as she prepared to make the transition.

Summary

Lisa's grief was delayed, perhaps in part because of the trauma of losing both her mother and grandmother in such a short time and because of the complexity of her relationship with her mother. The experience of mourning in the face of losing her mother, the secondary stress of losing her grandmother, and the obvious threat to her own survival were overwhelming. In addition, she faced two major life transitions: leaving home for college and the possibility that her father would remarry. Rather than feel excited about going to college as her friends were, she was filled with self-doubts and fear about her own vulnerability. Her concern about whether she would make it away from home the following year was realistic. Lisa's ability to share her feelings with her family was limited, in part because she may have been afraid of awakening their own fears, but especially because she was afraid of reawakening her father's grief.

Bruce began his mourning relatively soon after the death. His mother's death gave him no sense of relief, and his period of numbness was brief, if it happened at all. He and his mother had had a close bond, and he felt a great loss. His mourning was intense and much like adult mourning—full of a sense of helplessness and hopelessness. He was not certain he could go on without her, and his poor grades and lack of enthusiasm for athletics reflected his retreat.

All three children functioned well, at least in the three important domains of school, home, and peers. It was only in the stillness of their souls that we see sadness, apprehension, and perhaps fear. However when last seen, all the children remained within the boundaries of mourning rather than sinking into depression. Even Bruce's short-lived depression was reactive; it did not have persistent overtones. Lisa's depression was likely to be transient as well, although one would have liked to see her implement a counseling referral.

MOTHER AND 16-YEAR-OLD DAUGHTER

"You Can't Just Go on with Your Life!"

Robert met Ellen while consulting at her place of employment. He was recently divorced and was attracted to her competence and obvious managerial skills, and she was attracted to his artistic sensitivity. He was a well-known architect who worked for a large corporation. Ellen found his way of staging events irresistible: For example, he proposed to her on Christmas Eve "in a most romantic and beautiful setting." They married, and their daughter Shelby was born four years later. Ellen was a private person who had been raised by her mother to respect privacy and secrecy; Ellen's father had been an alcoholic. There was a rigid coldness in her parent's home that was also part of her upbringing. "Robert was the first person I was ever hugged by."

Marriage and the first years of Shelby's life were blissful for Ellen. To meet the recurring deadlines his growing success imposed, Robert was seldom home before 8 or 9 P.M. Ellen liked and respected his obvious success.

When Shelby entered school, problems soon surfaced. In fact, she never was successful in school, which gradually became a battleground. In the early grades, she had occasional bouts of refusing to go to school. By the time she was in sixth grade, there were battles over homework. In junior high school, she skipped school on occasion. At this point, she was found to have a specific learning disability and received some remedial education.

When she entered high school, Shelby liked school for the first time because she had discovered boys and social life and obviously was popular. As Ellen pointed out, "She has a lot of girlfriends and a boyfriend, who also adore Robert. Shelby and I have a good relationship, but we have a normal relationship. She is, after all, a teen-ager, and she goes through all the terrible things that teen-agers experience—smoking, sex, alcohol. We fight all the time: She wants to stay out, I want her home. But we know that we love one another." Ellen was the disciplinarian in the family, whereas Robert thought Ellen should praise first and discipline later. Although her father worked long hours, Shelby felt close to him and thought he understood her. For example, she said that if she begged, he would let her go to an important party for a couple of hours even if her activities had been restricted. "Dad's on my good side."

Illness

Robert's first symptom was blood in the urine. Ellen read everything she could get her hands on and found that painless hematuria is often the first symptom of bladder cancer. However, the diagnosis was not established until four months later because all the tests, including biopsies, were negative at first. Once the diagnosis was made, the doctors removed his bladder and also discovered that one lymph node was affected. Because Robert was not a candidate for a "new bladder," he wore a bag hidden by baggy pants. He had chemotherapy for four months, was extremely ill, lost what little hair he had left, but then made an excellent recovery. He had maintained an optimistic attitude throughout.

One month after his final treatment, Robert returned to work. In looking back on the period of Robert's diagnosis and treatment, Ellen felt that she had concentrated all her energy and concern on him and had more or less withdrawn from Shelby.

Both parents kept Shelby well informed and tried to maintain an atmosphere of normalcy. "Dad told me all the gory details. He knew I was interested in going into medicine." Shelby had a birthday party the day after Robert came home from the hospital. The illness had no effect on her grades. Ellen had sent Shelby for counseling before Robert's first symptom appeared because Shelby was dealing with her first relationship with a boy, and there was some smoking and drinking. Shelby went to the counselor twice, saying to Ellen: "I'll go if you want me to, but because I have my friends I can talk to, I feel I have nothing to say to him." Shelby believed that all her conflicts with her mother concerned school. "I did my homework, Ma." "No you didn't." Then she added: "We get along great much of the time, but when we have trouble, we fight hard." She thought the fighting had started before her father became ill, but had gotten worse afterward.

Terminal Illness

Six months after Robert went back to work, his doctors found that his disease had metastasized to lung and bone. The greatest problem was bone pain. He could no longer work. Although he participated in a number of clinical trials with experimental drugs, his disease progressed rapidly. When the metastases were discovered, Ellen decided not to talk to the doctors anymore because she could not face hearing about what she knew was happening. Robert remained optimistic to the end, so she tried to hide her own despair, which was fueled by her mother's recent death from cancer. Her mother had been terminally ill for three years and, until the end, preferred to suffer excruciating pain rather than experience the mental side effects of pain medications.

Robert's parents were devastated by his illness. Robert did not want them to visit him because he was afraid of their reaction to his changed state. When he stopped working, the family finances became extremely tight. His parents insisted on paying half of the family's monthly mortgage payments, and Ellen worked both a full-time and a part-time job. Seeing Robert at home all the time made Ellen feel sad. He was lonely, bored, and tired of being sick.

Shelby told the interviewer that she believed that her parents kept her well informed about her father's illness and its progression. She was aware of the changes not only in her father but in her mother as well. Although the conflicts with her mother about school and household chores continued, Shelby empathized with her mother's increasing sense of helplessness. "She does so much, but after a while she doesn't know what else to do." Shelby was more defensive when describing her interaction with her father, and reflected the fluctuation of empathy, self-centeredness, but also the worry about the passing of time. "Just because my dad has cancer, I'm not going to hide in a closet. I'm not going to ruin my teen-age years! I know that is pretty mean. But we spend time together. I sit there and watch the TV with him. All he does is watch TV. My dad and I never fight. He's always on my side."

Shelby said that she recently received a poor grade and her father had decided to ground her. She thought the mark her teacher had given her was unfair. Although he had grounded her, she persuaded him to let her go to a special party for a couple of hours. The next day he called the teacher and found out that her grade was a mistake; her actual grade was much better.

Shelby told the interviewer that her father's intervention made a big difference in how the teacher treated her and in how she felt about herself. In fact, she thought that his help had inspired her to work harder. Her father told the teacher that Shelby loved the class, was interested in medicine, and was upset about the grade. Her teacher was surprised because all he had observed was Shelby's anger and unhappiness, and he was unaware of her interest.

When the interviewer asked Shelby if she had any advice for other kids in a situation like hers, she said: "I'd tell them, first of all, don't jump to conclusions. Things you think are real bad or crazy won't really happen. Think of the good things, the bad things, but also think of yourself. I didn't dedicate 24 hours a day to Dad, because your friends are important too. You have to describe and explain the illness to your friends. Sometimes when I talk about it, it gets me scared, but now I'm used to it. My Dad's great. Just because he's going to be away for another week in the hospital doesn't mean he's never going to come back. He may not come back, but you never know. You have to be prepared; you have to know everything. All the time I ask questions. My Mom will tell me everything. My Dad will tell me everything, even the grossest things, and I go "Oh, my God!" He tells me because he knows I want to do something in medicine and he wants me to know what it's really like. You just ask a lot of questions. If my Dad dies, it will be like we did everything we could."

Shelby anticipated the future without her father. She had gotten to know him so much better since he was sick and stayed at home. "If I live with my Mom I'm in a jail cell. If I'm with my Dad, he'll let me do whatever I want. He was like a stranger, before he was sick; I felt strange around him. Now I'm around him a lot. He wants me to bring my friends in, but then he might get sick, and he understands that."

Death and Family Rituals

Six weeks before Robert died, he was hospitalized again because he needed pain management. He was unable to sleep, his temperament changed, and he seemed to be a different person. He was so heavily medicated that he hallucinated at times. Ellen explained to Shelby that her father's demanding and angry behavior was caused by the pain, the debility, and the drugs. She called her in-laws to tell them their son was dying. When they came she was careful to let them have time alone with their son.

Robert and Ellen had been married for 23 years when he died. The private viewing of his body by members of the immediate family, the funeral, and the burial seemed like a blur to Ellen. Typical of children her age, Shelby insisted on taking an active role in the rituals. She wanted to view the body, to be alone with her father, to pray, talk to him, cry a bit, touch him—all of which were helpful to her. Ellen was surprised by the number of Shelby's friends who came to her daughter's aid. Shelby even received telephone calls from friends she had not heard from since elementary school. Four days after Robert's death, Shelby went with her school team to a national cheerleading competition. She called home a few times, but otherwise did well.

Ellen needed to return to work quickly. Her only apprehension was that she might be overwhelmed by her colleagues' condolences. Six weeks after Robert's death, all she felt was numbness, although she expected to break down at some point. What surprised her was the strong fear that she would never again have a close physical relationship with a man she had come to need and appreciate so much.

Bereavement and Reconstitution

Shelby was beginning to establish a more mutual relationship with her mother. She showed a new sense of empathy for her mother's changed reality, and both of them noted a marked shift in their relationship toward greater intimacy and mutual respect. Shelby also explored age-appropriate existential questions concerning the value of religion: "If religion is so powerful, then why did he die?" She thought she might want to be a social worker because her friends and her mother were able to confide in her and enjoyed talking with her. She wanted her mother to be happy, even to date, so she would feel less guilty about being with her own boyfriend.

> In health class we talk about death a lot. I can't stand the kids in my class. The kids said you just go on with your lives, and I said: "You try! It doesn't work that way. I wish you could be in my house for a while and see how really hard it is; you can't just go on with your life! One kid was talking about his mother, who left her kids. She never came back; they don't know where she is. He and I are the only ones that understand how things are never really the same as they were before.

One subject that Shelby did not talk to her mother about or mention in the health class was her concern that she might be at risk for cancer herself. Her father also had been concerned about her for that reason.

The full impact of single parenthood emerged during the first several months after Robert died. With the interviewer, Ellen examined several factors that added to her difficulty. First, her own dysfunctional family, especially her cold mother and alcoholic father, resulted in a joyless adolescence that did not yield useful memories or guidelines for handling Shelby. Second, before Robert became ill, she had been thoroughly involved with Shelby, but all her daughter's school problems had made the relationship a conflicted one. Afterward, she had become extremely fearful of his dying and had therefore devoted herself fully to her husband for two years. She could always count on Robert to soften her disciplinarian approach and to support Shelby. That balance was no longer available, and it frightened Ellen.

An example of this complex balance was how to handle the whole issue of dating and sex—for herself as well as Shelby. As her numbness thawed, she was aware of an emerging need for closeness. Symbolically, this centered on wearing her wedding ring: "I feel like the longer I wear it, I'll never be able to take it off." Ellen's relationship with Shelby wavered between a sibling and a parent relationship. For example, Shelby invited her mother to come to her high-school prom, and Ellen, only partly in jest, warned her that if she came, she might show up with a date. At another point, Ellen asked Shelby if it was O.K. if she had a date, and Shelby said she would not mind. Privately, Ellen often thought about the issue of dating.

Ellen's mourning process deepened: During an interview, she said: "I'm coping very well and it frightens me. I go from listening to very sad, sensuous music to feeling good to feeling bad. Today, I heard some music that was upbeat and started to feel good. Then I thought, It's only been a few months, and I feel like a traitor to Robert." During the next interview, she said she was feeling real rage at Robert, and this finally made it possible for her to remove her wedding ring.

As was characteristic of so many adolescent girls, Shelby wanted to talk with Ellen about how much she missed her father and how, at times, she felt as if she were going crazy dealing with those feelings. Talking with Shelby about this was not easy for Ellen. Being confronted with the intensity of Shelby's feelings at a time when she herself was in such turmoil about her own feelings made it extremely difficult for her to listen. Ellen decided she needed to encourage Shelby to enter counseling.

Mid-Year Mark

Various factors coalesced that might have contributed to Shelby's spate of serious acting out over the next few months. First, she may have been partly responding to the depth of sadness often seen in adults and in older adolescents between four and eight months after the death of a loved one. Her discussions with her mother certainly seemed to reflect this more adult mourning process. Second, her mother worked at two jobs to maintain the family finances, which left Shelby without much supervision, and Shelby had always been an adolescent who needed supervision. Third, Shelby was 17 years old and beginning to think about the end of high school. Finally, Ellen had begun to date and had an active social life—a new experience that delighted her. Shelby's negative response to the fact that her mother was dating surprised Ellen. Having initially assented to the idea of Ellen's dating, Shelby now resented her mother going out all the time, and thought it was too soon after her father's death.

Shelby broke up with her boyfriend of several years and joined a new social group that was involved in drinking, drugs, and smoking. She cut school several times, received flunking grades, became defiant, and stayed out late. Ellen felt that the closeness they had developed was gone: "She no longer has any concern about me." When Ellen gave Shelby permission to invite a few friends to the house, 15 arrived and refused to leave when Shelby asked them to do so. Angry conflicts between Ellen and Shelby ensued, and the man Ellen was dating broke off his relationship with her as a consequence. Much of Shelby's misbehavior changed toward the end of the summer, when she broke up with her new boyfriend and distanced herself from the new social group.

Fourteen Months After the Death

Both Ellen and Shelby began to see a therapist on a weekly basis. They agreed that Shelby's plans for college after graduation should not be discussed until they had worked out the conflicts in their relationship that had defeated any reasonable planning. Neither one was ready to begin thinking about college and separation. Ellen believed that her relationship with Shelby was now on the mend. The love they felt for each other, although not freely expressed, seemed evident.

Summary

Shelby's mourning was complicated by her own pre-existing vulnerabilities and by secondary stressors related to her mother's troubled mourning and the deprivations her mother had experienced in her own youth. Shelby lost the parent who had been in her corner, had understood her problems with self-esteem, and had been patient with her. Although Ellen struggled to compensate for Shelby's loss, her own grief and lack of experience in being a parent of an adolescent led her to withdraw from Shelby and to violate mother-daughter boundaries in ways that reduced Shelby's self-esteem even more and made her feel more alone. Shelby also had a pre-existing problem, her academic difficulties, which fortunately hadn't stigmatized her with her peers (as such difficulties stigmatize so many adolescents). She had many good friends, both male and female—an important source of self-esteem for adolescent girls.

In retrospect, Shelby's two months of angry rebellion seemed to be an equivalent of mourning. The depth of her mourning overwhelmed her capacity to cope. Because her mother paid a price for her dysfunctional upbringing, she was at best an awkward filter for Shelby. However, the strength in their relationship was Ellen's commitment to her daughter, her persistence and self-reflection, and therapy that helped them to renegotiate a more mutually supportive and appropriate relationship.

Finally, mother and daughter shared a love for Robert and wanted to fulfill his legacy of commitment to Shelby's growth. Their effort to work out a different relationship shortly after his death also seemed to have helped. Finally, by seeking therapy for herself as well as Shelby, Ellen confronted her own troubled past. She supported, protected, and informed her daughter, and persisted in negotiating a better relationship with her.

OUTCOMES

By the final assessment, 8 to 14 months after the parent's death, 21 of the 36 adolescents had achieved their previous levels of functioning in all of the major areas: psychological state, relationships at home, academics, athletics and after-school activities, and developmentally appropriate peer relationships. Nine had a delayed reconstitution, three a compromised reconstitution, and three a symptomatic reconstitution.

Characteristics of Timely Reconstitution

The 21 adolescents who had a timely reconstitution had a history of considerable competence in at least one area of functioning that predated the parent's illness. Their accumulated successes, coupled with years of satisfactory parenting by either or both parents, seemed to have given them the security to cope with the loss of the parent. What was surprising were adolescents who adapted well after the death despite having relatively serious pre-existing personal problems or having parents whose problems affected their competence as parents.

Pre-existing Problems in Functioning

Among the 21 adolescents who did well, two became addicted to alcohol or drugs shortly after their parent's diagnosis, but responded well to intensive treatment. While the parent was dying, these two adolescents used therapy and were able to function well throughout the period of bereavement and reconstitution. Apparently, they had learned about how they functioned under stress and used this knowledge to master the stress of the death and their own mourning.

The previously diagnosed mental illness of another adolescent was briefly exacerbated. With therapy, and with his surviving mother's ability to set firm limits and his own considerable abilities, he was able to regain his previous level of functioning. Another child resolved her chronic and severe learning problem by embarking on a career as the housekeeper for her father and younger sisters. Rather than resenting this role, she was proud of her competence, and her father appreciated and supported her.

Serious Problems in Parenting

Surprisingly, serious family conflicts and parenting problems that might have been associated with a poorer outcome among children in earlier developmental stages did not have such an effect on these adolescents. It seemed like they were more reliant on their integrated sense of self and significant peer relationships and less affected by home conflicts. One father who died had a history of alcoholism; another had been severely mentally ill; and still another, although abusive to all family members, was particularly abusive to the adolescent. In these situations, the surviving parent functioned competently, acknowledged the dead parent's behavior and the negative feelings it provoked, but also encouraged realistic idealization of the dead parent. As described in earlier chapters, that approach was very successful with younger age groups as well. Among the surviving fathers, one was a recovered alcoholic and another had a history of severe mental illness. Both acknowledged their illness and their vulnerability as parents and sought additional help and support for themselves and their children.

Characteristics of Delayed Reconstitution

The nine adolescents who recovered more slowly were adapting relatively well to their parent's death but were still struggling to regain their equilibrium in at least one major area 14 months after the death of the parent. In all nine adolescents, the parents were less successful in discussing details of the patient's illness and probable death than were the parents of the timely reconstitution group. More specific factors associated with their slower reconstitution included a broad range of additional stressors.

Pre-existing Problems

Three girls and one boy had mild to moderate learning problems, health problems, or a severe previously diagnosed mental illness that predated the parent's illness. The surviving parents struggled with assuming the role of a single parent to a vulnerable adolescent. A common pattern became mutual provocative interactions. In these cases, the patient had been more successful in helping the adolescent and in defusing problematic interactions.

Marked Limitations of the Surviving Parent's Skills

In three families, the surviving father's parenting skills were markedly limited. These fathers were overwhelmed by the loss of their wife's crucial support, and their efforts to assume the role of single parent with their sons floundered.

Grief or Depression

The grief reactions of one boy and one girl were unusually strong and prolonged. This may have reflected an emerging depressive illness. Although neither adolescent had experienced previous episodes of depression, there was a history of depression in both families. The parenting skills of both surviving mothers were adequate, but both adolescents had always been less comfortable with the surviving parent. There were additional stressors in both. The boy was the eldest of four siblings and felt overwhelmed by his sense of responsibility. He had just entered a highly competitive private school where the faculty were not supportive, and he had difficulty confiding in newly made friends. Finally, his father died within six months of diagnosis, giving all a limited time to prepare. The girl felt betrayed by her boyfriend and a girlfriend who withdrew from her, and they began to date each other after her father died. In addition, her mother permitted regressive behaviors such as allowing her daughter to sleep with her for several months.

Characteristics of Compromised Reconstitution

Three girls showed no signs of improvement in internalizing and externalizing symptoms 14 months after the death. In all three, the patient, two mothers and one father, had had a close, supportive relationship with the girls. Both surviving fathers were distant, angry men. One girl began to sneak out of the house at night and became sexually involved with a divorced man many years her senior. Her father, an immigrant from a Mediterranean country, became enraged and refused to allow her ever to return home. Another adolescent had a series of additional stressors: She had a history of severe learning disabilities. Her favorite older brother left home and married after quarreling with his father, and an aunt the girl felt close to moved to a different state. When last seen, her behavior in school and with her peers continued to decline markedly. The third girl had progressive symptoms of depression. She had felt especially close to and supported by the patient, her father, who had a history of severe depression that had been controlled with medication. Despite ongoing therapy that began shortly after her father's death, her depression was unrelieved when she was last seen.

Characteristics of Symptomatic Reconstitution

After their parent's death, two boys and one girl developed new psychiatric symptoms that were severe and qualitatively different from the symptoms they had exhibited before. These symptoms included severe and dangerous aggressive behavior with peers, severe phobias that interfered with normal functioning, self-mutilation, clinical depression with suicidal behavior, and abuse of drugs and alcohol. Both parents of one adolescent had severe psychopathology: depression and constricting phobias. In another, the surviving parent tried hard to respond effectively to the adolescent's escalating pathological behaviors but became locked into negative, mutually provocative cycles. In the third, psychiatric treatment was delayed until the symptoms became blatantly self-destructive.

DISCUSSION

Three features stand out in this group of 36 adolescents: their mourning, their formal operational cognitive understanding, and their emotional development. They mourned more like adults. Although with most the period of mourning was shorter then that of the parents, it had other characteristics that were similar: the grief was intense and at times overwhelming, it could not be controlled by immersion in other activities, sadness permeated their lives, some responded with externalizing symptoms, and their functioning level in most areas was at least temporarily affected. This is a contrast to the mourning of their younger peers—the youngest mourned more with joy and pleasure in the memories of their parent, the older ones with clear boundaries between mourning and activities that allowed an escape from the grief. The grief seemed to be a different level of stress for these adolescents, perhaps contributing to some of the less optimal outcomes.

Another feature emerged in their cognitive development. Although formal operational thinking was present in some early adolescents, the automatic perspective on the past-present-future features of the illness and death, on the more comprehensive understanding of the death's effect on everyone's life without the parent were more evident in middle adolescence. These cognitive abilities made the reality of anticipatory grief more frequent in this group of adolescents.

Boys' emotional development continued the withdrawal of investment from the parents. Girls gave evidence of starting or continuing to change the relationship, rather than only detach. This, coupled with the new emphasis on loving friendships with peers, opened up an important avenue for support, which may have contributed to the relative independence from the need for more permeating parental support in some of the adolescents with a timely reconstitution. On the other hand, with several children we also saw that problems with loving friendships, including sexual acting out, was a greater potential source of stress. Two related areas, a reduction in their egocentrism and an increase in their ability to empathize, made the task of parenting them somewhat easier.

Finally, for many, thoughts about leaving home, often to go to college, presented a different set of stressors. Even in many of the youngsters with a timely reconstitution, the joy of the adventure of leaving home, seen in many nonbereaved children, was not there. With many, there was a level of apprehension about another separation; with some, a reawakening of the mourning. Their ecological world was expanding rapidly. Confronting the probability of a different type of independence was affected by their recent loss.

15

꙰

Conclusion

The findings presented in this book rest on the foundations of development and the continuum of reconstitution of the family after a parent's death. Effective healing processes that were identified included: understanding children's developmental needs; preparing, informing and guiding them through the experience; supporting and resonating with their unique expressions of grief; helping them construct a positive legacy; and reconstituting relationships without the day to day presence of the parent who died.

Increasing developmental specificity in studies of children's reactions to the death of a parent has been identified as an important direction for research (Clark et al., 1994; Roosa et al., 1997; Rutter, 1994; Tremblay & Israel, 1998). However, creating a methodology for incorporating developmental specificity has been a major challenge. The research presented here used a qualitative method, grounded in the data, to identify five groups of children with similar cognitive, emotional and social-ecological characteristics. These characteristics were drawn from theories of development that provided useful, comprehensive and pertinent attributes of development in these bereaved children.

Beginning the research during the parent's terminal illness emerged as an important design feature, because this period proved to be the time when most of the children and adolescents experienced the highest levels of depression and anxiety; levels that were higher than they experienced after the death (Siegel et al., 1996). The qualitative analysis allowed an exploration of children's anticipatory responses as well as their reactions after the death, thus providing a more complete understanding of how children experienced an anticipated death.

The developmental approach also made it possible to identify outcomes within each age-development group that described how children adapted more or less effectively to the parent's terminal illness and death. Both positive and negative mediating and moderating factors (different factors in each stage of development, during the periods before the death and during the reconstitution) were related to each outcome category. A four-dimensional bereavement outcome model, described in chapter 4, emerged that depicted the complex interactions among development, stages of a parent's illness, the structural-dynamic-interactive dimension, and the resulting outcome. Two findings, the differences in the mourning processes as children matured and the children's outcome category when last seen, illustrate the role of mourning in the process of healing children's grief and clarify factors that contributed to better and worse adaptation.

MOURNING

Mourning is the process by which children adapt to the death of their parent. Much was learned about the different manifestations of mourning in the five development derived age groups. It is perhaps this variation in the way children communicate their grief that has made it difficult for adults to respond to them in ways that acknowledge the reality of their grief, honor their varying expressions of it, and provide the resonance, empathy, solace, guidance, education, and support that promotes healing. The quest to understand the mourning process itself can be traced through most of this century, but the way children's development influences its manifestations has been elusive. It was a goal of this study.

Developmental Differences in Mourning

Ages 3 to 5 Years

Children in this age group expressed their grief in ways that were difficult to recognize. They certainly did not exhibit any signs of anticipatory mourning. Indeed, even after the death, their mourning became apparent only when they finally understood and accepted the fact that the parent would never come back, a realization that sometimes took several months. The children's manifestations of mourning included sleeping with the surviving parent, thumb sucking, bed wetting, clinging behavior, night terrors, whining, stomachaches, other physical symptoms, and worries about their own health. When these symptoms lasted too long, all was not well with the child.

Some young children asked questions and talked about the dead parent; others did so only rarely. One clear expression of the protest of the loss by children this age was their demand that the surviving parent find a replacement for the lost parent. They mourned the loss of the whole family as they had come to know it and their play was often replete with themes of restoration.

These young children reacted negatively to separations from the primary caregiver as well as to major mood changes in the caregiver. Healing interactions included providing a language and an emotional context they could use to communicate about the parent who died. This structure relieved their anxiety and improved their ability to talk about remembered positive interactions.

Ages 6 to 8 Years

The children in this age group experienced anticipatory anxiety rather than anticipatory grief; they feared the awesome event they knew was likely to occur. However, unlike their younger peers, as soon as they were told about the death, they knew that the dead parent was gone forever. Furthermore, they "knew" that the parent was in heaven looking down on them; they just could not see the parent. They felt the parent's presence and could talk to the parent. Unlike the older children, these children loved to talk about the parent, surround themselves with photographs of the parent, and incorporate the parent's clothing or other belongings into their play. Although they experienced moments of grief, anger, and sadness, sometimes connected with thoughts about the parent, the predominant affect of their mourning was pleasure in telling and retelling stories about what they and the parent had done together. The image of the dead parent they retained was usually that of a loving caregiver, protector, the provider of good things, of a strong, much admired hero or heroine.

Interactions that were healing to children of this age included consistent involvement with a primary caregiver who could support their self-esteem. The caregiver needed to provide continuous clarification of logical errors the children made that were based on magical thinking processes and excessive self reference leading to self blame and disturbing guilt. They needed warm empathic resonance to their disappointments and sadness, but also respect for their joyous remembrance which was the unique way of grieving for children this age.

Ages 9 to 11 Years

Older school aged children seemed to be so overwhelmed by their grief that they could not tolerate such feelings. Unlike the 6- to 8-year-olds, they did not like to talk about the dead parent. Instead, they compartmentalized their feelings, refused to express or experience their sadness by resorting to intellectualization. The children who were voracious learners sought information about the disease and wrote papers about it for school. Most of them also compartmentalized by escaping into school and after-school activities that would not remind them of, or force them to think about the dead parent.

Because of the age-related advances in their cognitive abilities, they were capable of experiencing anticipatory mourning during the parent's terminal illness. However, they worried about the surviving parent's health as a result. Like their 6- to 8-year-old counterparts, they described having a sense of the dead parent's presence. They felt that the dead parent was watching them and was pleased when they succeeded at school or in sports. They dreamed of doing things they had wanted to do with the parent while the parent was alive. The image of the parent retained by children this age emphasized the parent as the conveyor of knowledge and skills they needed for independence and achievement. They mourned the parent as a coach, advocate, "cheerleader," friend, and buddy.

Healing interactions required adults to provide a continuous flow of detailed information that gave them a sense of mastery, but permitted avoidance of emotional expression except on infrequent occasions. This more intellectual, non-emotional grieving needed to be honored as such. These children productively used opportunities to assist the patient and the family as long as the tasks were reasonable. Creating formal opportunities for remembering the parent who died helped them to give expression to feelings they often found too frightening to discuss.

Ages 12 to 14 Years

Children in this age group not only compartmentalized and avoided their feelings but avoided information about the parent's illness as well. The manifestations of their mourning merged with the emotional and behavioral upheavals associated with puberty and early adolescence. Although it seems paradoxical, what was very upsetting for them was the withdrawal and preoccupation of their parents during the terminal illness and after the death at the very time these children were themselves withdrawing and moving toward independence. Like the 9- to 11-year-olds, they worried about the surviving parent's health and escaped into school, after-school activities, and being with their friends. They grieved, but alone, in their room because they were preoccupied with controlling powerful emotions that threatened to overwhelm them in public places. The sense of the dead parent's presence was more prevalent and powerful to these early adolescents than it was for their younger counterparts. Although most of them said that they talked with the dead parent, they never doubted that the parent was in fact dead. This behavior seemed to reflect the process of internalizing the parent rather than avoiding the reality of the loss.

They grieved for a different parent than their younger peers did. They grieved for the loss of the parent's specific characteristics and his or her special functions in the family. The early adolescents mourned the parent as their mentor who would give them an "edge" in some important area. Girls mourned the loss of the mother who had begun to share with them and had enjoyed being with them during shopping excursions or slightly guilty ice cream splurges rather than the mother who only provided care. Importantly, the parent was mourned by children of this age as their gender and social role model. Both boys and girls missed the mother who had organized the family, had made it possible for them to spend time with their friends, had mediated conflicts, and had helped them cope with their volatile emotions. They mourned the parent who set limits on their outrageous behavior.

Young adolescents often needed more information about what was occurring than they wanted. Healing interactions included providing structure for limit setting, help with de-escalating conflicts, substitute social and gender role models, and understanding their need for time with peers. They also needed adults to express empathy for the conflict they confronted between the demands of their developmental level for emotional withdrawal from parents and the demands of the situation for greater emotional closeness. Formal opportunities for remembering helped early adolescents as well since expression of sad and lonely feelings was generally threatening.

Ages 15 to 17 Years

The mourning of middle adolescents differed markedly from the mourning of their younger peers. Because they received more preparatory information and understood the long-term implications of what was about to happen, their anticipatory grief was more focused and complex. What distinguished them most from younger children, however, was the intensity of their mourning after the death. They could become overwhelmed by their grief, and were unable to control it by immersing themselves in school and other activities. Because feelings of sadness, longing, despair, helplessness, and hopelessness permeated their lives, their functioning in most areas was temporarily seriously affected. In short, their mourning was more like that of an adult, but it did not last as long.

The aspects of the parent they mourned and wanted to retain included some of the parent's abstract characteristics. They spoke of the parent's sense of humor, and mourned the loss of their confidant and wise counselor. When they thought about the disease, they mourned the courageous fighter. Because they were in the process of separating from parent figures they mourned the parent as "believer" in their ability to succeed on their own. Their descriptions suggested that they already had a more internalized image of the parent than younger children did because they seemed less occupied with creating this image. Having internalized the parent's image, they also experienced a sense of losing a part of themselves. They thought about what the parent expected of them and how they would fulfill those expectations. They worried about the implications of the parent's illness and death on their own and the family's future.

Adults tended to underestimate the depth and intensity of the mourning of middle adolescents, especially when it was expressed by acting out, stubbornness, passivity, or anger. The mourning process itself needed to be explained to adolescents with opportunities to express their unique experience of it. They sometimes needed help with limit setting and conflict resolution, but they also responded to help with their increased fears of independence, separation from family, and their possible vulnerability to illness themselves. As they said often, "So much has changed, things will never be the same again".

The Legacy

Constructing a legacy is an important part of a child's mourning (Normand et al., 1996; Silverman et al., 1995). The legacy the ill parents left their children was generally much more than they had hoped for. They, and we, did not know just how much children collaborated in the final creation of the legacies. We learned that they worked consciously and unconsciously to construct a good 'memory,' a comforting representation of their dead parent. They were influenced by the memories of others as well as their own. We suspect that this representation will undergo revision as they mature. A longer term revision can be inferred from the 15-year follow-up of Rachel in Chapter 1, the changes we began to observe in the children in the sample, and the findings from other studies (Rizzuto, 1979; Shapiro, 1994; Silverman et al., 1995). Becoming like the dead parent, incorporating the parent as part of themselves, and living out the parent's dreams for them as they forged identities of their own shaped the children's evolving relationship with the parent. This process was an integral part of their mourning.

Many ill parents wanted to leave a positive legacy for their children. One father went on a final hunting trip to fill the freezer with venison for his family, another remodeled the house and created a beautiful stained-glass window for his young daughters. Other ill parents dedicated their final months to being with their children, teaching them, giving them an 'edge' in sports or schoolwork, or taking them on special trips as long as they were able. Still others wrote letters, made audiotapes, and told the children how much they loved them.

Because the ill parents worried that their children would remember them in their undignified decline, they struggled with the impact of their changed appearance. I wish we had known earlier what we learned subsequently. The legacy the parents left for their children—or more accurately, the legacy their children constructed—generally did not include memories of the ill and disfigured parent. Frightening reminders and negative images of the parent are more frequent when a parent has suffered a traumatic death (Pynoos, 1992). For the children and adolescents described in this book, negative images tended to occur when their relationship with the dead parent had been a negative one or when the relationship with the surviving parent was unsatisfactory. Dealing with the painful memories of the terminal illness was likely to characterize the mourning of the surviving spouses, but this was not the case for most children.

OUTCOME

Quantitative studies have used some combination of child, parent and teacher standardized measures to organize the outcome of children's adaptive effort along a meaningful continuum (Gray, 1987; Kranzler et al., 1990; Raveis et al., 1999; Sandler et al., 1992; Siegel et al., 1996; Silverman & Worden, 1993; Van Eerdewegh et al., 1985; Weller et al., 1991; Worden, 1996). Their relationship to a host of predictor variables yielded important findings that have been summarized in Chapter 2. Unfortunately, the relative weakness of the relationships between these outcome measures and the predictor variables limits the applicability of such findings at the individual case level (Rutter, 1983; Rutter, 1994).

Four categories of outcome provided a way to organize information about the children who were able to return to their previous level of functioning in a timely manner, those whose reconstitution was delayed to some extent, those whose reconstitution was compromised, and those who developed new symptoms compatible with a *DSM-IV* diagnosis after the death (symptomatic reconstitution) when seen at the time of the final evaluation. When last seen, 116 (83%) of the 139 children aged 6 to 17 years gave evidence of timely or delayed reconstitution. (These terms have been defined in Chapter 4 and are summarized in Table 4.3.) I interpret these two categories of outcome as variations in the more 'normal' outcomes among children who experience their parent's death.

The 23 children whose reconstitution was either compromised or symptomatic reflected situations in which the parent's death, although important, played a secondary role to the cascade of other stressors related to the death and the presence of unrelated but significant additional stressors, or both. What was apparent in most of these families was the multiplicity of stressful situations and events that added to the compromised or symptomatic outcomes: For example, the surviving parent's parenting skills were minimal or absent; other family members were ill or had recently died; the family was impoverished, had recently immigrated, or both; or the child had pre-existing problems. In short, the entire ecological system of the child and family conspired to add stresses and reduce supports.

It was not unusual for families to have one child who had a timely reconstitution and other children whose reconstitution was delayed or compromised.

Clearly, the parent's death had a different meaning and impact on different children within each family system.

Timely Reconstitution

The 84 children and adolescents whose reconstitution was timely experienced transient symptoms not only before the death but sometimes after the death as well. The specific symptoms varied by age and pre-existing problems, as has been reported in the chapters about the different age groups. Six months after the parent's death, many issues of reconstitution in the family had been settled, issues such as where the family would live, how the family would be supported financially, and how the roles and functions of the dead parent would be filled and by whom. What remained unclear six months after the death was how the young surviving parents would cope with their intense grief. Most of them were still unable to see, at this point, how they would reconstitute their lives in a satisfying and effective way.

The surviving parents of children who had a timely reconstitution had good problem-solving skills and were able to use a broad range of individuals and resources consistently to obtain help, and their children had many pre-existing strengths and abilities. Many of these parents had educational and economic assets. Others struggled effectively with the multiple stresses of poverty, immigration, and the illness or death of other family members. Surprisingly, several surviving parents who had histories of relatively severe psychiatric problems, such as clinical depression, schizophrenia, or alcoholism, coped well with their parenting role, and their children had either a timely or delayed outcome rather than a compromised or symptomatic one. These parents recognized their vulnerability, obtained timely and appropriate treatment for their own problems, reached out for additional resources and assistance, and sought substitute parenting when they believed that would help. In this way, they were able to provide adequate support for their children.

Another interesting finding was the parenting ability of some of the surviving fathers, an ability several learned while taking a half year leave from work to care for their children after the death of their spouse. Most of these men had minimal previous experience with the care-taking tasks traditionally provided by mothers, not only with the physical tasks but with the psychologically supportive and nurturing roles as well. Although some fathers never learned to fulfill these roles, a number of other fathers did learn to do so, even with their young daughters.

Although no divorced families were included in the intervention, several participating families were in the midst of separating when the patient was diagnosed. These families reunited during the terminal illness so that the ill spouse would receive adequate care. Most of such families had experienced considerable conflict before the diagnosis, and some even experienced domestic violence. However, many, but not all, of the children in these 'divorcing' families were able to cope without having a delayed or compromised outcome. The surviving spouses in these families apparently had resolved the marital conflict during the decision to divorce and therefore were able to support their children well during the family emergency. They appeared to be flexible and pragmatic people who were able to shift to a caregiving role after the acrimony of the planned divorce.

Delayed Reconstitution

On the whole, the 32 children whose reconstitution was delayed had more stresses and fewer protective factors than did the children whose reconstitution was timely. Underlying temperament, psychological problems, chronic learning problems or other vulnerabilities were sometimes apparent in these children as well. Some had an especially strong relationship with the parent who died and a less satisfactory relationship with the surviving parent. Added to this were other stresses, such as a lack of financial resources or large families with more than three children whose care overwhelmed the surviving parent's capacity to cope in a more satisfactory way.

The children whose reconstitution was delayed appeared to have the problem of a less "good fit" between their own vulnerabilities and their surviving parent's needs and abilities. However, the parents of these children, unlike the parents of children whose reconstitution was compromised or symptomatic, were generally able to change their dysfunctional patterns and correct their communication problems. Even if their children took longer to return to their previous level of functioning, the parents persisted in solving their problems. In addition, the children or adolescents themselves were beginning to mobilize their own strengths to make constructive changes.

Compromised Reconstitution

The 13 children whose reconstitution was compromised had not returned to their previous level of functioning by the final evaluation. Most were depressed and exhibited low self-esteem. The pre-existing problems of a few children were exacerbated after the parent's death, and their surviving parents had a more profound struggle regarding their competence as a parent.

The parents of the children in our study whose reconstitution was compromised confirmed findings of recent quantitative studies cited above which report that the parenting competence of the surviving parent has a significant impact on the child's ability to cope with the experience of the other parent's death. They either were overcome by their own grief or were unable to relate to the child in a way that provided support for the child's mourning, ongoing development, or both. They could neither filter the child's stress appropriately nor provide substitutes who could. Many were unable to moderate spiraling conflicts with their children. Thus, the children and the surviving parents in these families needed to be engaged in ongoing counseling or therapy.

Symptomatic Reconstitution

The 10 children who had a symptomatic reconstitution had far more difficult experiences than the children in the other three groups. In fact, they developed psychiatric symptoms that had not been present before the parent's death. This outcome was associated with one of two conditions. In the first condition, the surviving parents had severe psychopathology that seriously affected their function as a parent. In these situations, the children had lost the parent who had protected them from a detached, neglectful and/or psychologically abusive parent whose problems affected them directly. The second condition occurred when the child was reported to have preexisting problems that were severely affected and exacerbated by the stress of the parent's death which resulted in new symptoms.

Summary

These analyses showed that most surviving parents, both fathers and mothers, could be helpful, supportive, and encouraging to their children in many different ways that contributed to the children's timely or delayed reconstitution. On the other hand, the more deleterious interactions between surviving parent and child—interactions that probably contributed to the child's compromised or symptomatic reconstitution—were relatively few. The qualitative analyses yielded an equally important finding concerning surviving parents: even parents with major psychiatric disorders could deal with their difficulties so that their children experienced a timely or delayed reconstitution.

In some situations, the parent's illness and death released a cascade of stressors; in other situations, stressors unrelated to the death seemed to be more injurious to a child because of the death. However, the most striking finding was that the many factors that were different in each child's environment, rather than the death alone, seemed to be most powerfully associated with these outcomes. Despite the fact that many children were experiencing extraordinarily painful grief and mourning, most of them reconstituted in a timely way.

THE UNTOLD STORIES

Perhaps the most important finding, but one that cannot be summarized, are the narratives the families shared with all of us. They showed that surviving parents can grieve deeply but can still be available to their children, can support them and make it possible for them to continue with the tasks of ongoing development. I chose to speak about reconstitution rather than resilience in defining the post-death period. Neither the children nor the surviving parent will bounce back to the way they were before the death, as resilience implies. Rather, both must transform their relationship to the parent/spouse who died and work to build a life that incorporates the painful reality of the loss. Both can find a satisfying way of doing this. These stories show how reconstitution was possible for families and how they achieved personal growth through the process. Reconstitution implies this.

These stories also make clear that there is no one way to reconstitute: The parents described in this book show us that there are many different "roads to Rome." Parents reading these narratives should not view them or the recommendations listed in the cross sectional chapters as offering a formula for helping children. Instead, the untold stories should be viewed as offering support to parents in finding their own way of dealing with their children that is syntonic with their family's situation and background, using the provided material as a source of ideas, not of methods.

Combining Qualitative and Quantitative Approaches

This report of findings generated by the qualitative analyses of the data obtained from a parent guidance intervention complements the findings from quantitative analyses (Siegel et al, 1992, 1995, 1996). Together they provide a more comprehensive understanding of a life event as complex as the effect of a parent's death on the lives of surviving family members. The analysis of the previously untold stories are humbling as reminders of the complexity of the lives of the families, the multiplicity of influential variables that emerge, and the presence of surprising and unexpected factors.

Subjective interpretation and judgment are required to reduce the data and to interpret its meaning in qualitative analyses. The provision of the detailed information provided in this book was my effort to permit the reader to make an independent judgment. Replication of findings is another challenge for qualitative analyses. Triangulation, that is, the presence of results from different sources may strengthen confidence in research outcomes. For example, both the qualitative and the quantitative analyses of these data found that from 14 percent to 17 percent of children fell outside the range of the normal outcome. Along with other prospective quantitative studies, this study found the relationship to the surviving parent was closely related to better or worse outcome.

Although our ultimate goal is to generate information that has application to a much wider population, that goal may be premature in the study of children's bereavement. The description of the range of responses of a fairly homogenous population such as the one presented in this book with very few confounding variables like serious psychopathology in the children; a fairly constricted social class variance which reduces the confounding problems of poverty; the death of one of two parents rather than the cauldron of issues so common following the death of a single parent, begins to clarify the impact of the death of a parent even in an otherwise fairly idealized situation. The proportion of less favorable outcomes, the effectiveness of positive and negative mediators and moderators, may present a different picture of bereavement in situations that included these other variables. Yet some of the similarities and differences, so critical in planning interventions, could be lost if samples of bereaved populations were not fairly homogenous, at least during the early stages of research into such a complex area.

Future Directions

The findings from this study, together with those from studies of traumatic stress, suggest the need to compare and contrast at least five groups of bereaved children: (1) children whose single parent dies, (2) children of poverty, (3) children whose parent dies unexpectedly from natural causes, such as stroke or heart disease, (4) children whose parent dies unexpectedly and traumatically from an accident or from suicide or homicide, and (5) children whose parent dies of an anticipated death, such as the deaths that occurred in our study population. One purpose for these distinctions is to document the presence or absence of a traumatic stress response in each population because the intervention required for children with a traumatic stress reaction is indeed different. A more systematically derived understanding of the effect of poverty on the bereavement process and the differing needs of children whose only parent dies is required. Only longitudinal studies will determine whether the problems are doubled after two years as reported by one study (Worden, 1996), or whether symptoms that persist five years after a traumatic stress may be the fate of some children whose parent died from an unexpected cause (Terr, 1990).

Finally, it may be useful to include a qualitative component, not just as a pilot to generate a workable hypothesis to be tested quantitatively, but as a serious partner to quantitative studies. These can be complementary approaches each of whose findings enriches the other. To understand complex life issues such as the effect of the death of a parent, the previously untold stories that describe these intricate interactions can make quantitative outcomes more meaningful and understandable.

Bibliography

Abraham, K. (1927). A short study of the development of the libido, viewed in the light of mental disorders. In S. Troop & W. Green (eds.), *Selected Papers* (pp. 248–279). London: Hogarth Press.

Arthur, B., & Kemme, M. (1964). Bereavement in childhood. *Journal of Child Psychology and Psychiatry*, 5:37–39.

Balk, D.E. & Corr, C.A. (1996). Adolescents, development, tasks, and encounters with death and bereavement. In C.A. Corr & D.E. Balk (eds), *Handbook of adolescent death and bereavement* (pp. 3–24). New York: Springer.

Bandura, A. (1989). Social cognitive theory. In R. Vasta (ed.), *Six theories of child development: Annals of child development.* (Vol. 6, pp. 1–60). Greenwich, CT: JAI Press.

Becker, D., & Margolin, F. (1967). How surviving parents handle their young children's adaptation to the crisis of loss. *American Journal of Orthopsychiatry*, 37:753–757.

Berlinsky, E., & Biller, H. (1982). *Parental death and psychological development.* Lexington MA: Lexington Books.

Berlinsky, E., & Margolin, F. (1982). *Parental death and psychological development.* Lexington MA: D. C. Heath.

Bifulco, A., Brown, G., & Harris, T. (1987). Childhood loss of parent, lack of adequate parental care and adult depression: A replication. *Social Psychology*, 16:187–197.

Birtchnell, J. (1972). Early parent death and psychiatric diagnosis. *Social Psychiatry*, 7:202–210.

Black, D. (1978). The bereaved child. *Journal of Child Psychology and Psychiatry*, 19:287–292.

Black, D., & Urbanowicz, M. (1987). Family intervention with bereaved children. *Journal of Psychology and Psychiatry*, 28:467–476.

Blos, P. (1962). *On adolescence.* New York: Macmillan.

Bowlby, J. (1969). *Attachment and loss: Attachment.* New York: Basic Books.

Bowlby, J. (1973). *Attachment and loss: Separation anxiety and anger.* New York: Basic Books.

Bowlby, J. (1980). *Attachment and loss: Loss, sadness and depression.* New York: Basic Books.

Breier, A., Kelsoe, J., Kirwin, P., Wolkowitz, O., & Pickar, D. (1988). Early parental loss and development of adult psychopathology. *Archives of General Psychiatry*, 45:987–993.

Bronfenbrenner, U. (1979). *The ecology of human development: Experiments by nature and design.* Cambridge MA: Harvard University Press.

Bronfenbrenner, U. (1989). Ecological systems theory. In A. Vesta (ed.), *Six theories of child development: Annals of Child Development.* (Vol. 6, pp. 187–249). Greenwitch, CT: JAI Press.

Bronfenbrenner, U. (1993). The ecology of cognitive development: Research models and fugitive findings. In R. H. Wozinak & K. Fisher (eds.), *Scientific environments.* Hillsdale, NJ: Erlbaum.

Brooks-Gunn, J. Growing up female: Stressful events and the transition to adolescence. In T. M. Field, P. M. McCabe, & N. Schneiderman (Eds.), *Empathy and its development* (pp. 119–148). Hillsdale, NJ: Erlbaum.

Brown, F. (1961). Depression and childhood bereavement. *Journal of Mental Science*, 107:754–777.

Brown, G., Harris, T., & Bifulco, A. (1986). Long-term effects of early loss of parent. In M. Rutter, C. Izard, & P. Read (eds.), *Depression in young people* (pp. 251–296). New York: Guildford Press.

Brown, G., Harris, T., & Copeland, J. (1977). Depression and loss. *British Journal of Psychiatry*, 130:1–18.

Cella, D., Tan, C., Sullivan, M., Weinstock, L., Alter, R., & Jow, D. (1987). Identifying pediatric Hodgkin's Disease survivors in need of psychological interventions. *Journal of Psychosocial Oncology*, 5(4):83–96.

Cerel, J., Fristed, M., Weller, E., & Weller, R., 1999. Suicide-bereaved children and adolescents: a controlled longitudinal examination. *Journal of the American Academy of Child and Adolescent Psychiatry*. 38:672–679.

Christ, G. (1987). Social consequences of the cancer experience. *American Journal of Pediatric Hematology/Oncology*, 9:84–88.

Christ, G. (1991). Principles of oncology social work. In A. Holieb, D. Fink, & G. Murphy (eds.), *American cancer society textbook of clinical oncology* (pp. 594–605). Atlanta, GA: American Cancer Society.

Christ, G., Lane, J., & Marcove, R. (1995). Psychosocial adaptation of long-term survivors of bone sarcoma. *Journal of Psychosocial Oncology*, 13(4):1–22.

Christ, G., Siegel, K., Freund, B., Langosch, D., Henderson, S., Sperber, D., & Weinstein, L. (1993). Impact of parental terminal cancer on latency-age children. *American Journal Orthopsychiatry*, 63:417–425.

Christ, G., Siegel, K., Mesagno, F., & Langosch, D. (1991). A preventive intervention program for bereaved children: Problems in implementation. *American Journal of Orthopsychiatry*, 61:168–178.

Christ, G., Siegel, K., & Sperber, D. (1994). Impact of parental terminal cancer on adolescents. *American Journal Orthopsychiatry*, 64:604–613.

Cicchetti, D., Rogosch, F., Lynch, M., & Holt, K. (1993). Resiliance in maltreated children: Processes leading to adaptive outcome. *Development and Psychopathology*, 5:629–647.

Clarke, A. D., & Clarke, A. M. (1984). Consistency and change in the growth of human characteristics. *Journal of Child Psychology and Psychiatry*, 25:191–210.

Clark, D., Pynoos, R., & Gobel, A. (1994). Mechanisms and processes of adolescent bereavement. In R. Haggerty, N. Garmezy, M. Rutter, & L. Sherrod (eds.), *Stress, risk and resilience in children and adolescents: Process mechanisms and interventions* (pp. 100–146). Cambridge, UK: Cambridge University Press.

Cohen, P., Dizenhaus, I., & Winget, C. (1977). Family adaptation to terminal illness and death of a parent. *Social Casework*, 58:223–228.

Compas, B., Malcarne, V., & Fondacaro, K. (1988). Coping with stressful events in older children and young adolescents. *Journal of Consulting and Clinical Psychology*, 56:405–411.

Compas, B., Worsham, N., Epping-Jordan, J., Howell, D., Grant, K., Mireault, G., & Malcarne, V. (1994). When mom or dad has cancer: Markers of psychological distress in cancer patients, spouses, and children. *Health Psychology*, 13:507–515.

Cresswell, J. (1998). *Qualitative inquiry and research design: Choosing among five traditions.* Thousand Oaks, CA: Sage Publications.

DSM-IV (1994). American Psychiatric Association: *Diagnostic and Statistical Manual of Mental Disorders*, Fourth Edition. Washington D.C.: American Psychiatric Association.

Edelman, H. (1994). *Motherless daughters: The legacy of loss.* New York: Dell.

Elizur, E., & Kaffman, M. (1982). Children's bereavement reactions following death of the father. *Journal of the American Academy of Child Psychiatry*, 21:474–480.

Elizur, E., & Kaffman, M. (1983). Factors influencing the severity of childhood bereavement reactions. *American Journal of Orthopsychiatry*, 53(4):668–676.

Erikson, E. (1963). *Childhood and society.* 2nd ed. New York: W. W. Norton.

Erikson, E. (1968). *Identity: youth and crisis.* New York: Norton.

Eth, S., & Pynoos, R. (1985a). Children and psychic trauma: A brief review of contemporary thinking. In S. Eth & R. Pynoos (eds.), *Post-traumatic stress disorder in children* (pp. 3–15). Washington, D.C.: American Psychiatric Press.

Eth, S., & Pynoos, R. (1985b). Developmental perspective on psychic trauma in childhood. In C. Figley (ed.), *Trauma and its wake.* New York: Brunner Mazel.

Eth, S., & Pynoos, R. (1985c). Interaction of trauma and grief in childhood. In S. Eth & R. Pynoos (eds.), *Post-traumatic stress disrder in children* (pp. 171–186). Washington, D.C.: American Psychiatric Press.

Figley, C., Bride, B., & Mazza, N. (eds.). (1997). *Death and trauma: The traumatology of grieving.* Washington, DC: Taylor & Francis.

Finkelstein, H. (1988). The long-term effects of early parent death. *Journal of Clinical Psychology,* 44:3–9.

Fisher, C., & Wertz, F. (1975). Empirical phenomenological analyses of being criminally victimized. In A. Giorgi (ed.), *Phenomenology and psychological research* (pp. 135–158). Pittsburgh: Duquesne University Press.

Flavell, J. H. (1963). *The developmental psychology of Jean Piaget.* Princeton, NJ: D. Van Nostrand.

Flavell, J. H. (1977). *Cognitive development.* Englewood Cliffs, NJ: Prentice-Hall.

Flemming, S.J. & Adolph, R. (1986). Helping bereaved adolescents: Needs and responses. In C.A. Corr & J.N. McNeil (eds), *Adolescence and death* (pp. 97–118).

Fobair, P., Hoppe, R., Bloom, J., Cox, R., Varghese, A., & Spiegel, D. (1986). Psychosocial problems among survivors of Hodgkin's disease. *Journal of Clinical Oncology,* 4:805–814.

Freud, A. (1958). Adolescence. *Psychoanalytic Study of the Child,* 13:255–278.

Freud, A. (1960). Discussion of Dr. John Bowlby's paper. *Psychoanalytic Study of the Child,* 17:53–62.

Freud, A., & Burlingham, D. (1974). *Infants without families and reports on the Hampstead nurseries (1939–1945).* London: Hogarth.

Freud, S. (1905). *Three essays on the theory of sexuality.* Vol. VII. London: Hogarth.

Freud, S. (1915/1957). *Mourning and melancholia.* Vol. 14, pp. 273–302. London: Hogarth.

Fristad, M., Jedel, R., Weller, R., & Weller, E. (1993). Psychosocial functioning in children after the death of a parent. *American Journal of Psychiatry,* 150:511–513.

Furman, E. (1974). *A child's parent dies: Studies in childhood bereavement.* New Haven: Yale University Press.

Furman, E. (1978). Some developmental aspects of the verbalization effects. *Psychoanalytic Study of the Child,* 33:187–211.

Furman, E. (1983). Studies in childhood bereavement. *Canadian Journal of Psychiatry,* 28:241–247.

Garmezy, N. (1983). Stressors in childhood. In N. Garmezy (ed.), *Stress, coping and development in childhood.* New York: McGraw Hill.

Gilligan, C. (1979). Women's place in man's life cycle. *Harvard Educational Review,* 49:431–446.

Gilligan, C. (1982). *In a different voice: Psychological theory and women's development.* Cambridge MA: Harvard University Press.

Ginsburg, H., & Opper, S. (1979). *Piaget's theory of intellectual development.* 2nd ed. Englewood Cliffs, NJ: Prentice-Hall.

Gotay, C. (1987). Quality of life among survivors of childhood cancer: A critical review and implications for intervention. *Journal of Psychosocial Oncology,* 5(4):5–32.

Gray, R. (1987). Adolescent response to the death of a parent. *Journal of Youth and Adolescence,* 16:511–525.

Gray, R. (1989). Adolescents' perceptions of social suport after the death of a parent. *Journal of Psychosocial Oncology,* 7(3):127–144.

Harris, T. (1991). Adolescent bereavement following the death of a parent: exploratory study. *Child Psychiatry and Human Development,* 21:267–279.

Harris, T., Brown, G., & Bifulco, A. (1986). Loss of parent in childhood and adult psychiatric disorder: The role of lack of adequate parental care. *Psychological Medicine,* 16:641–659.

Harris, T., Brown, G., & Bifulco, A. (1987). Loss of parent in childhood and adult psychiatric disorder: The role of social class position and premarital pregnancy. *Psychological Medicine,* 17:163–183.

Heinicke, C. (1956). Some effects of separating two-year-old children from their parents: A comparative study. *Human Relations,* 9:105–176.

Hetherington, E. (1993). An overview of the Virginia longitudinal study of divorce and remarriage with a focus on early adolescence. *Journal of Family Psychology,* 7:39–56.

Hilgard, J., Newman, M., & Fisk, J. (1960). Strength of adult ego following childhood bereavement. *American Journal of Orthopsychiatry,* 30:788–799.

Huberman, A., & Miles, M. (1998). Data management and analysis methods. In N. Denzin & Y. Lincoln (eds.), *Collecting and interpreting qualitative materials: Book 2.* Vol. 2, pp. 179–210. Thousand Oaks, CA: Sage Publications.

Inhelder, B., & Piaget, J. (1958). *The growth of logical thinking from childhood to adolescence.* New York: Basic Books.

Jordan, J. (1991). The meaning of mutuality. In J. Jordan, A. Kaplan, J. Miller, I. Striver, & J. Surrey (eds.), *Women's Growth in Connection* (pp. 81–96). New York: Guilford Press.

Jordan, J., Kaplan, A., Miller, J., Striver, I., & Surrey, J. (eds.). (1991). *Women's growth in connection: Writings from the Stone Center.* New York: Guilford Press.

Kaffman, M., & Elizur, E. (1983). Depression related symptoms among preschool-age children. *Child Psychiatry and Human Development,* 13:233–238.

Kaffman, M., Elizur, E., & Gluckson, L. (1987). Bereavement reactions in children: Therapeutic implications. *Israeli Journal of Psychiatry,* 24(1–2):65–76.

Kalter, N. (1990). *Growing up with divorce: Helping your child avoid immediate and later emotional problems.* New York: Free Press.

Kaplan, A., Gleason, N., & Klein, R. (1991). Women's self development in late adolescence. In J. Jordan, A. Kaplan, J. Miller, I. Stiver, & J. Surrey (eds.), *Women's growth in connection* (pp. 122–140). New York: Guilford Press.

Kliman, G. (1965). *Psychological emergencies of childhood.* New York: Grune & Stratton.

Koocher, G.P. (1983). *The Democles syndrome: Psychological consequences of surviving childhood cancer.* New York: McGraw-Hill.

Kornblith, A.B. (1998). Psychosocial adaptation of cancer survivors. In J. Holland & W. Breitbard (eds). *Handbook of psychooncology* (pp. 223–254). New York: Oxford Press.

Kranzler, E., French, N., Unis, A., & Esveldt-Dawson, K. (1983). Assessment of childhood depression. *Journal American Academy of Child Psychiatry,* 22:157–164.

Kranzler, E., Shafer, D., & Wasserman, G. (1989). Early childhood bereavement. *Journal of the American Academy of Child and Adolescent Psychiatry,* 29(4):513–520.

Kranzler, E., Shaffer, D., Wasserman, G., & Davies, M. (1990). Early childhood bereavement. *Journal of the American Academy of Child/Adolescent Psychiatry,* 29:513–520.

Krupnick, J. (1984). Bereavement in children and adolescents. In M. Osterweiss, F. Solomon, & M. Green (eds.), *Bereavement reactions, consequences and care* (pp. 99–141). Washington, D.C.: National Academy Press.

Lewis, F. M., Hammond, M., & Woods, N. (1993). The family's functioning with newly diagnosed breast cancer in the mother: The development of an explanatory model. *Journal of Behavioral Medicine,* 16:351–370.

Lewis, M. (1997). *Altering fate: Why the past does not predict the future.* New York: Guilford Press.

Lifshitz, M., Berman, D., Galili, A., & Gilad, D. (1977). Bereaved children: The effect of mother's perception and social system organization on their short term adjustment. *Journal of the American Acedemy of Child/Adolescent Psychiatry,* 16:272–284.

Luria, A. R., & Vygotsky, L. (Cole, M., trans.). (1976). *Cognitive development: Its cultural and social foundations.* Cambridge MA: Harvard University Press.

Lutzke, J., Ayers, T., Sandler, I., & Barr, A. (1997). Risks and interventions for the parentally bereaved child. In S. Wolchik & I. Sandler (eds.), *Handbook of children's coping: Linking theory and intervention* (pp. 215–243). New York: Plenum Press.

Mahler, M., Pine, F., & Bergman, A. (1975). *The psychological birth of the human infant.* New York: Basic Books.

Masterson, J. (1972). *Treatment of the borderline adolescent: a developmental approach.* New York: Wiley Interscience.

Mellette, S., & Franco, P. (1987). Psychosocial barrier to employment of the cancer survivor. *Journal of Psychosocial Oncology,* 5(4):97–115.

Miller, J. (1991). The development of women's sense of self. In J. Jordan, A. Kaplan, J. Miller, I. Striver, & J. Surrey (eds.), *Women's growth in connection* (pp. 11–26). New York: Guildford Press.

Mischel, H., & Mischel, W. (1983). The development of children's knowledge of self-control strategies. *Child Development,* 54:603–619.

Mischel, W. (1968). *Personality and assessment.* New York: Wiley.

Mischel, W. (1973). Toward a cognitive social learning reconceptualization of personality. *Psychological Review,* 80:252–283.

Mischel, W., Shoda, Y., & Rodriguez, M. (1989). Delay of gratification in children. *Science,* 244:933–938.

Mishne, J. (1984). Trauma of parent loss through divorce, death and illness. *Child and Adolescent Social Work Journal,* 1:74–88.

Muuss, R. (1996). *Theories of adolescence.* 6th ed. New York: McGraw-Hill.

Nader, K., Pynoos, R., Fairbanks, L., & Frederick, C. (1990). Children's PTSD reactions one year after a sniper attack at their school. *American Journal of Psychiatry,* 146(11): 1526–1530.

Normand, C., Silverman, P., & Nickman, S. (1996). Bereaved children's changing relationships with the deceased. In D. Klass, P. Silverman, & S. Nickman (eds.), *Continuing bonds: New understandings of grief* (pp. 87–111). Washington D.C.: Taylor & Francis.

Offer, D. (1987). In defense of adolescence. *Journal of the American Medical Association,* 257:3407–3408.

Osterweis, M., Solomon, F., & Green, M. (eds.). (1984). *Bereavement, reactions, consequences and care.* Washington D.C.: National Academy Press.

Parker, G., & Manicavasagar, V. (1986). Childhood bereavement circumstances associated with adult depression. *British Journal of Medical Psychology,* 59:387–391.

Parkes, C. (1972/1986). *Bereavement: Studies of grief in adult life.* London: Penguin.

Piaget, J. (Cook, M., trans.). (1952). *The origins of intelligence in children.* New York: International Universities Press.

Polack, P., Egan, D., Vandenberg, R., & Williams, W. (1975). Prevention in mental health: A controlled study. *American Journal of Psychiatry,* 132:146–149.

Pynoos, R. (1992). Grief and trauma in children and adolescents. *Bereavement Care,* 11:2–10.

Pynoos, R., & Nader, K. (1990). Children's exposure to violence and traumatic death. *Psychiatric Annals,* 20:334–344.

Pynoos, R., Nader, K., & March, J. (1991). Post-traumatic stress disorder. In J. Weiner (ed.),

Textbook of childhood and adolescent psychiatry (pp. 339–348). Washington, D.C.: American Psychiatric Press.

Pynoos, R., Steinberg, A., & Wraith, G. (1995). A developmental model of childhood traumatic stress. In D. Cicchetti & D. Cohen (eds.), *Manual of developmental psychopathology* (pp. 72–95). New York: Wiley.

Raphael, B. (1982). The young child and the death of a parent. In C. Parkers & J. Stevenson-Hinde (eds.), *The placement of attachment in human behavior* (pp. 131–150). New York: Basic Books.

Raveis, V., Siegel, K., & Karus, M. (1999). Children's psychological distress following the death of a parent. *Journal of Youth and Adolescence*, 28:165–180.

Riessman, C. (1993). *Narrative analysis*. Newbury Park, CA: Sage Publications.

Rizzuto, A. (1979). *The birth of the living God: A psychoanalytic study*. Chicago: University of Chicago Press.

Robertson, J. (1953). *A two year old goes to the hospital* [University Film Library: Film]. London: Tavistock Clinic.

Roosa, M., Wolchik, S., & Sandler, I. (1997). Preventing the negative effects of common stressors. In S. Wolchik & I. Sandler (eds.), *Handbook of children's coping* (pp. 515–533). New York: Plenum Press.

Rosenthal, P. (1980). Short-term family therapy and pathological grief resolution with children and adolescents. *Family Process*, 19:151–159.

Runyan, W. (1982). *Life histories and psychobiography*. New York: Oxford University Press.

Rutter, M. (1966). *Children of sick parents*. London: Oxford University Pess.

Rutter, M. (1983). Stress, coping and development: Some issues and some questions. In N. Garmezy & M. Rutter (eds.), *Stress, coping and development in children*. New York: McGraw Hill.

Rutter, M. (1989). Pathways from childhood to adult life. *J. Child Psychology and Psychiatry*, 30(1):23–51.

Rutter, M. (1990). Psychosocial resilience and protective factors. In A. Rolph, A. Masten, D. Cicchetti, K. Nuechterlein, & S. Weintraub (eds.), *Risk and protective factors in the development of psychopathology* (pp. 181–214). New York: Cambridge University Press.

Rutter, M. (1994). Stress research: Accomplishments and tasks ahead. In R. Haggerty, L. Sherrod, N. Garmezy, & M. Rutter (eds.), *Stress, risk and resilience in children and adolescents* (pp. 354–385). Cambridge, UK: Cambridge University Press.

Saldinger, A., Cain A., Kalter, N. & Lohmes, K. (1999). Anticipating parental death in families with young children. *American Journal of Orthopsychiatry*, 69(1):39–48.

Saler, L., & Skolnick, N. (1992). Childhood parental death and depression in adulthood: Roles of surviving parent and family environment. *American Journal of Orthopsychiatry*, 62:504–516.

Sanchez, L., Fristad, M., Weller, R., Weller, E., & Moye, J. (1994). Anxiety in acutely bereaved prepubertal children. *Annals of Clinical Psychiatry*, 6(1):39–42.

Sandler, I., West, S., Baca, L., Pillow, D., Gersten, J., Rogosch, F., Virdin, L., Beals, J., Reynolds, K., Kallgren, C., Tien, J. K., G., Cole, E., & Ramirez, R. (1992). Linking empirically based theory and evaluation: The family bereavement program. *American Journal of Community Psychology*, 20:491–521.

Sandler, L., Wolchick, S., & Braver, S. (1988). The stressors of children's post-divorce environments. In S. Wolchick & P. Karoly (eds.), *Children of divorce: Empirical perspectives on adjustment* (pp. 111–144). New York: Gardner Press.

Saucier, J., & Ambert, A. (1982). Parental marital status and adolescents' optimism about their future. *Journal of Youth and Adolescence*, 11:345–354.

Sears, R. R. (1951). A theoretical framework for personality and social behavior. *American Psychologist,* 6:476–483.

Sears, R. R., Maccoby, E. E., & Levin, H. (1957). *Patterns of child rearing.* Evanston Ill: Row, Peterson.

Seidel, J., Kjolseth, R., & Seymour, E. (1988). *The Ethnograph.* Amherst, MA: Qualis Research Associates.

Shafer, R. (1968). *Aspects of internalization.* New York: International Universities Press.

Shapiro, E. (1994). *Grief as a family process: A developmental approach to clinical practice.* New York: Guilford Press.

Siegel, K., & Christ, G. (1995). Social work research in hospital settings: Strategies for implementation. *Social Work in Health Care,* 21(2):55–69.

Siegel, K., Karus, D., & Raveis, V. (1996). Adjustment of children facing the death of a parent due to cancer. *Jornal of the American Academy of Child and Adolescent Psychiatry,* 35:442–450.

Siegel, K., Mesagno, R., & Christ, G. (1990). A preventive program for bereaved children. *American Journal of Orthopsychiatry* 60:168–175.

Siegel, K., Masagno, F., Karus, D., Christ, G., Banks, G., & Moynihan, R. (1992). Psychosocial adjustment of children with a terminally ill parent. *Journal of the American Academy of Child/Adolescent Psychiatry,* 31:327–333.

Siegel, K., Raveis, V., & Karus, D. (1996). Patterns of communication with children when a parent has cancer. In L. Baider, C. Cooper, & A. DeNour (Eds), *Cancer in the Family* (pp. 109-128). New York: John Wiley & Sons.

Silverman, P. (1986). *Widow to widow.* New York: Springer.

Silverman, P. (1989). The impact of parental death on college age women. *Psychiatric Clinics of North America,* 10:387–404.

Silverman, P., Nickman, S., & Worden, J. (1995). Detachment revisited: The child's reconstruction of a dead parent. In K. Doka (ed.), *Children mourning, mourning children* (pp. 131–148). Washington, D.C.: Hospice Foundation of America.

Silverman, P., & Worden, J. (1992a). Children's reactions in the early months after the death of a parent. *American Journal of Orthopsychiatry,* 62:93–104.

Silverman, P., & Worden, J. (1992b). Children's understanding of funeral rites. *Omega,* 25:319–331.

Silverman, P., & Worden, J. (1993). Children's reactions to the death of a parent. In M. Stroebe, W. Stroebe, & R. Hansson (eds.), *Handbook of bereavement: Theory, research and intervention* (pp. 300–316). Cambridge, UK: Cambridge University Press.

Sood, B., Weller, E., Weller, R., Fristad, M., & Bowes, J. (1992). Somatic complaints in grieving children. *Comprehensive Mental Health Care,* 2:17–25.

Spitz, R. (1946). Anaclitic depression. *Psychoanalytic Study of the Child,* 2:313–342.

Stake, R. (1998). Case studies. In N. Denzin & T. Lincloln (eds.), *Strategies of qualitative analysis.* Vol. 2, pp. 86–109. Thousand Oaks, CA: Sage Publications.

Strength, J. (1991). *Factors influencing the mother-child relationship following the death of the father and how that relationship affects the child's functioning.* Unpublished doctoral dissertation, Rosemead School of Psychology, La Mirada, CA.

Tebbi, C., & Mallon, J. (1987). Long-term psychosocial outcome in adolescent cancer amputees. *Journal of Psychosocial Oncology,* 5(4):69–82.

Tennant, C. (1988). Parental loss in childhood: Its effect in adult life. *Archives of General Psychiatry,* 45:1045–1049.

Terr, L. (1983). Chowchilla revisited: The effects of psychic trauma four years after a school-bus kidnapping. *American Journal of Psychiatry,* 140:1543–1550.

Terr, L. (1990). *Too scared to cry.* New York: Basic Books.

Terr, L. (1995). Childhood traumas: An outline and overview. In G. Everly & J. Lantin (eds.), *Psychotraumatology* (pp. 301–320). New York: Plenum Press.

Thomas, A., & Chess, S. (1977). *Temperament and development.* New York: Brunner/Mazel.

Tremblay, G., & Israel, A. (1998). Children's adjustment to parental death. *Clinical Psychology: Science and Practice,* 5(4):424–438.

Tweed, J., Shoenback, V., George, L., & Blazer, D. (1989). The effects of childhood parental death and divorce on six-month history of anxiety disorders. *British Jounal of Psychiatry,* 154:823–828.

Van Eederwegh, M., Bieri, M., Parilla, R., & Clayton, P. (1982). The bereaved child. *British Journal of Psychiatry,* 140:23–29.

Van Eerdeweigh, M., Clayton, P., & Van Eerdewegh, P. (1985). The bereaved child: Variables influencing early psychopathology. *British Journal of Paychiatry,* 154:823–828.

Volkan, V. (1981). *Linking objects and linking phenomena: A study of the forms, symptoms, metapsychology, and therapy of complicated mourning.* New York: International Universities Press.

Wallerstein, J., & Blakeslee, S. (1989). *Second chances: Men, women and children a decade after divorce.* New York: Ticknor and Fields.

Walsh, F. (1998). *Strengthening family resilience.* New York: Guildford Press.

Weller, R., Weller, E., Fristad, M., & Bowes, J. (1991). Depression in recently bereaved prepubertal children. *American Journal of Psychiatry,* 148:1536–1540.

Wolfenstein, M. (1966). How is mourning possible? *Psychoanalytic Study of the Child,* 21:93–123.

Worden, J. (1991). *Grief counseling and grief therapy: A handbook for the mental health practitioner.* 2nd ed. New York: Springer.

Worden, J. (1996). *Children and grief: When a parent dies.* New York: Guilford Press.

World Health Organization (1991). *1990 World health statistics annual.* Geneva: World Health Organization Office of Publications.

Author Index

Subject Index